Creative Expression and Wellbeing in Higher Education

This volume focuses on individual and collective practices of creativity, embodiment and movement as acts of self-care and wellbeing.

Creative Expression and Wellbeing in Higher Education positions creative and movement expression as an important act for professionals working in higher education, as a way to connect, communicate, practice activism or simply slow down. Through examples as diverse as movement through dance and exercise, expression through drawing, writing or singing and creating objects with one's hands, the authors share how individual and collective acts of creativity and movement enhance, support and embrace wellbeing, offering guidance to the reader on how such creative expression can be adopted as self-care practice. This book highlights how connection to hand, body, voice and mind has been imperative in this process for expression, flow and engagement with self and wellbeing practices.

Self-care and wellbeing are complex at the best of times. In higher education, these are actions that are constantly being grappled with personally, collectively and systematically. Designed to support readers working in higher education, this book will also be of great interest to professionals and researchers.

Narelle Lemon is an interdisciplinary researcher in the fields of education, positive psychology and arts, holding the positions of Associate Professor in Education and Associate Dean (Education) for the School of Social Sciences, Media, Film and Education at Swinburne University of Technology in Melbourne, Australia.

Wellbeing and Self-care in Higher Education
Editor: Narelle Lemon

Healthy Relationships in Higher Education
Promoting Wellbeing Across Academia
Edited by Narelle Lemon

Creating a Place for Self-care and Wellbeing in Higher Education
Finding Meaning Across Academia
Edited by Narelle Lemon

Creative Expression and Wellbeing in Higher Education
Making and Movement as Mindful Moments of Self-care
Edited by Narelle Lemon

Reflections on Valuing Wellbeing in Higher Education
Reforming our Acts of Self-care
Edited by Narelle Lemon

For more information about this series, please visit: www.routledge.com/Wellbeing-and-Self-care-in-Higher-Education/book-series/WSCHE

Creative Expression and Wellbeing in Higher Education

Making and Movement as Mindful Moments of Self-care

Edited by Narelle Lemon

LONDON AND NEW YORK

Cover image: © Getty Images

First published 2023
by Routledge
4 Park Square, Milton Park, Abingdon, Oxon OX14 4RN

and by Routledge
605 Third Avenue, New York, NY 10158

Routledge is an imprint of the Taylor & Francis Group, an informa business

© 2023 selection and editorial matter, Narelle Lemon; individual chapters, the contributors

The right of Narelle Lemon to be identified as the author of the editorial material, and of the authors for their individual chapters, has been asserted in accordance with sections 77 and 78 of the Copyright, Designs and Patents Act 1988.

All rights reserved. No part of this book may be reprinted or reproduced or utilised in any form or by any electronic, mechanical, or other means, now known or hereafter invented, including photocopying and recording, or in any information storage or retrieval system, without permission in writing from the publishers.

Trademark notice: Product or corporate names may be trademarks or registered trademarks, and are used only for identification and explanation without intent to infringe.

British Library Cataloguing-in-Publication Data
A catalogue record for this book is available from the British Library

Library of Congress Cataloging-in-Publication Data
Names: Lemon, Narelle, editor.
Title: Creative expression and wellbeing in higher education : making and movement as mindful moments of self-care / edited by Narelle Lemon.
Description: Abingdon, Oxon ; New York, NY : Routledge, 2023. | Series: Wellbeing and self-care in higher education | Includes bibliographical references and index.
Identifiers: LCCN 2022007770 (print) | LCCN 2022007771 (ebook) | ISBN 9781032076010 (hardback) | ISBN 9781032076027 (paperback) | ISBN 9781003207863 (ebook)
Subjects: LCSH: College teachers—Psychology. | College teachers—Job stress. | College teachers—Mental health. | Arts—Therapeutic use. | Well-being. | Self-care, Health. | Work-life balance.
Classification: LCC LB2333.2 .C74 2023 (print) | LCC LB2333.2 (ebook) | DDC 378.1/2—dc23/eng/20220617
LC record available at https://lccn.loc.gov/2022007770
LC ebook record available at https://lccn.loc.gov/2022007771

ISBN: 978-1-032-07601-0 (hbk)
ISBN: 978-1-032-07602-7 (pbk)
ISBN: 978-1-003-20786-3 (ebk)

DOI: 10.4324/9781003207863

Typeset in Bembo
by Apex CoVantage, LLC

Contents

List of illustrations vii
List of contributors x
Series preface xv
Acknowledgements xviii
Review team xix

1 Poetic inquiry: transformational representations of wellbeing and self-care in higher education 1
NARELLE LEMON

SECTION 1
Making and creating as a representation of self-care 19

2 The feeling of doing*thinking* and thinking*doing* of making processes 21
MEGAN MCPHERSON

3 Journaling right and left 33
JANET SALMONS

4 Meditative math-making 53
MELISSA SILK

SECTION 2
Collaborative expression, embodiment, and the power of relationships 71

5 Stepping off the edge: circles of connection and creativity for wellbeing in the academy 73
CATHERINE E. HOYSER

6 Running, writing, resilience: a self-study of
collaborative self-care among women faculty   87
SANDRA L. TARABOCHIA, KRISTY A. BRUGAR AND JULIE ANN WARD

7 Making mindful moments: made artefacts as a form
of data visualisation to monitor and respond to
self-care and wellbeing   105
SHARON MCDONOUGH AND NARELLE LEMON

SECTION 3
Creative practice as interruption   119

8 Using arts-based and feminist methodologies to slow
the wear and tear/s of academic work/life   121
ALISON L. BLACK

9 Playing with pictures to make sense and interrupt the
hurly-burly university game   137
MARK SELKRIG

10 Self-care in the time of crisis: an *a/r/tographic*
conversation to explore self-care as academics that
took an unexpected turn   153
NICOLE BRUNKER AND ROBYN GIBSON

SECTION 4
Mind, body, and movement as acts of self-care   183

11 Kia kōrero te tinana katoa (The whole body must
speak): Māori early-career academics and performing
one's cultural self for hauora   185
JANI KATARINA TAITUHA WILSON

12 Cycling as a form of self-care: incorporating and
sustaining purposeful movement practices to support
wellbeing   199
NADINE CRANE

13 Anatomy of a burnout: walking, reading and journal
writing as practices of self-care to support intellectual life   211
LYNELLE WATTS

Index   226

Illustrations

Figures

9.1　Traditional relationship between artist and audience by Willats (1976) — 143

Images

2.1　The breadth of it is astounding. Relief printed etching on rice paper, pigment ink, glues 1.2 m × 1 m × 0.3 m (3 bags, installation variable) 2020 — 22

2.2　Three bags full of that affect, while in anxious times. Relief printed etching on rice paper, pigment ink, glues 2 m × 1 m × .30 m (3 bags, installation variable) 2020 — 26

2.3　Shallow breathing through fog, snap. Relief printed etching on rice paper, pigment ink, glues, pins 1.2 m × 1 m × 0.3 m (3 bags, installation variable) 2021 — 28

3.1　Journaling right and left means using both practical and creative ways to make progress with your research and practice self-care — 33

3.2　When I use my planning journal to capture and close the proverbial book on work demands, I enjoy my creative space for art. I am so engrossed the cares of the world are set aside — 36

3.3　Sometimes, my art journaling involves reflection, when I try to represent the beauty of the natural world around me. I use observational skills to note colours, shapes, and the quality of the light. Other times, I reflexively write in an effort to make sense of thorny social issues in current projects — 38

3.4　It is funny how journaling can sometimes blur what is outside and what is on the page. The journal takes on its own reality — 40

3.5　When I look at the world around me with paints in hand, I note details I might not otherwise see — 40

3.6　There is no right or wrong mix of words and images. I use both, sometimes incorporating words into visual diagrams or adding illustrations or doodles to pages of text — 44

viii *Illustrations*

3.7	I appreciate my tech tools, but I love my art supplies!	45
3.8	A waterbrush is great for on-the-go journaling and works well with paints or water-soluble pencils	47
3.9	Keyboards and fountain pens co-exist on my desk	48
3.10	In the midst of a busy project, the handwritten memos to self keep me centred and on track	49
4.1	Making and flexing a hyperbolic paraboloid	55
4.2	Fold lines for creating a paper hyperbolic paraboloid	63
4.3	Opposite corners	64
4.4	HP folding completed	65
4.5	The HP form showing the location of parabolic and hyperbolic surface curves	65
4.6	HP embodiment	66
4.7	Playful polyhedral construction	66
4.8	HP-inspired story writing	67
5.1	The tactile organic shapes that help centre and ground me	77
6.1	Parking lot light	87
6.2	Map	92
6.3	Kristy and Sandy just before running the Dallas Marathon	93
6.4	Bicycle	94
6.5	Prairie Fire	96
6.6	Skunk	98
6.7	Bridge	99
6.8	Sunset	101
7.1 and 7.2	Photo of Sharon's data visualisation scarf and a snapshot of the meeting logs that forms the pattern for the scarf (on the left), with each colour representing the different number of meetings held on a day. Narelle's blanket and virtual meeting log (on the right) represents the total number of hours per day in virtual meetings	106
7.3	#10minsofmaking	109
7.4	Mindfully reflecting on patterns of work	110
7.5	I began knitting a scarf . . .	111
7.6	Growing slowly	112
7.7	Sparking a conversation	112
7.8	Representing growth	113
7.9	My data dump	114
7.10	Being present with the representation	115
7.11	Recording hours to make the colour pattern	115
8.1	Exploring feminist snap	130
9.1	Photographic collage: Community engagement is . . .	137
9.2	Renderings for sculptures made to reflect my doctoral journey	141
9.3	Four examples of the passageway posters	145
9.4	Posters that resulted from the postcard project	146

9.5	Collage of various Zoom backgrounds	148
10.1	'Sitting in the bush that surrounds us'	155
10.2	'To afford myself the luxury of time'	157
10.3	'I'm far from alone in this experience'	158
10.4	'I yearn for the warm embrace'	160
10.5	'In being prepared I was proactive'	161
10.6	'Self-care came from the universe today'	163
10.7	'Embrace the chaos'	164
10.8	'Hold tight to the memories'	165
10.9	'Bittersweet memories of my mother'	166
10.10	'I'm done. I need a break'	168
10.11	'This week is reflective of the Tree of Yggdrasill'	169
10.12	'It is an individual responsibility'	171
10.13	'The stability of the familiar'	172
10.14	'Consider images through an artistic lens'	175
10.15	Robyn's collage	178
10.16	Nikki's collage	179
11.1	The art of kapa haka	185
12.1	Bicycle on track	199
13.1	Walking shoes	211
13.2	Trajectory of a burnout	214
13.3	Recovery from burnout	216
13.4	Anatomy of a burnout	220

Tables

| 13.1 | Symptoms of burnout | 215 |

Contributors

Alison L. Black is an arts-based/narrative researcher in the School of Education, University of the Sunshine Coast, Australia. She uses feminist, creative and contemplative research methodologies to understand lived lives, to engage in collaborative work and to critique, contest and resist the intolerable and injurious agendas of neoliberal institutions.

Kristy A. Brugar is an associate professor of social studies education and Huddleston Presidential Professor of Education at the University of Oklahoma. Her research interests include elementary social studies education; interdisciplinary instruction and opportunities including history and literacy; and teacher development. Brugar's work has been published in *Theory and Research in Social Education, Journal of Social Studies Research, The History Teacher, The Journal of Teacher Education,* and *Social Studies and the Young Learner.* She received the College and University Faculty Assembly, National Council for the Social Studies, Early Career Award, 2017, for her contributions to social studies education. She regularly works with pre-service and in-service teachers in the field. She is an avid "fun runner" and has participated in several marathons including in Boston and Houston, and the Marine Corps Marathon in Washington D.C. (1995 and 2018).

Nicole Brunker is a lecturer in the Sydney School of Education and Social Work, the University of Sydney, responsible for convening the foundation units in the Masters of Teaching. Nicole has taught in alternative and mainstream schools, with experience in early childhood, primary and secondary schooling as a teacher and principal. Her research interests centre around children's social and emotional wellbeing, initial teacher education pedagogy, alternative schooling and innovative qualitative methodologies. Current research projects include an exploration of children's experiences when school has not 'fit'; school–teacher and teacher educator alignment on student-centred practice; and schools' shift away from behaviour management. Nicole is interested in post-qualitative and arts-informed inquiry approaches to research.

Nadine Crane is a lecturer and PhD candidate at the Melbourne Graduate School of Education (MGSE). Prior to joining the MGSE, Nadine was a primary school teacher and education consultant with an interest in student voice. She has worked extensively with schools on how to develop and enact integrated curriculum and inquiry-based learning approaches, with a particular emphasis on the inclusion of student voice by negotiating the curriculum. Nadine's PhD research is focussed on how primary schools sustain the pedagogical practice of negotiating the curriculum with students. Her other current research interests and projects are centred around pre-service teacher education.

Robyn Gibson is an associate professor visual and creative arts education and deputy head of school at Sydney School of Education and Social Work, University of Sydney. Robyn has been a primary school teacher, art/craft specialist and tertiary educator in Australia and the US. Her doctoral thesis explored the relationship between surrealism and fashion, specifically the creative collaborations between the surrealist Salvador Dali and fashion designer Elsa Schiaparelli. Her research has focused on children's attitudes to art, art making and art education. Currently she is examining the role of arts education in academic motivation, engagement and achievement as part of a large ARC funded research project. Her other academic research – which utilises interdisciplinary methodologies such as arts-informed inquiry and a/r/tography – concerns art as research; research as art particularly the connection between clothes and memory.

Catherine E. Hoyser, PhD, is professor of English at the University of Saint Joseph in West Hartford, Connecticut, USA, where she teaches British cultural studies, including postcolonial literature and gender studies. Hoyser's research includes the American missionary impact on the Indigenous people of Hawaii and the British feminist activist for Indian independence and leader of the International Theosophical Society, Annie Besant. Besides publishing scholarly articles and books, Hoyser is a published poet. She is the recipient of the Connecticut Women's Network American Council of Education Distinguished Woman in Higher Education Leadership Award, as well as honourary membership in Alpha Sigma Lambda, the national honour society for adult learners, for her support of non-traditional students in higher education. She also publishes about holistic, transformative, embodied pedagogy. Her latest book is the co-edited volume *The Whole Person: Embodying Teaching and Learning Through Lectio and Visio Divina* (2019, Rowman & Littlefield).

Narelle Lemon is an interdisciplinary researcher in her fields of education, positive psychology and arts, holding the position of associate professor in education and associate dean (education) for the School of Social Sciences, Media, Film and Education at Swinburne University of Technology in Melbourne, Australia. Narelle is a researcher who focuses on translating theory and evidence into practice to enhance engagement and participation for teachers and students across all fields of education. Recent research has investigated mindfulness in education, self-care and wellbeing to empower educators, arts and cultural education and her award-winning scholarship of learning and teaching in the integration of social media for learning and professional development. Narelle is currently the series editor with Routledge for the series called *Wellbeing and Self-Care in Higher Education: Embracing Positive Solutions*. More recently Narelle has co-authored the books: *Building and Sustaining a Teaching Career: Strategies for Professional Experience, Wellbeing and Mindful Practice* (Lemon & McDonough, 2020, with Cambridge University Press); and *Reframing and Rethinking Collaboration in Higher Education and Beyond: A Practical Guide for Doctoral Students and Early Career Researchers* (Lemon & Salmon, 2021, as part of the Insider Guides to Success in Academia Series with Routledge).

Sharon McDonough is a researcher in teacher education with advanced disciplinary knowledge of sociocultural theories of teacher emotion, resilience and wellbeing at Federation University, Ballarat, Victoria, Australia. Dr. McDonough brings these to explore how best to prepare and support teachers for entry into the profession, how to support the professional learning of teachers and teacher educators across their careers and how to support wellbeing in education and in community. Sharon's research expertise lies in methods of phenomenology and self-study. She is co-author of the recent text *Building and Sustaining a Teaching Career: Strategies for Professional Experience, Wellbeing and Mindful Practice* (Cambridge).

Megan McPherson is a settler artist, educator and researcher based at the Wilin Centre for Indigenous Art and Cultural Development, the University of Melbourne. Megan's overarching creative practice research emphasis is in printmaking, textiles and installations. She publishes in the areas of the academic identity, social media use, Indigenous knowledges and pedagogies and educator and student experience in the creative arts. Megan uses ethnographic, sociological and creative practice methodologies to focus on identity, subjectivities, affect and agency. She studies the intersections of pedagogical and material engagements in artistic, social and cultural productions.

Janet Salmons, PhD, is a free-range scholar, writer, coach and artist through Vision2Lead. She serves as the methods guru for SAGE Publications' research community, www.MethodSpace.com. Janet blends imagination with curiosity in an eclectic life–work mix. One minute, she is writing an academic book or blog post; the next, she is painting and art journaling. Areas of interest include emerging research methods and teaching and collaborative learning in the digital age. Her most recent books are *Doing Qualitative Research Online,* 2nd edition (2022); *What Kind of Researcher Are You?* (2021); *Reframing and Rethinking Collaboration in Higher Education and Beyond: A Practical Guide for Doctoral Students and Early Career Researchers* with Narelle Lemon (2021); *Publishing From Your Doctoral Research: Create and Use a Publication Strategy* with Helen Kara (2020); *Learning to Collaborate, Collaborating* to Learn (2019); *Find the Theory in Your Research* (2019); and *Gathering Your Data Online* (2019). She lives and works in Boulder, Colorado.

Mark Selkrig is an associate professor in education at the University of Melbourne. His research and scholarly work focus on the changing nature of educators' work, their identities, lived experiences and how they navigate the ecologies of their respective learning environments. He also has an interest in the ways the arts and creativities are interpreted and promoted in education contexts. Mark engages with arts-informed methodologies in these areas to probe the uneasy tensions and intersections that influence change, capacity building and agency of individuals and communities. He is always keen to work, talk and collaborate with others who have an interest in these areas. Mark has received awards for university teaching and research and is a practising artist, having participated in numerous solo and group exhibitions and several community-based arts projects. He is a Churchill Fellow, in recognition of his contribution and research related to regional arts development and education.

Melissa Silk is a Sydney educator, working in a variety of contexts to encourage transdisciplinarity through doing, being and becoming. Melissa collaborates with many thinkers and makers to design experiences that embed the arts in science, technology, engineering and mathematics (STEAM). Melissa is currently co-director of STEAMpop.zone and national head of design at JMC Academy while also engaged in research that contributes to learning ecologies spanning creative intelligence and innovation, transdisciplinary education and designing for preferred futures. Melissa enjoys being part of a bold community of multipotentialites intent on developing and sharing unique learning experiences for everybody.

Sandra L. Tarabochia is an associate professor of English and core affiliate faculty in Women's & Gender Studies at the University of Oklahoma. Her research focuses on the intersection of teaching, learning and writing. Her recent book, *Reframing the Relational: A Pedagogical Approach to Cross-Curricular Literacy Work* (National Council of Teachers of English, 2017), offers discursive strategies and a pedagogical ethic for faculty collaboratively developing writing curriculum across disciplines. Her work appears in *WPA: Writing Program Administration*, *Across the Disciplines*, *Writing Across the Curriculum Journal*, *Composition Forum*, *Writing & Pedagogy*. Her co-edited collection *Making Connections: WAC and the Search for the Common Ground* is forthcoming with the WAC Clearinghouse and University Press of Colorado Press. She is founding co-editor of the journal *Writing: Craft & Context*, an open-access interdisciplinary journal dedicated to inclusive publishing and focused on writers: the work they do, the contexts in which they compose and circulate their work and how they develop across the life span. She has run several half-marathons including OKC Memorial, Cowtown, Madtown and Sarasota, for which she earned the largest dolphin medal in the state of Florida. The 2019 Dallas BMW Marathon was her first marathon!

Julie Ann Ward is assistant professor of 20th- and 21st-century Latin American literature and culture at the University of Oklahoma. Her research focuses on contemporary Mexican theatre and narrative. Her book, *A Shared Truth: The Theater of Lagartijas Tiradas Al Sol* (University of Pittsburgh Press, 2019), is the first book-length study of the autobiographical and documentary work of Mexican theatre company Lagartijas Tiradas al Sol. Her current project is a study of contemporary representations of national borders in Mexican cultural production. Her work has appeared in *Theatre Journal, TransModernity, Latin American Theatre Review, Revista de Literatura Mexicana Contemporánea* and *Paso de Gato*, as well as the *Routledge Companion to Dramaturgy* and the *Routledge Companion to Gender, Sex and Latin American Culture*. She is the general editor of student-generated *Open Educational Resource*, the *Antología abierta de literatura hispana* (*Open Anthology of Hispanic Literature*) and a publication on the anthology, co-authored with an undergraduate student, is forthcoming in *InSight: A Journal of Scholarly Teaching*. She completed her first half-marathon in Madrid in 2004, and completed the Surf City Marathon in 2014.

Lynelle Watts is a senior lecturer in social work at Curtin University. Lynelle has conducted research in the areas of family and domestic violence, extended care for care-experienced young people, reflective practice and critical reflexivity in social work, teaching and learning in higher education, social work curriculum and assessment tools for carers of people experiencing mental distress. At the time of writing, Lynelle is the serving President of Australia New Zealand Social Work Welfare Education & Research (ANZSWWER) – a peak body for social work and welfare educators. Lynelle is social media editor for the journal *Australian Social Work*. In addition to teaching and researching in social work, Lynelle is the co-author of two books, *Key Concepts and Theory in Social Work* (2017, Palgrave) and *Social Justice Theory and Practice for Social Work* (2019, Springer). Lynelle is active on Twitter – you can find her @watts_lj.

Jani Katarina Taituha Wilson (Ngāti Awa, Ngā Puhi, Mātaatua) hails from Pāroa on the outskirts of Whakatāne and has a PhD in film, TV and media studies from the University of Auckland and is senior lecturer/school research co-ordinator. All of her research and classroom teaching pivots on Indigenous academic excellence and the integration of mātauranga Māori into media/screen studies, with a lofty aspiration to influence screen production on and off screen. A longtime kaihaka and kaitito, Jani's current research focuses on the ongoing evolution of screened kapa haka as a central component of 'Māori popular culture', with a critical focus on the impact of screen production demands on the art.

Series preface

As academics, scholars, staff and colleagues working in the context of universities in the contemporary climate, we are often challenged with where we place our own wellbeing. It is not uncommon to hear about burnout, stress, anxiety, pressures with workload, having too many balls in the air, toxic cultures, increasing demands, isolation and feeling distressed (Berg & Seeber, 2016; Lemon & McDonough, 2018; Mountz et al., 2015). The reality is that universities are stressful places (Beer et al., 2015; Cranton & Taylor, 2012; Kasworm & Bowles, 2012; Mountz et al., 2015; Ryan, 2013; Sullivan & Weissner, 2010; Wang & Cranton, 2012). McNaughton and Billot (2016) argue that the "deeply personal effects of changing roles, expectations and demands" (p. 646) have been downplayed and that academics and staff engage in constant reconstruction of their identities and work practices. It is important to acknowledge this, as much as it is to acknowledge the need to place wellbeing and self-care at the forefront of these lived experiences and situations.

Wellbeing can be approached at multiple levels including micro and macro. In placing wellbeing at the heart of the higher education workplace, self-care becomes an imperative both individually and systemically (Berg & Seeber, 2016; Lemon & McDonough, 2018). Self-care is most commonly oriented towards individual action to monitor and ensure personal wellbeing; however, it is also a collective act. There is a plethora of different terms that are in action to describe how one approaches their wellbeing holistically (Godfrey et al., 2011). With different terminology comes different ways self-care is understood. For this collection self-care is understood as "the actions that individuals take for themselves, on behalf of and with others in order to develop, protect, maintain and improve their health, wellbeing or wellness" (Self Care Forum, 2019, para. 1). It covers a spectrum of health-related (emotional, physical and/or spiritual) actions including prevention, promotion and treatment, while aiming to encourage individuals to take personal responsibility for their health and to advocate for themselves and others in accessing resources and care (Knapik & Laverty, 2018). Self-love, -compassion, -awareness and -regulation are significant elements of self-care. But what does this look like for those working in higher education? In this book series, authors respond to the questions: *What do you do for self-care? How do you position wellbeing as part of your role in academia?*

In thinking about these questions, authors are invited to critically discuss and respond to inspiration sparked by one or more of the questions of:

> How do we bring self-regulation to how we approach our work?
> How do we create a compassionate workplace in academia?
> What does it mean for our work when we are aware and enact self-compassion?
> What awareness has occurred that has disrupted the way we approach work?
> Where do mindful intentions sit?
> How do we shift the rhetoric of "this is how it has always been" in relation to overworking and indiscretions between workload and approaches to workload?
> How do we counteract the traditional narrative of overwork?
> How do we create and sustain a healthier approach?
> How can we empower the "I" and "we" as we navigate self-care as a part of who we are as academics?
> How can we promote a curiosity about how we approach self-care?
> What changes do we need to make?
> How can we approach self-care with energy and promote shifts in how we work individually, collectively and systemically?

The purpose of this book series is to:

> Place academic wellbeing and self-care at the heart of discussions around working in higher education.
> Provide a diverse range of strategies for how to put in place wellbeing and self-care approaches as an academic.
> Provide a narrative connection point for readers from a variety of backgrounds in academia.
> Highlight lived experiences and honour the voice of those working in higher education.
> Provide a visual narrative that supports connection to authors' lived experience(s).
> Contribute to the conversation on ways that wellbeing and self-care can be positioned in the work that those working in higher education do.
> Highlight new ways of working in higher education that disrupt current tensions that neglect wellbeing.

References

Beer, L. E., Rodriguez, K., Taylor, C., Martinez-Jones, N., Griffin, J., Smith, T. R., Lamar, M., & Anaya, R. (2015). Awareness, integration and interconnectedness. *Journal of Transformative Education*, *13*(2), 161–185.

Berg, M., & Seeber, B. K. (2016). *The slow professor: Challenging the culture of speed in the academy*. University of Toronto Press.

Cranton, P., & Taylor, E. W. (2012). Transformative learning theory: Seeking a more unified theory. In E. W. Taylor & P. Cranton (Eds.), *The handbook of transformative learning* (pp. 3–20). Jossey-Bass.

Godfrey, C. M., Harrison, M. B., Lysaght, R., Lamb, M., Graham, I. D., & Oakley, P. (2011). The experience of self-care: A systematic review. *JBI Library of Systematic Reviews, 8*(34), 1351–1460. http://www.ncbi.nlm.nih.gov/pubmed/27819888

Kasworm, C., & Bowles, T. (2012). Fostering transformative learning in higher education settings. In E. Taylor & P. Cranton (Eds.), *The handbook of transformative learning* (pp. 388–407). Sage.

Knapik, K., & Laverty, A. (2018). Self-care individual, relational, and political sensibilities. In M. A. Henning, C. U. Krägeloh, R. Dryer, F. Moir, D. R. Billington, & A. G. Hill. (Eds.), *Wellbeing in higher education: Cultivating a healthy lifestyle among faculty and students*. Routledge.

Lemon, N., & McDonough, S. (Eds.). (2018). *Mindfulness in the academy: Practices and perspectives from scholars*. Springer.

McNaughton, S. M., & Billot, J. (2016). Negotiating academic teacher identity shifts during higher education contextual change. *Teaching in Higher Education, 21*(6), 644–658.

Mountz, A., Bonds, A., Mansfield, B., Loyd, J., Hyndman, J., & Watton-Roberts, M. (2015). For slow scholarship: A feminist politics of resistance through collective action in the neoliberal university. *ACME: An International E-Journal of Critical Geographies, 14*(4), 1235–1259.

Ryan, M. (2013). The pedagogical balancing act: Teaching reflection in higher education. *Teaching in Higher Education, 18*, 144–155.

Self Care Forum. (2019). *Self care forum: Home*. Retrieved July 27, 2019, from http://www.selfcareforum.org/

Sullivan, L. G., & Weissner, C. A. (2010). Learning to be reflective leaders: A case study from the NCCHC Hispanic leadership fellows program. In D. L. Wallin (Ed.), Special issue: *Leadership in an era of change: New directions for community colleges* (No. 149, pp. 41–50). Jossey-Bass.

Wang, V. C., & Cranton, P. (2012). Promoting and implementing self-directed learning (SDL): An effective adult education model. *International Journal of Adult Vocational Education and Technology, 3*, 16–25.

Acknowledgements

Thank you, dear colleagues, for your vulnerability, openness, and insights that help us all grow.

Much appreciation to my dear colleague and friend Catherine Hoyser for the ongoing inspiration.

Review team

Marni J. Binder, Toronto Metropolitan University, Canada
Alison L. Black, University of the Sunshine Coast, Australia
Kristy A. Brugar, University of Oklahoma, USA
Nicole Brunker, The University of Sydney, Australia
Anuja Cabraal, independent researcher and consultant, Melbourne, Australia
Mim Fox, University of Wollongong, Sydney, Australia
Robyn Gibson, The University of Sydney, Australia
Monica Green, Federation University, Australia
Kay Hammond, Auckland University of Technology, Auckland, New Zealand
Amira Hassouna, Auckland University of Technology, Auckland, New Zealand
Catherine E. Hoyser, University of Saint Joseph, West Hartford, Connecticut, USA
Aaron Jarden, The University of Melbourne, Australia
Rebecca J. Jarden, The University of Melbourne, Australia
Ljiljana Jowett, Auckland University of Technology, Auckland, New Zealand
Amanda Lees, Auckland University of Technology, Auckland, New Zealand
Nadine LeMescum, The University of Melbourne, Australia
Patricia Lucas, Auckland University of Technology, Auckland, New Zealand
Sherie McClam, Manhattanville College, USA
Sharon McDonough, Federation University, Australia
Megan McPherson, The University of Melbourne, Australia
Michelle Newcomb, Queensland University of Technology, Brisbane, Australia
Jonathan O'Donnell, RMIT University, Melbourne, Australia

Nicola Power, Auckland University of Technology, Auckland, New Zealand

Ajit Pyati, University of Western Ontario, London, Ontario, Canada

Aimee Quickfall, Sheffield Hallam University and Bishop Grosseteste University, UK

Janet Salmons, independent scholar, USA

Mark Selkrig, the University of Melbourne, Australia

Melissa Silk, JMC Academy, Sydney, Australia

Caroline Stretton, Auckland University of Technology, Auckland, New Zealand

Sandra L. Tarabochia, University of Oklahoma, USA

Julie Trafford, Auckland University of Technology, Auckland, New Zealand

Julie Ann Ward, University of Oklahoma, USA

Lynelle Watts, Curtin University, Australia

Jani Katarina Taituha Wilson, Massey University, New Zealand

1 Poetic inquiry

Transformational representations of wellbeing and self-care in higher education

Narelle Lemon

Introduction

Self-care requires us to engage with different and diverse types of practices and strategies to help us with our wellbeing. We can think of these as a menu of items that are informed by wellbeing science. They are completed across and within the variable of time. That is, some practices may be completed regularly or some once every now and then. And some practices may be micro-moments completed in as quick a time frame as 30 seconds, while others may be sustained practices that require long lengths of time. What we do know is that what we need changes. This is due to context, situation, and our own growth. Additionally, what works for one may not work for another.

This complexity is intriguing to many of us who work in the area of wellbeing. But it is also a motivator to explore further and find out what and how we can learn with and from one another. There is scope for interventions which address wellbeing from a positive lens. The removal of negative emotion is not the only focus, rather what is illuminated are positive emotions and experiences can serve as a means to wellbeing (Lambert et al., 2016; Schueller et al., 2014). So it is with this mindset that this book as an edited collection brings together a variety of international scholars who engage with their wellbeing across the areas of creativity, making, and movement. This is a way to feature a certain perspective and variety of approaches to enhance us. As a reader you may be inspired or find the visual narratives and narratives empowering or confronting, but most importantly you will be reflexive and as such consider what is possible with your own self-care.

Poetic representations

In the spirit of creatively expressing ourselves and exploring different ways of representing our lived experiences, I have responded to each of the authors' chapters in poetry rather than the traditional way of introducing chapters that often occurs in book collections. This is to honour the spirit of the book but also to engage in a way of writing and representation that "encourage[s] deep listening and dialogue . . . [and to promote] self-reflection and empathy building" (Hoyser, 2019, p. 37).

DOI: 10.4324/9781003207863-1

Sarah Wardle reminds us that before we approach the reading of a poem, we come with assumptions, and we need to "re-open the discussion" (Wardle, 2015, para 1). And it is with this perspective I invite you to engage with the poems I have created as one response to the authors of this book. It is a representation, a crafting of the authors' words and intentions in a way that represents a taster of what is to come. I don't reveal all, I merely touch on moments of tension, insights, and what I am calling pause-able moments that draw your attention to representations of creativity, making, movement, flow, and expression as forms of wellbeing and acts of self-care that empower.

> Poetry, I propose, has a value today both for individuals and society for the way it can help us to process dysfunctional responses and to emphasize and accentuate healthy responses, and for the way in which its positive humanism can enhance mindfulness and reinforce calm, non-aggressive rhetoric in our repertoire.
>
> (Wardle, 2015, para 69)

Poetry helps us voice messages. It highlights negative and positive. You are invited to engage both emotionally and cognitively with concepts (Januchowski-Hartley et al., 2018). Poetry helps us capture and explore experiences in ways that compel us to respond (Faulkner, 2019; Hoyser, 2019; Lemon, 2021). We are invited to be curious (Lemon, 2021). Engaging with poetry is positioned and embodied both in our sharing and in the responses to our lived experiences. Poetry can enhance us, change us, and touch our hearts (Faulkner, 2019; Leggo, 2018). It can leave us richer in a way that any form of creative expression can support us to process, shift, or become content with an idea (Faulkner, 2019; Hall et al., 2016). We are able to discuss "identity and communication in a more nuanced fashion" (Fidyk, 2016, p. 4), and we can reveal the physicality, emotionality, relationality, contextual influences of our lived experiences. Poetry can help us recover as much as it "is a site for dwelling, for holding up, for stopping" (Leggo, 2008, p. 167). It is transformational.

Poetic inquiry as one way of "offering new insights that may inform professional practice" (Rapport & Hartill, 2016, p. 213). In this chapter I respond through poetry to some of the tensions of being an academic in the academy, where the place of self-care requires a curious stance that supports ongoing reflection. We are required to be courageous. And the system is invited to also be courageous with how it needs to change its perspective and (lack of) action. The poems are thus artistic expressions and representations of each of the chapters in this collection. Each poem is constructed from the exact words, wording, or phrases. I take fragments of key moments that resonated with me as the editor and colleague while also tuning into the main throughline(s) of the chapter focus. As such I have aligned with Glesne's way of working with the creation of poetry and worked from predeterminate rules (Glesne, 2016). On this occasion my rules for poetry construction are: (1) the words must be the author's own, (2) the words or phrases can be taken from anywhere in the chapter, and (3) the words and phrases maintain the author(s) rhythm.

The poems are expressions. You can read them as creative interpretations that draw your attention to key moments of navigation of wellbeing and self-care in the academy. The bold and italics plus the layout of the words are my capturing and framing. In this way, poetic representation "is not simply an alternative way of presenting the same information; rather, it can help the researcher evoke different meaning from the data, work through a different set of issues, and help the audience receive that data differently" (Leavy, 2020, p. 64). Emotional meaning is rich for me. It maybe for you as well. And the poems are presented in non-linear ways, igniting performance, energy, passion, and (re)focus of our attention. The construction of each poem, and also collective bringing together in this edited collection, is "seen as critical moments to build bridges between experience and reframing that scaffold a journey of self-care for one and many to flourish physically, emotionally, mentally and spiritually" (Lemon, 2021, p. 173).

As I have written these poems to introduce the chapters, I too have had to reflect on my interpretations, subjectively while compassionately making sure I ethically (re)present each author and chapter with an accuracy that honours, values, and respects their lived experiences. In this way I have been clear about my intent and made sure I have proceeded "ethically to build in the safeguards, boundaries and protocols which are required" (Evans, 2016, pp. 47–48). I have processed, healed, reflected, and been inspired and confronted with each of the chapters. I hope you are as well. With this comes the caveat that poetic inquiry allows for a "crafting of richly textured pieces that can do justice to the matter in hand and/or to what participants have generously shared" (Rapport & Hartill, 2016, p. 213). We are led as readers "to a place of self-discovery and the ethical production of what is uniquely my [our/their] practice" (Porter, 2016, p. 260).

Poetry as a methodology and/or method enhances our teaching, research, and practice. It enhances us in the academy in how we see, experience, consider our wellbeing. It also offers leaders and those policymakers in our sector to (re)consider.

As you engage with this book, the authors' chapters, and my poems, I invite you to consider the following questions:

How is self-care an action of activism?
How is self-care a relational act?
How have we been empowered?
What do we need to do further do to value self-care as worthy of our attention?
Where is the system we work in?
How can we interrupt, extend, and be more visible as advocates of care and change?

In the next section of this chapter, I present each poem. They can be read independently, in different orders, or as collective bundles across the four sections of the book or, indeed, as a whole collection.

Section 1

Making and creating as a representation of self-care

In response to Megan McPherson's chapter:

Making, doing . . .
        Responding . . . thinking . . . doing
        doing*thinking*
          and thinking*doing*

artist, practitioner, knowledge maker.
Research-creation
Practices
  Process
    Product

Intersections
Unheard,
Unseen,
Unfelt,
Unnoticed,
Unappreciated.

Looping **care**, **care-fullness** and **self-care**
Movements of care
        wellness
        wellbeing
            holding together self
            wholeness
            whole – ness

                agency
                reflexivity
                      welcome, unwelcome

pause
        making
        remaking
        reframing
        rediscovering
        responding

In response to Janet Salmons' chapter:

                Right
                Left
       Whole brain journaling

              imagination
                curiosity
            observational
            meaning making

a time to practice being mindful
        writing by hand
           physical
             release
               expression
                  embodied

handwriting as movement creates the thought that it inscribes

              scribble
               sketch
          stress release
               process
               ponder
               outline
                plan
                notes

                ideas
                ideas
                ideas
            expression
     make a mark on the page

Narelle Lemon

In response to Melissa Silk's chapter:

making with mathematics
a transformative human experience
extending the interconnectedness of ideas investigated in my external world

thinking and making being as inextricably linked
powerful connections
arts and sciences

play
risk
embracing curiosity
fearlessness

fear
joy
fear *and* **joy**

self-discovery
transformation
It is within this collective math-making experience that I feel most wellbeing.

Section 2

Collaborative expression, embodiment, and the power of relationships

In response to Catherine E. Hoyser's chapter:

Exhaustion, burnout, increasing pressures
Values clash
Personal and professional conflict

    Tension
            Stress
   Alienation

              Shall I leave?
              Can I leave?
              Leave . . .

                    A fractured world
                      Interruption
                        Pause

Path to wellbeing
Writing
Poetry

    Collaborative community
    Like-minded colleagues
    Trying new creative activities

Expression . . . a creative outlet
Nurturing
Embrace my creativity and acknowledge its importance to my wellbeing

path of self-care
path to self-care
a continual process of balance, imbalance . . .

                          re-balance

**Catherine,
Calm,
Creativity,
Collaborative community.**

connect with your creativity.
challenge yourself to find flow and wellbeing. Step off the edge into creativity and community.

In response to Sandra L. Tarabochia, Kristy A. Brugar, and Julie Ann Ward's chapter:

"publish or perish"
Struggle,
Oppressive systems
Competition
Measured
Rush to publish
Quality verses quantity
Engagement verses citation counts and metrics

Interruption
Transformation
Movement
Running
Marathon
Nurturing personal and professional identities

running together as a deep,
        dynamic,
                resistant act of care.
                        Together
                        Supporting
                        Mentoring
                        Self-care
                        Other-care

        building a healthy, sustainable writing life
        humanise faculty development,
          attending to **holistic** wellbeing
    embodied activity of running with others.
promoting the authentic, relational work scholars need to navigate
                academic spaces.

        We are writers.
        We are runners.
Navigating academic expectations **and** prioritising wellbeing and self-care.

Forging space through running,
being **vulnerable**, cultivating relational **resilience**
rooted in **mutuality** and **connection**

                Pushing back
                surface a path to wellbeing that goes beyond
                the corporate slogans that identify self-care as
                an individual responsibility,
                we celebrate holistic, sustainable
                wellbeing.

In response to Sharon McDonough and Narelle Lemon's chapter:

Making
Knitting
Returning to our hands
An embodied practice
Takes us away from being in our head constantly
        after being absorbed
            in the cognitive work of academia.

the touch,
medium
mindful moments
interruptions

Knitting as a form of data visualisation
A response to our self-care and wellbeing needs
monitor our working practices
pandemic project

    working hours
    zoom hours
    pandemic working hours

        represented
        line
        stich
        pattern
        textile with embedded social meaning
        exploring patterns of work

Section 3

Creative practice as interruption

In response to Alison L. Black's chapter:

> finding channels of expression
> to make visible our "hidden injuries"
> stress and distress,
> the detrimental effects of excessive overwork,

Sharing	the fear
We speak	shame.
Inviting collaborative work	Offering
Contesting these conditions	vulnerable stories
Collective analysis	representations of
Reimaging universities	scholarly life are
Is this possible?	ways of ensuring
	history and
I lost my way	context are not
Duped by the "productivity imperative"	erased by a
where I thought I could "prove my value"	climate of
The trauma of career games	continuously
Not enough	raised
depletion,	expectations of
disillusionment,	achievement.
and emptiness	

> goal postings shifting
> I am so tired of this game!
> ***I have been trying to do academia differently***

Snap	a way of saying NO MORE
sNaP	as an opening,
snAp	a new way of proceeding
snaP	refusal,
Snap – as a	revolution,
feminist	seeing through the daze/haze of neoliberal
pedagogy of	production and surveillance.
slowing down,	To hear snap, one must thus slow
learning	down.
to hear	I have decided to resign in a way that
exhaustion,	feels doable and right for me, a
when it is all	necessary and **nourishing gesture**
too much.	**of refusal**.

12 *Narelle Lemon*

In response to Mark Selkrig's chapter:

the arts or image-making
    an inherent way for me to make meaning
        present ideas that are "hard-to-put-into-words"
        force myself and others
            to pay attention to things in new ways

I engage in aesthetic modes of interruption
    to make sense,
    I want to share some particular events
        where this meaning making occurred.

        I, attempted to explore,
            address and represent
                the challenges and concerns
                facing those who work in
                universities,
                to let voices and experiences
                be heard
                and provide opportunities to
                bring
                the emotional or affective
                aspects to the fore.

            advance ideas about de-centring the notion of wellbeing
                thinking in terms "of dynamic relationalities
                    instead practice well-be(com)ing

                        continually changing
                  created as a result of being practised
                      remain wide-awake
                        being curious,
                          often furious,
                            take risks.

In response to Nikki Brunker and Robyn Gibson's chapter:

A/r/tography

relational,
aesthetic inquiry,
a coming together of image and word.

Through engaging in *a/r/tographic* conversation,
we share our experience of self-care,
the pressures that increase the need for self-care,
those that potentially inhibit self-care,
our increased responsibility for self-care
        institutional pressure
        individual self-care;
        to care
        or not to
          care;
        the toxic
          and the
            healthy.

Section 4

Mind, body, and movement as acts of self-care

In response to Jani Katarina Taituha Wilson's chapter:

>rhythmical movements
>limbs and body
>sound
>shape
>flow

>Haka is a moment to restore,
>reclaim,
>celebrate one's cultural identity.

>Kapa haka,
>a time where we make room.
>in our skin for the wairua (spirit) of our mātua tīpuna (ancestors)
>to perform through our bodies.

>How do we make time to restore,
>reclaim,
>celebrate?

>intensity,
>unrelenting,
>tumultuousness,
>mis-managed,
>mis-guided . . .

>damaged pillars of my own depleted hauora (wellbeing),
>Mine is not an isolated case;
>there are many other Māori and Indigenous academics who are (mis)managed
>in such a way that our hauora is at severe risk.
>We must address this.

In response to Nadine Crane's chapter

Intentionally make space for wellbeing

> *disrupt* approaches to my work
> > *disconnect* from my work,
> > > then *reconnect with clarity and passion*

the click of my shoes
connecting into the pedals
> *push off down the road*
> > I know the next couple of hours
> > are mine to think,
> > to breathe,
> > to notice.
> >
> > *physical work*
> > *time to be in the moment*
> > *appreciate my surroundings*
> > *repetition soothes me*
> > > *allows my mind to clear*
> > > *I focus on the now*

> > > > > My self-care is centred around
> > > > > *mind,*
> > > > > *body* and
> > > > > *movement*
> > > > > through cycling.
> > > > > Continue to find balance
> > > > > in my work as an academic.
> > > > > By freeing my mind
> > > > > for the time it takes to ride,
> > > > > I feel more focused
> > > > > and refreshed
> > > > > when work is required.

16 *Narelle Lemon*

In response to Lynelle Watts's chapter:

Burnout
overwhelming exhaustion,
cynicism,
feelings of ineffectiveness associated with perceptions of a lack of accomplishment.

Burnout
affected my sense of the right
    good in myself,
             amongst people around me.

Burnout
profound loss of intellectual affect
    about my place within academia
    extended beyond work
    into
        every
            area
                of
                    my
                        life.

walking,
rebuilding connections with
others,
reading,
writing and   Self-tending practices
spirituality   **reseating**
                                      connections to
learning self-compassion   **myself,**
these practices contributed   **others and**
to my   **the wider world**
recovery,   through walking,

of compassion,   reading,
towards others too.   writing and learning
                                and spending time in
essential self-tending   natural spaces.
                practices   **These practices**
     foundational   **continue to form a**
to enacting an academic life   **route through which**
set in the **right proportion** **to balance my life**
to the **rest of my life**.   **and work.**

Final remark

This book is part of a series called *Wellbeing and Self-Care in Higher Education: Embracing Positive Solutions*. This fourth volume within the series focuses on individual practices and collective actions as acts of self-care and wellbeing. Creative expression through using your hands and making is a creative act embodied in flow, being in the moment, with connection to the heart seen as an important act for many who work in higher education. Likewise, using your body, whether it be through dance, meditative movement, cycling, running, or through more commonly considered acts of creativity such as writing, knitting, folding, drawing, writing, singing, or acting, for example, opportunity presents itself to slow down. With this slowing down comes a connection to the mind and body. This creating for those working in higher education can be an expression of self, a moment of bringing others together, or a way to communicate and explore a topic. It can be an act of identity formation. It can also be an act of activism. Or it can be an act just to stop, be, and rejuvenate. In this edited collection, authors share how individual and collective acts of creativity enhance, support, and embrace self-care and wellbeing.

This book aligns to the series rationale by illuminating other ways we can explore acts of self-care and wellbeing as educators, researchers, students, and staff in higher education.

Self-care is not something we do in emergencies, when we are already in the midst of burnout, stress, or feelings of total exhaustion. It is something we need to do every day. But for those who work in and across higher education, self-care is something that is not illuminated in the academy as something that is celebrated or of value. It is something that is an addition, a good thing to do if you can, but unlikely to be achieved. This way of thinking needs to change. It is not sustainable. And as a result of this type of thinking there is a problem in the system.

Self-care becomes an imperative both individually and systemically when working in higher education as an academic, leader, teacher, PhD student, research assistant, librarian, or support staff member. There is no doubt universities are stressful places, and as such, revealing narratives of coping, how wellbeing is approached, and self-care strategies are enacted is vital. In this fourth book as part of the collection I illuminate how those who work in higher education engage in constant reconstruction of their identities and work practices and place self-care at the centre of the work they do. In this book are positive acts of using one's mind and body through movement and expression that demonstrate individual and collective embodiment. Through image and word narratives that form visual narratives, a common factor present in all books of the series, highlighted are realities that position a shift in what is possible when we care for ourselves and others. Strategies, approaches, and philosophies are shared to support how self-care is understood and can be enacted and embodied.

References

Evans, K. (2016). A/R/T(Herapist)-ography: Examining the weave. In K. T. Galvin & M. Prendergast (Eds.), *Poetic inquiry II – seeing, caring, understanding* (pp. 41–50). Sense Publishers. https://doi.org/10.1007/978-94-6300-316-2_3

Faulkner, S. L. (2019). *Poetic inquiry: Craft, method and practice*. Routledge.

Fidyk, A. (2016). Seeing with an unconscious eye: The poetic in the work of Emily Carr. In K. Galvin & M. Prendergast (Eds.), *Poetic inquiry II – seeing, caring, understanding* (pp. 3–20). Sense Publishers. https://doi.org/10.1007/978-94-6300-316-2_1

Glesne, C. (2016). That rare feeling: Re-presenting research through poetic transcription. *Qualitative Inquiry*, 3(2), 202–221. https://doi.org/10.1177/107780049700300204

Hall, M., Hoyser, C., & Brault, A. (2016). Embodying performativity in story-to-poem conversion. *Ubiquity: The Journal of Literature, Literacy, and the Arts, Praxis Strand*, 3(2), 43–69. http://ed-ubiquity.gsu.edu/wordpress/hall-hoyser-and-brault-3-2/

Hoyser, C. (2019). Lectio Divina and story-to-poem conversion as tools for transformative education. In J. E. Dalton, M. P. Hall, & C. E. Hoyser (Eds.), *The whole person: Embodying teaching and learning through lectio and Visio Divina* (pp. 37–49). Rowman & Littlefield Publishers.

Januchowski-Hartley, S. R., Sopinka, N., Merkle, B. G., Lux, C., Zivian, A., Goff, P., & Oester, S. (2018). Poetry as a creative practice to enhance engagement and learning in conservation science. *BioScience*, 68(11), 905–911. https://doi.org/10.1093/biosci/biy105

Lambert, L., D'Cruz, A., Schlatter, M., & Barron, F. (2016). Using physical activity to tackle depression: The neglected positive psychology intervention. *Middle East Journal of Positive Psychology*, 2(1), 42–60. https://www.middleeastjournalofpositivepsychology.org/index.php/mejpp/article/view/46/39

Leavy, P. (2020). *Method meets art: Arts-based research practice* (3rd ed.). Guildford Press.

Leggo, C. (2008). Astonishing silence: Knowing in poetry. In J. G. Knowles & A. L. Cole (Eds.), *Handbook of the arts in qualitative research: Perspectives, methodologies, examples, and issues* (pp. 165–174). Sage Publications Inc. https://www.google.com.au/books/edition/Handbook_of_the_Arts_in_Qualitative_Rese/srUCmBP98dEC?hl=en&gbpv=1&dq=Poetry+(Leggo,+2008,+p.+167)&pg=PA165&printsec=frontcover

Leggo, C. (2018). Poetry in the academy. *Canadian Journal of Education*, 41(1), 69–97. https://www.jstor.org/stable/90019780

Lemon, N. (2021). Holding the space: A teacher educator's poetic representations of pre-service teachers acts of self-care. In M. P. Hall & A. K. Brault (Eds.), *Academia from the inside* (pp. 169–193). Palgrave Macmillan. https://doi.org/10.1007/978-3-030-83895-9_8

Porter, L. A. (2016). Unnamed moments, transformation and the doing and making of trauma therapy practices. In K. T. Galvin & M. Prendergast (Eds.), *Poetic inquiry II – seeing, caring, understanding* (pp. 255–272). Sense Publishers. https://doi.org/10.1007/978-94-6300-316-2_19

Rapport, F., & Hartill, G. (2016). Making the case for poetic inquiry in health services research. In K. T. Galvin & M. Prendergast (Eds.), *Poetic inquiry II – seeing, caring, understanding* (pp. 211–226). Sense Publishers. https://doi.org/10.1007/978-94-6300-316-2_16

Schueller, S. M., Kashdan, T. B., & Parks, A. C. (2014). Synthesizing positive psychological interventions: Suggestions for conducting and interpreting meta-analyses. *International Journal of Wellbeing*, 4(1), 91–98. https://doi.org/10.5502/IJW.V4I1.5

Wardle, S. (2015). The mindfulness of poetry. *The Journal of Creative Writing Research*, 1. https://www.nawe.co.uk/DB/wip-editions/articles/the-mindfulness-of-poetry.html

Section 1
Making and creating as a representation of self-care

2 The feeling of doing*thinking* and thinking*doing* of making processes

Megan McPherson

Academic practice as care-ful practice

Dot dot dot.
I dot the glue on the paper weft on my studio table.
Dot dot dot.
Another three lines of the mesh are laid down.
Dot dot dot.

This chapter is speculative thinking through artwork and theory, in particular affect theory as resonates in the in-between and a force that is one that is care-ful (Price & Hawkins, 2018b; Ingold, 2010). It is a different line of thought to add to Gregg and Seigworth's eight 'blurry' orientations of affect (2010) and maybe not so different but an example of one line on its way through and in the midst of affect. It is about the acts of feeling. It is about what I call 'doing-*thinking* and thinking*doing*'; the work that is done in the making and in the practice in research-creation. Just the term 'research-creation' places the work I do in the academy. 'Research-creation' is a term used in the Canadian Social Sciences and Humanities Research Council of Canada (SSHRC) to describe what we would call in Australia creative practice research or non-traditional research outcomes. Research-creation is both created in and problematised by being situated in the academy, where the "analytically communicative" (Loveless, 2019, p. 29) disciplines and traditions do the work of depreciating forms of discipline research from feminism and Indigenous scholarship that is considered care work or personal voice as "nonresearch" (Loveless, 2019). I like using the term 'research-creation,' as it places research first and locates the action of creation in the academy. For me, research is intimately linked with creation that Natalie Loveless argues is a commitment to 'a feminist university of creativity, experiment and . . . a mode of *eros* that is committed, cathected, and sustaining." (Loveless, 2019, p. 3).

> Tell the story of the work. People want the story.
> A professor once told me, just before my masters' artwork was examined, "Tell the story of the work. People want the story."

DOI: 10.4324/9781003207863-3

I always wondered what story I should tell. It will always be a "partial-story" (Richardson, 2006, p. 2).

Dot dot dot.

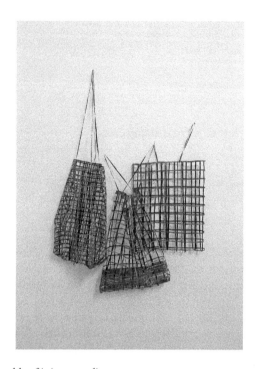

Image 2.1 The breadth of it is astounding

Relief printed etching on rice paper, pigment ink, glues 1.2 m × 1 m × 0.3 m (3 bags, installation variable) 2020

> *In my practice I attend to the emotional and cognitive affects of being in a place and space. In these bag works I work with the notion of unease, how it is carried with us, and how it is measured. I am considering how this affective heaviness permeates and measures what we do. Voluminous and weighty, the anxiety is the exact opposite of the paper bags made to carry it. Anxiety's breadth is astounding.*

I am an artist.

I introduce myself as an artist when I meet people, and this causes confusion. I work in the academy, now in an academic team of Indigenous and non-Indigenous artists-educators-researchers, but before that in research roles and even before that as an art lecturer teaching in printmaking. It's a long history of working in the academy. It is not necessarily comfortable. It has been precarious, but now with longer fixed-term contracts than the semester-long ones

I began with. Still unstable enough to not know if I'll be working like I am now this time next year. My research-creation practice is a care-ful countering and the repeated encounter of this unstableness.

In this chapter, I am setting down a narrative of practice. A practice in research-creation which is inherently situated in and with the academy. It is a practice of making and research which includes an embedded practice of self-care. This practice uses doing*thinking* and thinking*doing* in the ways the body and mind in movement responds to making practices as a form of engagement that encourages moments of flow and expression (McPherson & Lemon, 2018, 2022). It is a practice that is in constant movement through actions of translating and transforming practices (Bennett, 2010) that make research-creation discernible in the academy.

What we do as artist-researchers needs translating into wider tertiary academic cultures, just as the knowledge we produce in the creative practice discipline can be a struggle to translate. I am an artist who does research through my practice of making and teaching. Doing research informs both what I do and how I do it. My research does not fit easily either in a faculty of education or art but is informed by and does both. I realise I am already doing this academic thing a bit wonky. My practice's transdisciplinary-ness needs translating and transforming into something discernible in the academy in ways other research practices do not. This research practice brings with it a demand on the academy to respond and confirm that it is new knowledge. It needs to be recognised and accredited as a way of doing research inquiry (Irwin, 2013; Sullivan, 2010; Smith & Dean, 2009; Barrett & Bolt, 2010) not only by non-traditional outcomes – the artworks – we make but also by the texts we write to justify how the non-traditional outcomes fit as research. This research text is the translation of the new, the fit and the value of the research. It is something that other disciplines don't have to do.

Artist-researchers address issues of identity in the disciplines of creative art practice that are untold and unaddressed in terms of wider tertiary academic cultures. These issues of identity "as bearers of professional expertise" (Burnard, 2016, para. X) are increasingly important and relevant in the sector (Burnard, 2016; Shreeve, 2007). It is the identity of the maker, the artist-researcher, and the creation of unwieldy research. The identity work we do, "combined with the view of academics as agents of learning and change, contributes to the complex labyrinth of expectations and change demands for academia in the 21st century" (Burnard, 2016, para. 5). It is research that is doing*thinking* and thinking*doing* work.

There is movement already in the phrase – doing*thinking* and thinking*doing*. And it is in this movement that I think through when care-ful making, in conjunction with writing. In my PhD thesis (McPherson, 2018) I wanted to present my artwork in tandem in the written work; this practice was somewhat outside the practice of the faculty I was in. I added artwork in; it was artwork that had already been selected for juried exhibitions, included in national survey awards to show its currency as non-traditional research outcomes. It was artwork I made in response to the action of doing the research and the research with people in complex relations. The thesis artworks are meshwork nets and grid made for gathering ideas and measuring affects. Made from paper, in the meshwork the text may slip, stutter, and bump up and wear against other texts just as it was doing in my research. This focus infuses the act of looking, visibility, and recognition of academic practices of research. The possibilities and encounters of looking, visibility, and recognition aids us to think past the experience to contend with the more "vague, diffuse or unspecific, slippery, emotional, ephemeral, elusive or indistinct" (Law, 2004, p. 2) partial-ness, actions, and doings.

The artwork is not the data of the research but, rather, was made in relation to the experience of 'doing' research; the physical, the material and its materiality, the emergent analysis of thinking-feeling through and with the practice and theory. The artwork in the thesis is situated in the in-between of the research. In the practice of a/r/tography, the a/r/tographer, Rita Irwin (2013) asks, "what does this [art education] practice set in motion do?" (Irwin, 2013, p. 198) rather than what an art education practice means. In rephrasing this question, Irwin prompts an understanding of praxis – that is, an activation of both theorising and practicing in an exchange:

> Theorizing rather than theory, and practicing rather than practice, transforms the intention of theory and practice from stable abstract systems to spaces of exchange, reflexivity, and relationality found in a continuous state of movement.
>
> (Irwin, 2013, p. 199)

The visual language of art and making steps away from the canon of sociology and educational research through its actions. It makes actions visible in other ways. It makes the movement in the care-ful action and the encounter visible. The artwork is an iterative response to the actions, doing research, and becoming a researcher on my terms. I see the artwork as a doing*thinking* and thinking*doing*. Artworks do the work and embody a call for response and a mode of address (Ellsworth, 1997).

In Elizabeth Ellsworth's terms (2005), using artwork in this way is both a call for response and a mode of address. Ellsworth chooses the artful spaces in *Places of Learning* for their "qualities of the sensations of learning that they generated" and the "qualities of their pedagogical volition" that appear to her (Ellsworth, 2005, p. 7). In using images of the artwork in my thesis, I make a difference visible. They are a different emergent response that does not line up in the linear way a text can. bell hooks (1995) argues that making, selling, valuing, and writing about art is defined by race, class, and gender. The artwork is both knowledge making and contextualised by the personal, the institution, and cultural norms and values (Leavy, 2009). The artworks' action as I position them into texts is contributing to research and questions the ways we 'do' research in higher education with race, class, and gender. It is, as Carol Taylor argues, a way of attending to "the messy embodied practices, actions and doings rather than a focus on epistemological correspondence of constructivist approaches and post-structuralism" (Taylor, 2017, p. 3). I placed the artworks in the thesis as material-discursive enactments and not as data. They are much more that data awaiting findings. The artwork enacts as a reprise, an echo or multiple of doing and thinking. They are already doing the doing*thinking* and thinking*doing. They are the movement of making and the movement of thinking entwined.* The artworks here in this chapter are a way to consider how to "see[s] the future as radically open" (Taylor, 2017, p. 3) and who and what can contribute to the discussion.

In the next section I continue to add artworks to text. In doing so I reprise that call for an academy that is creative and generative, where research extends our knowledges in ways that can be elusive, a bit messy, and non-conclusive. In these spaces in the academy that afford the fraying of the edges, the centre, the whole, we get to unmake and remake care-fully anew in ways which can question we 'do' research.

Doing*thinking* and thinking*doing* with affect, space, and movement

Disciplinary understandings aside, art making is how we see the action in the generative movement. Art is, and is in action, as the production of knowledge. It is theory and practice which situates and locates its theoretical and philosophical paradigms (Barrett, 2010) through agentic movements and materialities. In art making, as in the production of knowledge, Barrett (2010) calls for revealing what new knowledge is generated that is uncovered in studio and post-studio enquiry that may have been overlooked in other disciplines. Furthermore, Hawkins and Price (2018) argue research making needs "research and writing methods that make space for explorations of embodied and often unconscious practices, and that are able to take account of the messy, unpredictable and agentive materialities of making" (Hawkins & Price, 2018, p. 20).

In the literature in artmaking and geography, affect, space, and movement are pivotal concepts on/with making in geography. A newer field of research examining how artmaking practices intersect with geography in studio practices (Bain, 2004, 2005; Hawkins & Price, 2018; Sjoholm, 2018) "requires a series of understandings that unmake and remake making, such that it evolves as a nimble and agile concept that refuses to settle out into accepted spaces and practices" (Hawkins & Price, 2018, p. 20). It is these intersections of making and geography and vis à vis that require care-ful unmaking and remaking. Moreover, Hawkins and Price argue that it requires methods and methodologies that afford us "to *grasp* matter and materiality" (Hawkins & Price, 2018, p. 21). This grasping may take place in different spaces to where written texts normally inhabit – artworks in galleries and public spaces, in private-practice workplaces, or in studio teaching and learning spaces. And mindfully and care-ful reckoning with, as this grasping will be in conversation and collaboration with the materials themselves and present the affordances of the expert-material/s, and the artist/maker/researcher and however many entities are involved in each of those categories.

In this chapter, I now turn to the series of artworks I have been making through the period of 2019–2021, what I call my "paper bags" to discuss materiality, affect, and making. I focus on the notion of expert-material/s and how this is developed through studio making practice, working with, responding to, and observing how materials work in space.

Image 2.2 Three bags full of that affect, while in anxious times

Relief printed etching on rice paper, pigment ink, glues 2 m × 1 m × .30 m (3 bags, installation variable) 2020

Working with, responding to, and observing how expert-material/s work

While the artwork, *Three bags full of that affect, while in anxious times* (2020) was on display at the Fremantle Art Centre (FAC) Print Award in 2021, I made an Instagram post inviting people to go visit and added some text provided for social media purposes by the art centre. I added a call to action:

> Go drop some deep thoughts into the bags. They won't mind. They've got a lot of mine.
>
> (McPherson, 2021)

A part of my research practice is working closely with materials over time. I use paper. It is directly influenced by its environment. You can see when the paper becomes damp from its atmosphere, its limpness tells tales of the seasonal, moist or dry, non-archival situations of uninsulated unregulated studio spaces. I posted this call to action and then reflected – they are leaky bags. Maybe the bags will mind? Maybe they are full already? What if people realise the bags are porous? I hoped the bags are keeping their form as they hang in the exhibition – keeping the forms of the breath and had not yet been deflated by humidity and environment conditions. I hoped that the material, the inked and printed paper, hadn't torn with air movement.

Dot dot dot.

To make the paper bag works, the paper is handprinted, dried, and saturated with pigment ink, dried, cut, glued with an archival glue into long thread-like strips, and dried. The bags are formed by making a grid-like meshwork on a table, glued with dot, dot, dot, another type of archival glue. Then the grid is cut again, formed and glued into the voluminous bag shapes with handles for hanging from the long pins.

Dot dot dot.

The paper can tear easily if my cutting knife blade is blunt; it can tear again in the etching press if the press pressure is not set right. And tear again when it is most fragile when it is saturated with ink. The gluing can go wrong, too much glue, and it sits on the surface. Too little glue and the grid falls apart. The grid can stick to the table, get caught on a corner, or tear with too much weight put on the point by the intersection with the bag's handles.

Dot dot dot.
Dot dot dot.
Dot dot dot.

What is left is the encounter and sensation of the work in the making. The making of the grids, where I sit putting dots of glue on to long strips of paper. The sensation of running the thread through my finger and thumb to straighten and flatten any creases and folds. The glue that gathers on the finger that presses the grid intersections together. Moving through the grid, over the surface, checking intersections, removing glue with a bamboo point. Doting glue on with the other end of the bamboo stick.

Dot dot dot.
Dot dot dot.
Dot dot dot.

All the while breathing. Moving. The movement in doing*thinking* and thinking*doing* in action, and in practice.

28 *Megan McPherson*

Image 2.3 Shallow breathing through fog, snap

Relief printed etching on rice paper, pigment ink, glues, pins 1.2 m × 1 m × 0.3 m (3 bags, installation variable) 2021

Movement in doing*thinking* and thinking*doing*

In 2019 as I started thinking and making the paper bags, I also started a new artistic ecosystems research project. The research project considers how artistic practices, career knowledges, and capacities are taught and learnt, formally and informally, in the academy, in Indigenous art centres, artist-run initiatives, over time, and throughout practice. It is a mix of scholarly and creative practice that questions how research is done and how knowledge, art-making knowledge, Indigenous Knowledges, queer knowledge, and feminist knowledge fits into the academy. The paper bags are my doing*thinking* and thinking*doing* through how to conduct the research into artistic ecosystems.

As 2020 began and the impact of COVID-19 was beginning to be felt throughout the Australian research sector, my thinking through how to carry the research through continued through the making of the paper bags. When my fieldwork/art residency was cancelled and the remote community partners were no longer available, being behind closed interstate borders, I questioned how to conduct the research as an art residency. With making artworks as a focus, and conversation-in-the-making studio a key methodological feature, all of the conversationists – artists, practice, action, materials, storytelling, and ecosystems – all had a force in this methodological approach.

Dot dot dot.
Dot dot dot.
Dot dot dot.

Then, when my art studio was no longer accessible (it has shared bathrooms) and was closed for four months during Melbourne's hard lockdown, I kept making parts of the paper bags on my kitchen table. I joked to myself and my anxiety that I could always use the paper bags to unsuccessfully regulate hyperventilation and balance my unbalanced breathing. Or not.

Dot dot dot.
Dot dot dot.
Dot dot dot.

To grasp at matter and materiality, in this section is a return to the embodied action and the matter of making. The material acts in ways unexpected, with agency and capacity, and accounting for wellbeing, ways of being and becoming, and of activism, answering back, responding forward, generating thinking and doing.

Being care-ful

> Care comes together with making in myriad ways, attuning us to practices of those we study and ourselves, engaging in complex questions of gender relations, fluid boundaries between home and work, between capital and creativity, between economic and leisure. Care also calls us towards an appreciation of how making cultivates ethical relations between human, and between humans and non-humans (living and non-living).
>
> (Price & Hawkins, 2018a, p. 238)

Where does care fit into this research-creation? Care generates boundaries; it points us to where practice becomes uncomfortable. Care is the mediator of practice; it is the jolt of reckoning when the materials fall apart in your hands, slides off the wall, or just no longer wants to stick together. Care is an instigator, problematising what we think we are doing, and in practice questioning how – how does this work? With care is how we respond to our expert-materials as they tear, adding support, letting it go, and remaking. Self-care then is a part of this practice in the ways where boundaries are established and maintained, where risk is encountered and meets and greets practice. Self-care is sometimes unwelcomed, sometimes disparaged, and sometimes unacknowledged. It is a force that affects the ecosystem of the academy in ways that might be unseen. Practice makes this self-care see-able.

Care is a force. Affect is a force. Affect is what we feel in our bodies and in our movements.

Affect is not necessarily forceful (Seigworth & Gregg, 2010), nor is it necessarily care-ful. Seigworth and Gregg describes affect as sometimes as the "subtlest of shuttling intensities: all the minuscule or molecular events of the unnoticed" (2010, p. 2). In the affect and care of making practices, subtle movements in the body respond to expert materials in conversation. Unspoken yet with action, the conversation continues through making. And once the making is over, this conversation still remains and continues through the encounter of others with the making. Furthermore, this conversation continues as the making makes its way through the research statement process. It continues through as it is considered as research or non-research in the academy. This recognition is bound in the encounter with the action and practice of making, with materials, and with praxis. It is in care-ful process that it then becomes a part of this encounter into the future.

Practicing strategies of wellbeing

In stating "practice makes this self-care see-able," I propose a call for making self-care see-able. This is risky. However, research-creation encourages risks in ways that extend what we think is research. It allows the messier presentation of fluidity; a less fixed notion of what research should look like. What research-creation in the academy wants is new knowledge. That in itself is a risk. Strategies inherent in research-creation practices should look to developing ways of managing the demands of the new and the balances of value to self, wellbeing, and looking towards the practice, what this practice generates. It is in the movements of practice that hold together sense of self, identity, and agency that engages practice in spaces that allow and afford reflexivity and relationality. In this movement there is space for exchange, encounter, risk, and experimentation which is both the practice and the research-creation.

Conclusion

Returning then to the academy and process of recognition of research-creation, the place where I started. Loveless calls for the "insertion of voices and practices that trouble the relays of knowledge/power that figure the disciplines impacted the any given research-creation practice" (Loveless, 2019, p. 28). How the academy generates research-creation is as much about itself as it is the practices entailed in research-creation. How the academy recognises research-creation is a part of the practice of research creation. It is one of those events of the unnoticed and the extra labour of writing research statements, of translating sometimes messier outcomes that do not fit so easily.

In the relay of the practice, that movement between research and creation, there are spaces and intersections where embodiment, practice, and matter and the intersections of ways of knowing, being, and doing come together in moments of care, care-fulness, and self-care. It is in these spaces that include voices and research practices as yet unheard, unseen, unfelt, that we can start to consider doing*thinking* and thinking*doing* as a looping, amplifying part of practice that is becoming in movement.

Acknowledgement of Country

Narrm (Melbourne) occupies the unceded Lands of the Wurundjeri and Boon Wurrung peoples of the Kulin Nations. I give thanks and pay my respects to the traditional custodians and Elders past and present of these Lands, Waters, and Skies. As a non-Indigenous settler, I undertake to uphold my responsibilities of being on Country.

References

Bain, A. L. (2004). Female artistic identity in place: The studio. *Social & Cultural Geography*, *5*(2), 171–193. https://doi.org/10.1080/14649360410001690204

Bain, A. L. (2005). Constructing an artistic identity. *Work, Employment and Society*, *19*(1), 25–46. https://doi.org/10.1177/0950017005051280

Barrett, E., & Bolt, B. (Eds.). (2010). *Practice as research: Approaches to creative arts enquiry* (Paperback ed.). I.B. Tauris.

Bennett, J. (2010). *Vibrant matter: A political ecology of things*. Duke University Press.

Burnard, P. (2016, September 26). *The imperative of creative teaching in relation to creative learning for artist-scholars working in higher education [website]*. https://nitro.edu.au/articles/edition-3/the-imperative-of-creative-teaching-in-relation-to-creative-learning

Ellsworth, E. (1997). *Teaching positions; Difference, pedagogy and the power of address*. Teachers College Press.

Ellsworth, E. (2005). *Places of learning: Media, architecture, pedagogy*. Routledge Falmer.

Hawkins, H., & Price, L. (2018). Towards the geographies of making: An introduction. In L. Price & H. Hawkins (Eds.), *Geographies of making, craft and creativity* (pp. 1–30). Routledge.

hooks, b. (1995). *Art on my mind: Visual politics*. The New Press.

Ingold, T. (2010). The textility of making. *Cambridge Journal of Economics*, *34*(1), 91–102. https://doi.org/10.1093/cje/bep042

Irwin, R. (2013). Becoming a/r/tography. *Studies in Art Education*, *54*(3), 198–215. http://www.jstor.org/stable/24467860

Law, J. (2004). *After method: Mess in social science research*. Routledge.

Leavy, P. (2009). *Method meets art: Arts-based research practice*. The Guilford Press.

Loveless, N. (2019). *How to make art at the end of the world: A manifesto for research-creation*. Duke University Press.

McPherson, M. [@meganjmcpherson]. (2021, June 6). If you're in Fremantle, my work is a finalist in the Fremantle art centre print award. *Instagram*. https://www.instagram.com/p/CPwoe4FDcGC

McPherson, M., & Lemon, N. (2018). It's about the fun stuff! Thinking about the writing process in different ways. In N. Lemon & S. McDonough (Eds.), *Mindfulness in the academy – practices and perspectives from scholars* (pp. 113–127). Springer.

McPherson, M., & Lemon, N. (2022). Table chats: Research relations and the impact on our wellbeing as academics. In N. Lemon (Ed.), *Healthy relationships in higher education: Promoting wellbeing across academia* (pp. 132–142). Routledge.

Price, L., & Hawkins, H. (2018a). Geographies of making: Matter, transformation and care. In L. Price & H. Hawkins (Eds.), *Geographies of making, craft and creativity* (pp. 231–240). Routledge.

Price, L., & Hawkins, H. (Eds.). (2018b). *Geographies of making, craft and creativity*. Routledge.

Richardson, L. (2006). Skirting a pleated text: De-disciplining an academic life. In S. Hesse-Biber & P. Leavy (Eds.), *Emergent methods in social research* (pp. 2–12). Sage.

Seigworth, G. J., & Gregg, M. (2010). An inventory of shimmers. In M. Gregg & G. Seigworth (Eds.), *The affect theory reader* (pp. 1–25). Duke University Press.

Shreeve, A. (2007). Learning development and study support – an embedded approach through communities of practice. *Art, Design & Communication in Higher Education*, 6(1), 11–25. https://doi.org/10.1386/adch.6.1.11_1

Sjoholm, J. (2018). Making bodies, making space and making memory in artistic practice. In L. Price & H. Hawkins (Eds.), *Geographies of making, craft and creativity* (pp. 31–43). Routledge.

Smith, H., & Dean, R. (2009). *Practice-led research, research-led practice in the creative arts*. Edinburgh University Press.

Sullivan, G. (2010). *Art practice as research: Inquiry in visual arts* (2nd ed.). Sage.

Taylor, C. A. (2017). Rethinking the empirical in higher education: Post-qualitative inquiry as a less comfortable social science. *International Journal of Research & Method in Education*, 40(3), 311–324. http://doi.org/10.1080/1743727X.2016.1256984

3 Journaling right and left

Janet Salmons

Journaling Can Be Practical or Creative, or Both

Image 3.1 Journaling right and left means using both practical and creative ways to make progress with your research and practice self-care.

DOI: 10.4324/9781003207863-4

Journaling invites us to exercise both sides of our brains. Betty Edwards, author of the book *Drawing on the Right Side of the Brain*, popularised the notion that "for a majority of individuals, information-processing based primarily on linear, sequential data is mainly located in the left hemisphere, while global, perceptual data is mainly processed in the right hemisphere" (Edwards, 1999, p. xxii). I echo Edwards's perspective: the precise location of these modes in the brain is less important than a recognition that as humans, we handle information in different ways. Researchers use analytical skills associated with the left brain and creative abilities associated with the right. This chapter charts my observations about ways journaling allows researchers to integrate these modes of processing and generating information so we can use all our strengths and build new ones.

What Is a Research Journal?

Qualitative and quantitative researchers use different kinds of record-keeping to track their process and progress. "Journaling right and left" extends the typically functional style. It is rooted in the idea that journaling has beneficial potential for the researcher as well as for their inquiries. As Bacon (2014) notes, the research journal is "a flexible instrument of personal and scholarly insights. Journaling informs the mapping of self and research" (Bacon, 2014, p. 1). Qualitative researchers are familiar with the view that the self cannot be fully separated from the roles we take and recognise that we are instruments (Pezalla et al., 2012). However, *all* researchers are deeply engaged with and impacted by experiences associated with the conduct of scholarly studies. In a quantitative example from computational biology, Schnell advocates an expanded view of laboratory notebooks in which researchers organise ideas while keeping track of what they gain from other sources (Schnell, 2015).

Research journals are not limited to written expressions, as Brown observes:

> Research entries may be reflections written in prose, but if we are looking to other disciplines and contexts, the process of journaling does not necessarily entail words at all.
>
> (Brown, 2021)

With the increasing use of visual (Pink, 2021), arts-based (Leavy, 2020), and creative methods (Kara, 2020), researchers need to include sketches, paintings, photographs, or collages in their journals. Shields explains her experience with visual research journaling:

> I found myself using the visual journal to make sense of ideas and concepts. . . . This is the movement of research, both making sense of and making visible; however, in traditional research we are often first making sense of and then through our writing making our understanding visible. As an arts-based practice for researchers to engage in, I believe the power of the

visual journal is the opportunity to engage in practice that works through both of these processes together.

(p. 181)

Shields points to the journal as occupying spaces between *doing* research, writing it up, and publishing it. They draw on this observation by Irwin to argue that the visual research journal is "an active space for knowledge creation, and particularly, an active space for unfolding aesthetic sensibilities" (Irwin, 2003, p. 64). Clearly a journal can provide space for both self- and scientific awareness. While research journals are as unique as the researchers who keep them, for the purpose of this chapter we will define the term as:

> A collection of written and/or visual entries created to document, understand, and/or to further the research process and wellbeing of the researcher.

Right-and-Left Journaling Forms

Left-brain journaling allows us to stay organised and to manage the myriad details associated with projects that involve multiple stages over a period of time. We can create records of key experiences, notes, plans, and memos that help us feel confident about moving forward. Right-brain journaling allows us to record perceptions of ourselves in our roles as researchers, portray environments, and express thoughts and feelings. We can view problems from new angles or just step away for a creative break that heals the stress associated with difficult research or common tensions of academic life. In other words, journaling allows us to think more deeply about research specifics or to not think at all, just be present in the moment. In this chapter we will explore three of the many possible reasons to journal: for self-care and creative expression, for reflective and reflexive purposes, or to plan and manage research or projects.

DIY Art Therapy: Journaling and Mindful Self-Care

Research and academic work are stressful occupations. Budget cuts, dropping enrollments, and even natural disasters can drastically increase the levels of volatility and uncertainty within an institution and, subsequently, our own work contexts (Sam & Gupton, 2021, p. 80). Many academic positions are highly competitive, with expectations for productivity and service. The publishing process brings its own stressors with deadlines, ongoing reviews, and revisions.

Researchers frequently work in difficult settings or with people who are experiencing painful, sad, conflict-ridden, traumatic situations. Action researchers might be able to offer participants ways to make a difference, but for many of us, findings reveal root causes and point to solutions, but we typically miss the gratification that comes from seeing transformative changes implemented.

36 *Janet Salmons*

Meanwhile, life goes on, with families and children and dishes and laundry. The world outside is full of conflicts and challenges. We hear the clock ticking in our ears for the next deadline to be met. We sense that we could be more ingenious, if only we could catch our breath. Institutions and their leaders can take steps to make the academic workplace more supportive of positive work–life balance. However, on a personal level, we must do what we can to can take care of ourselves. If we don't, we are the ones who suffer. As illustrated in Image 3.2, journaling can be a way to create some revitalising space.

Image 3.2 When I use my planning journal to capture and close the proverbial book on work demands, I enjoy my creative space for art. I am so engrossed the cares of the world are set aside.

For me, right- and left-brain journaling fills the need for staying on track and organised while prioritising self-care. Years ago, I attended a professional workshop that advised a strategy I adopted: when you end work for the day, jot down any unfinished business and to-do items for the next day. That way, you can close without a nagging sense that you have missed something important. I use my planner journal for that purpose. On the other side, creative journaling allows me the space to focus on colour and form, to be aware and creative. I am not trying to sell my artwork; my journal is just for me, so I am not worried about perfection. I return to my work life refreshed. Let's explore how and why journaling is beneficial for busy academics and researchers.

Why Use Journaling for Reflection and Reflexivity?

Consistent definitions often elude academic writers, so let's begin by defining the terms *reflection* and *reflexivity*. It is not unusual to see the terms conflated, as in this discussion from *The SAGE Encyclopedia of Social Science Research Methods*:

> The most fundamental and straightforward [understanding of reflexivity] is that research is a complex and difficult activity that cannot be reduced to following a set of preestablished rules. Rather, deciding how best to do it requires continual reflection on what has been done, how successful it has been, and how best to pursue it further. . . . It is argued that researchers are always part of the social world they study; they can never step above it in order to gain an Olympian perspective or move outside it to get a "view from nowhere." It is taken to follow from this that they should continually reflect on their own role in the research process and on the wider context in which it occurs.
>
> (Hammersley, 2004, p. 934)

From this definition, we could understand *reflection* as an activity one carries out in order to be a *reflexive* researcher. For our purposes, the terms have distinctive meanings. *Reflection* occurs when we document our observations, thoughts, or ideas. We think through key characteristics and try to accurately explain significant elements. *Reflexivity*, then, is the next step we take when we scrutinise and question. By these definitions, reflection could answer the question, "what is?" and reflexivity could answer the more critical questions, "why?" "what if?" "how could it be different?" For example:

> The ethnographer's diary or field notes not only provide an account of events but support the development of their wisdom about those events through engaging reflexively with the various data.
>
> (Atkinson et al., 2010, p. 462)

Using our definitions, we could say that the "account of events" is reflective, and the "development of wisdom, developing understanding" is reflexive.

For researchers working with new methods or settings, reflexive journaling can generate insights into how they will shape interactions with participants

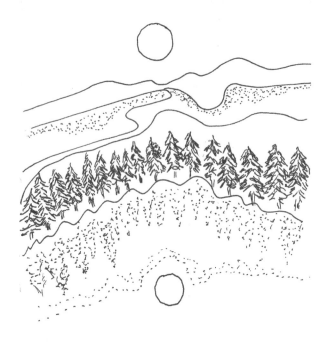

Image 3.3 Sometimes, my art journaling involves reflection, when I try to represent the beauty of the natural world around me. I use observational skills to note colours, shapes, and the quality of the light. Other times, I reflexively write in an effort to make sense of thorny social issues in current projects.

and deal with challenging situations (Meyer & Willis, 2018). Journaling offers a space to think through options and brainstorm strategies. The process of journaling can unwrap "a heightened awareness of both differences and similarities between the researcher and participant" (Oliphant & Bennett, 2020, p. 600). Journaling reflexively is particularly important when we are an outsider or "a stranger to the culture" (Berger, 2015, p. 228). We may be unable to recognise or interpret clues that would be easily discerned by an insider (Oliphant & Bennett, 2020, p. 602). Reflexive journaling can help us rethink the way we position ourselves and the way our positions and actions reflect dominant discourses and practices when studying situations of economic, gender, and political inequalities (Gilbert & Sliep, 2009, p. 468).

To use an artistic analogy, reflection is like representational art that, whether realistic or impressionistic, presents an image recognisable as a flower or tree. Reflexivity is like non-representational art, abstract art, in which concepts or emotions are described in colours and shapes. The artist must think differently when trying to show what is versus trying to distill *what is* into a new representation. One is not better than the other; together, the processes associated with reflective and reflexive journaling can help us document and interpret our research experiences.

Journaling = A Time to Practice Being Mindful

Whether we are mapping out the next stage of a project, sketching features of a research setting, or taking a half hour to paint the rose that just bloomed, journaling invites us to mindful awareness. The term *mindful* originated in the Buddhist concept of sati and is being redefined for Western understanding. In the process, the term is increasingly used in a secularised way, with meanings that diverge from the original basis in meditation (Arat, 2017). Arat says, "mindfulness is simply defined as the quality or state of being conscious or aware of something. . . . Mindfulness does not merely designate a proxy for self-awareness or self-focused attention per se, but rather a unique form of consciousness in and of itself" (p. 173). Prominent theorists trying to define the term draw a clear link between mindfulness and creativity:

> Langer (2005) argued that mindfulness and creativity are natural partners, because the key feature of mindfulness – the openness to new ideas – invokes the types of cognitive processes that are essential for creativity (e.g., curiosity, insight, analogical reasoning, remote associations, ideational productivity, divergent and convergent thinking, flexibility, critical thinking).
>
> (Hart et al., 2013)

The four components of mindfulness identified by Langer align well with the practice of journaling (Langer, 2004):

- **Engagement:** being aware of changes that take place in the environment;
- **Seeking novelty:** having an open and curious orientation to one's environment;
- **Novelty producing:** the capacity to construct new meanings or experiences; and
- **Flexibility:** the tendency to view experiences from multiple perspectives and to adjust one's behaviour accordingly.

While Langer chose the term *novelty*, which could seem to describe something superficial or frivolous, here we will hold to the Oxford Dictionary definition: "the quality of being new, different and interesting" (Soanes & Stevenson, 2004). To see something new and interesting, even in familiar places and faces, we need to approach each situation with a fresh perspective. To the best of our ability, we should try to set aside preconceived notions and avoid pre-judgements.

40 *Janet Salmons*

Image 3.4 It is funny how journaling can sometimes blur what is outside and what is on the page. The journal takes on its own reality.

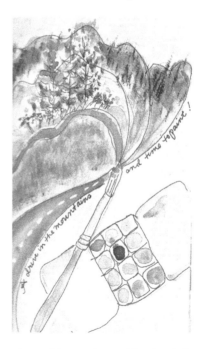

Image 3.5 When I look at the world around me with paints in hand, I note details I might not otherwise see.

Journaling can bridge inner and outer awareness, as illustrated in Image 3.4. When we journal, we are deeply aware of the environment and engaged with our responses to it. We build and use our research skills as curious, open-minded observers. We might choose our workplace or research setting for the journaling activity or find a place where we can relax. Weather and circumstances permitting, I prefer to journal outdoors, or at least away from my work desk. A walk or a drive, a change of scenery, a little art time, and I am ready to tackle whatever languishing project when I return. (See Image 3.5.)

Using written or creative expressions, we practice mindfulness when we sharpen our awareness and construct our own interpretations of the world and our place in it. Sometimes, we want to reflect on what we are seeing by recording what we see or think. Other times, we reflexively dig below the surface, ask hard questions, and look for new meanings. These processes may unfold over time in the pages of our journals.

Types of Journals

What Is Your Focus?

There is no right or wrong way to journal, and you are not limited to one. You might decide to use different types for your right- or left-brain, reflective, reflexive journaling activities. You will also want to think about what fits given the scope and focus of your content. I categorise four levels not as rigid parameters but as starting points:

- ***Intimate:*** Do you want to use your journal to record personal thoughts and feelings? For example, you are involved with stressful projects or sensitive research and need space to decompress. Intimate journals offer a getaway, pages for art, affirmations, and poems that inspire you.
- ***Immediate:*** Do you want to use your journal to record aspects of your surroundings and everyday life and work, your home, workplace, or research setting? For example, you want to record your own process for research, or outside of your academic life, you want to keep track of your garden, a quilt project, or your baby's first year.
- ***Local:*** Do you want to use your journal to record details of the community, including cultural or natural environments? For example, you want to document observations related to the context for the problems or phenomena you are studying.
- ***Big picture:*** Do you want to use your journal to record ideas, thoughts, or plans at the societal or global level? For example, you want to make note of future directions or implications of your study or wrestle with questions about social justice issues.

With these thoughts in mind, there are many ways to fill your journal:

- ***Planner*** journaling refers to practical techniques for keeping track of schedules, ideas for new projects, steps, and to-do lists.

- ***Memoir*** refers to diaries or travel or event journals. Such journals can be ongoing, or chart responses to a particular time frame, journey, or project. You might think of a *memoir* as an autobiographical form, but you can also use this type to think through and document your experiences with a specific study, site, or population.
- ***Nature*** journaling involves written, photographed, or drawn observations of settings and the natural world. Researchers in environmental or biological sciences might use nature journaling to draw or write about plants, animals, or habitats. Social researchers might want to look at natural features too, as related to health or risk. Alternatively, you might look to nature for your own reset button, immersing yourself in a beautiful place so you can shift your mind away from pressures that are weighing you down.
- ***Art*** journaling encompasses creative expressions through drawing, painting, or collage. There are two broad reasons for using art journaling. The first is art-to-journal, and the second is journal-to-art.
    - *Art-to-journal:* This type involves visual storytelling. Drawing and painting are not merely a means to an end, they are valuable in and of themselves. Allen suggests that:

    Making images is a way of breaking boundaries, loosening outworn ideas, and making way for the new images are not all please beautiful; often they are raw and mysterious. . . . Art making is a way to explore our imagination and begin to allow it to be more flexible, to learn how to see more options.

    (Allen, 1995, pp. x, 4)

    Think of art making as development of the soft skills of research: imagination, flexibility, and openness to the unknown.
    - *Journal-to-art:* This type is used by artists to create visual records of work in progress including sketches, studies, tests, and colour swatches. Entries are not considered the complete or finished piece of art. You might use your journal in this way when planning presentations, research posters, or materials to use in creative methods research projects.

Fortunately, you do not have to choose one! Try a variety of approaches and see what fits with your projects and your current circumstances.

Do You Want to Go Digital?

An electronic journal, using an app or program, can work on your mobile devices and computers. It can be a self-contained, centralised space where your calendar, gleanings from web pages or social media, examples, or articles can co-exist with your own entries, artwork, photographs, notes, and memos. There are many advantages of electronic journals. Researchers can easily become overwhelmed with the many details associated with a research project. A journal as personal/research hub can help. You can create an index of sorts to keep track of literature, data, and art files. The ability to sync means you can access it anywhere. You can easily pull relevant ideas to incorporate into other writings or to upload materials into your data analysis software. The main disadvantage is that it is yet another computer- or device-based project, another effort that requires us to look at a screen.

Choosing an Electronic Journal

Some diary or journal applications are free, while others require a subscription. Characteristics of and options for an electronic journal include:

- **Simple entry:** Is it easy to set up and use? If adding a journal entry takes time and effort, you probably won't keep up a regular practice with it.
- **Varied entries:** Can you enter images, drawings or photos, audio, or video, as well as writing? Can you use voice-to-text or capture online pages or posts?
- **Shared or private options:** Will you share journal entries with collaborative partners, co-researchers, students, or followers or keep it private?
- **Visually-appealing layout:** Does it offer an attractive, pleasant experience for journaling?
- **Sync across computers and devices:** Can you keep your journal up to date regardless of the device you use? You might want the ability to capture thoughts or images on the go, then spend more time when you have a keyboard for more substantive writing.
- **Daily reminders or prompts:** Are there options for reminders, either built in or customised by you, to help you stay engaged?
- **Organisational features:** Does it offer checklists, templates, or other ways to manage your entries?

My Experience

I use online calendars for the scheduling part of my journal activities. I make notes in the description area, primarily as reminders associated with a task or event. I create "albums" of photos and scanned journal pages or artwork to share what I am doing. However, I do not make substantive entries in any of these programs. For original entries, I prefer old-school analog journaling.

Do You Want to Go Analog?

If you desire time away from a screen, a paper journal might be best. A paper journal can help if you are in the habit of making notes on bits of paper that get lost in the shuffle. A paper journal lends itself to the creative side but can serve practical purposes as well. We may expect ubiquitous access, but there are still many places where cell phone service and Internet are limited. If you are in such a location or will be conducting field work as a part of your research, having a paper journal will be essential.

You have many possibilities and considerations. One involves thinking through the balance of written and visual content. Will your journal be primarily used for written entries, with some drawings or illustrations? Alternatively, will it be primarily visual, a place for sketches, drawings, paintings, photographs, and/or maps? (See Image 3.6.) Or do you want an eclectic mélange for all kinds of entries?

Image 3.6 There is no right or wrong mix of words and images. I use both, sometimes incorporating words into visual diagrams or adding illustrations or doodles to pages of text.

Choosing a Paper Journal

Once you know how you want to use your journal, you are ready to purchase the right one that fits your purpose. (Of course, you may decide you need more than one!) Characteristics include:

- **Paper that fits your entries:** If you are planning entries based on writing, you might want lined paper. If you want to mix writing and drawing, you might want dot or graph paper. If you want to use your journal primarily for drawing and painting, you will want blank pages.

- **Suitable paper weight:** Many journals come with paper intended for written entries, and some are adequate only for pencils, ballpoint, or roller-ball pens. If you want to do more than that, you will need to take care in selecting the proper paper. Fountain pens do not work well on coated or shiny paper or paper that feathers and bleeds. Choose a journal that is fountain pen friendly, and if labelling is not clear, look up the brand or ask a knowledgeable shopkeeper.

    When you are using your journal for artistic purposes, the weight of the paper becomes an important consideration. If you want to mix written entries with sketches in pen and ink, pastels, graphite, or coloured-pencil drawings, a journal labelled as "sketch paper" will work. Sketch paper can range from 50–80 lbs, (approximately 75–90 gsm). If you want to add light washes and/or collage, then select paper labelled "mixed media." Mixed-media paper can range between 90–110 lbs. (approximately 180–260 gsm). However, if you want to do more water media, you will find that pages will wrinkle and buckle, and the journal will not li flat. If you want to include watercolour as part of your journaling practice, then you need to select watercolour paper, which is usually at least 130 or 140 lbs. (approximately 300 gsm).

Image 3.7 I appreciate my tech tools, but I love my art supplies!

- **Binding that fits your style:** Do you want to keep a journal with entries in chronological order? A spiral or hardbound journal allows you to keep all of the pages together so you can see how entries evolve over a period of time. In addition to chronological entries, you can use a bound journal for a more specific topic or theme. For example, you might want a journal dedicated to your entries from fieldwork on location. If you want the ability to add or rearrange pages or add different kinds of paper – lined paper for writing, and art paper for drawing and painting – select a loose-leaf type of journal.

Choosing Your Tools

You might find that you develop a fondness for your art journaling supplies. The tactile feel of the pen or brush in hand and the colours of the paints are appealing in ways quite different from a computer keyboard. How will you make entries in your journal? Most journalers use a mix of methods and tools. Here are some options:

- **Writing.** If you are planning to write in your journal, you can use the humble pencil, your everyday ballpoint or roller-ball pen, a marker or art pen, or a fountain pen. What writing utensil is comfortable for you? Note that you can also paste printed pieces of writing into your journal. You could add verbiage from a brochure, a poem, some necessary information you have printed out, or other source material it would be too labour-intensive to handwrite.
- **Drawing and Painting.**
    - *Graphite pencils.* Graphite pencils are described as various grades or degrees according to the softness or hardness of the material. Different grades produce darker or lighter marks. The typical #2 pencil is an HB according to this scale and is a tried-and-true pencil for writing. If you want to sketch, keep in mind that hard pencils create a light line, while softer pencils create a darker line. A medium-range pencil will be best for writing, while having a collection of different grades will allow you to create variations and subtleties in your drawings.
    - *Coloured pencils.* Coloured pencils are a great choice for journaling, whether you are creating artwork or simply want to add highlights. Coloured pencils also come in harder or softer shades and offer variation in transparency versus opacity. You will need to look at the packaging or do some research before you shop.

        You certainly don't need expensive pencils, but the difference between student and artist grade is significant. If possible, avoid purchasing inexpensive pencils intended for children, because the pigments are less intense, and you will have fewer options for shading and blending colours.

Journaling right and left 47

- **Watercolour pencils.** Watercolour pencils work like standard coloured pencils, with an added twist. With the addition of water, they act more like watercolour paint, allowing you to blend and mix colours. You can also find water-soluble graphite pencils that give you shades of brown and grey.
- **Watercolour paints.** Watercolour paints can be used for fine art or for adding artwork to your journal. Watercolour paints are sold in tubes or palettes. Artists enjoy the flexibility and cost-effectiveness of watercolour tubes, but as a beginner, find a small ready-made set of basic colours. Again, while you don't need the most expensive professional paints, avoid the most basic student grade.
- **Brushes.** If you are using watercolour paints or watercolour pencils, you will need a brush. As with any art supply, you can find a wide range of prices and qualities. A waterbrush is an option for mobile journaling. As the name suggests, the plastic brush has a water reservoir so you can add water to your page.

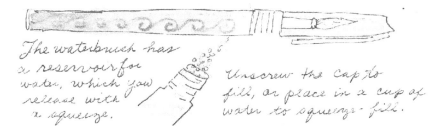

Image 3.8 A waterbrush is great for on-the-go journaling and works well with paints or water-soluble pencils.

- **Photographs and collage means paste.** You might want to add artifacts or photographs to your journal, so a simple glue stick is useful and portable.

One question when trying to choose journaling tools: where do you plan to journal? Do you plan to journal on the go, or in your home or office? If you plan to be a mobile journaler, create a compact toolkit, perhaps a pen, small set of coloured pencils or watercolour pencils, and a waterbrush. If you always journal in the same place, have as many supplies as you like!

My Experience

I have an eclectic, all-of-the-above approach. I dedicate journals for specific purposes, such as a travel journal, a book or research project journal, or a seasonal

48 *Janet Salmons*

nature journal. I use hardbound or spiral-bound watercolour and mixed media journals. I also use a customisable style of notebook that allows me to add printouts, lined paper, handwritten pages, sketch, or watercolour paper. My journals include mostly *immediate* and *local* types of entries. I teach journaling and share my journals as examples, so I include fewer *intimate* entries. I primarily create entries with watercolour and fountain pens, so I choose mixed-media or watercolour paper. My main practice is mostly art-to-journal, that is, the journal itself is the "product."

Why Do I Pick Up a Pen, a Paintbrush, and a Paper Journal?

Image 3.9 Keyboards and fountain pens co-exist on my desk.

I am a digital person, engaging with work, family, and friends online. I have a desktop computer with a fancy 32-inch monitor, a laptop, a tablet, and a smartphone. Why do I pick up a pen and a paintbrush to use with a paper journal?

I use a daily planner for the organisational side and unlined journals for the creative side of self-care and artwork. There is a physicality to writing by hand that connects with different parts of the brain than does typing; a pen seems to release the right-brain's creativity. "The hand and its method of thinking draw words into the body. Handwriting as movement creates the thought that it inscribes. . . . It sources the power of an ancient spatial-temporal evolution that the body experiences as movement, which is central to the way we are as human beings" (Saner, 2014, p. 118). As Philip Hensher observed in *The Missing Link: The Lost Art of Handwriting*, "handwriting is what registers our individuality . . . it involves us in a relationship with the written word which is sensuous, immediate and individual" (Hensher, 2012, p. 17). I value the ability to bring that kind of personality and power to my writing.

I typically use a hybrid approach, with a screen in front of me and paper journals at hand. If I am feeling intimidated by the awesome where-to-start moment or a new blank document, I might look away from the monitor and pick up a pen. I might scribble to tone down the stress or sketch ideas into a diagram, make a simple mind map, or outline next steps, then turn back to the screen to move forward. Some pen noodlings will become usable figures when transferred into a graphics program. Often, I open a journal to jot down an idea without turning on the computer with its rabbit-hole temptations.

Image 3.10 In the midst of a busy project, the handwritten memos to self keep me centred and on track.

As with many things in life, what one person considers a pleasure another considers an annoyance. Fountain pen lovers find the caretaking involved to be small rituals that serve as a pause for reassessing what direction to take when my fingers hit the keyboard. Apparently, I am not alone in my enjoyment of pen on paper as a complement to technology. David Sax described his surprise at seeing Silicon Valley technology professionals with Moleskin journals rather than computer notebooks:

> A paper notebook is a walled garden, free from detours (except doodling), and requiring no learning curve. . . . Moves back toward analog methods and tools seek, in a way, to undo many of the most heralded productivity advances of the digital era, which have morphed into vast time sucks. The same individuals and companies who once touted multi-tasking and 'round-the-clock connectivity are now actively searching for solutions that return work methods to a scale better adapted to human needs and traits.
>
> (Sax, 2015)

To adopt human-scale work methods and practice self-care, I do art and nature journaling.

Getting Started

"I can't draw."

"I have writer's block when I look at a blank page."

These and numerous other excuses can keep you from starting a journal. It takes courage to try something new. I bought journals and supplies and looked at them on my shelf for months before taking coloured pencils in hand and allowing myself the time and space to use them.

We started with this definition:

> A collection of written and/or visual entries created to document, understand, and/or to further the research process and wellbeing of the researcher.

Now, think about the basis for your collection, the kinds of entries you want to include, and the ways you want to improve your wellbeing as a person and a researcher. Do you want to focus on the left-brain side in order to create a consistent system for keeping track of notes? Do you want to focus on the right-brain side so you can build a space where you can retreat from the everyday details and just play with colours? Or will you weave varied kinds of journaling together in your own signature style? Find the approach that works for you. Make a mark on the page. Now you have begun your journal.

References

Allen, P. B. (1995). *Art is a way of knowing*. Shambala Press.

Arat, A. (2017). "What it means to be truly human": The postsecular hack of mindfulness. *Social Compass, 64*(2), 167–179. https://doi.org/10.1177/0037768617697390

Atkinson, P., Coffey, A., & Delamont, S. (2010). Ethnography: Post, past, and present. In Atkinson, P. & Delamont, S. (Eds.), *Sage qualitative research methods* (pp. 461–471). Sage Publications, Inc. https://dx.doi.org/10.4135/9780857028211

Bacon, E. (2014). Journaling-a path to exegesis in creative research. *Text Journal, 18*(2).

Berger, R. (2015). Now I see it, now I don't: Researcher's position and reflexivity in qualitative research. *Qualitative Research, 15*(2), 219–234. https://doi.org/10.1177/1468794112468475

Brown, N. (2021). *Making the most of your research journal*. Policy Press.

Edwards, B. (1999). *The new drawing on the right side of the brain*. Penguin Putnam.

Gilbert, A., & Sliep, Y. (2009). Reflexivity in the practice of social action: From self-to inter-relational reflexivity. *South African Journal of Psychology, 39*(4), 468–479. https://doi.org/10.1177/008124630903900408

Hammersley, M. (2004). *The Sage encyclopedia of social science research methods*. Sage Publications, Inc. https://doi.org/10.4135/9781412950589

Hart, R., Ivtzan, I., & Hart, D. (2013). Mind the gap in mindfulness research: A comparative account of the leading schools of thought. *Review of General Psychology, 17*(4), 453–466. https://doi.org/10.1037/a0035212

Hensher, P. (2012). *The missing ink: The lost art of handwriting* Farrar, Straus and Giroux.

Irwin, R. (2003). Toward an aesthetic of unfolding in/sights through curriculum. *Journal of the Canadian Association for Curriculum Studies, 1*(2), 63–78.

Kara, H. (2020). *Creative research methods in the social sciences: A practical guide* (2nd ed.). Policy Press.

Langer, E. J. (2004). *Langer mindfulness scale user guide and technical manual*. IDS Publishing.

Langer, E. J. (2005). *On becoming an artist: Reinventing yourself through mindful creativity*. Ballantine Books.

Leavy, P. (2020). *Method meets art: Arts-based research practice* (3rd ed.). Guilford Press.

Meyer, K., & Willis, R. (2018). Looking back to move forward: The value of reflexive journaling for novice researchers. *Journal of Gerontological Social Work, 62*(5), 578–585. https://doi.org/10.1080/01634372.2018.1559906

Oliphant, S. M., & Bennett, C. S. (2020). Using reflexivity journaling to lessen the emic – etic divide in a qualitative study of Ethiopian immigrant women [Article]. *Qualitative Social Work, 19*(4), 599–611. https://doi.org/10.1177/1473325019836723

Pezalla, A. E., Pettigrew, J., & Miller-Day, M. (2012). Researching the researcher-as-instrument: An exercise in interviewer self-reflexivity. *Qualitative Research, 12*(2), 165–185. https://doi.org/10.1177/1468794111422107

Pink, S. (2021). *Doing visual ethnography* (4th ed.). Sage Publications.

Sam, C. H., & Gupton, J. T. (2021). Ethical mindfulness: Why we need a framework for ethical practice in the academy [Article]. *Journal of the Professoriate, 12*(1), 80–103. http://search.ebscohost.com/login.aspx?direct=true&db=a2h&AN=150268236&site=ehost-live

Saner, B. (2014). Handwriting is xphysicalx visual thinking. *Visual Arts Research, 40*(1), 118–120. https://doi.org/10.5406/visuartsrese.40.1.0118

Sax, D. (2015, June 14). Why startups love moleskins. *The New Yorker*. https://www.newyorker.com/business/currency/why-startups-love-moleskines?reload=true

Schnell, S. (2015). Ten simple rules for a computational biologist's laboratory notebook [Editorial]. *PLoS Computational Biology, 11*(9), 1–5. https://doi.org/10.1371/journal.pcbi.1004385

Soanes, C., & Stevenson, A. (Eds.). (2004). *Concise Oxford English dictionary* (11th ed., Vol. 2005). Oxford University Press.

4 Meditative math-making

Melissa Silk

Introduction – the pursuit of newness

Encouraging peers to divert from knowledge expertise and pedagogical comfort zones affords us all new capabilities related to ways of knowing, being, and becoming. Meditative math-making might sound like an oxymoron. The action of making, in collision with mathematics, cycles through concrete to abstract thinking and back again. For many, this is a novel and sometimes frightening concept. I consider, however, the action of making through mathematics as a direct conduit to sensing joy in discovery that leads to a state of *promisingness* (Koestler, 1967). As Maeda (2012) says, there is no greater integrity, no greater goal achieved, than an idea articulately expressed through something made with your hands. Yet this articulation of integrity is difficult to activate because it requires a fearless *pursuit of newness* (Paavola et al., 2004; Ritchhart, 2015). Such pursuit is often fraught with anxiety and resistance. Conversely, resistance can also fuel intention to play, risk, and embrace curiosity in the face of 'not knowing' (Ritchhart, 2015). To be challenged through play strongly emphasises the power of risk and fearlessness in any pursuit of newness. For me, the contributory actions of play, curiosity, and fearlessness have led unswervingly into a world of self-discovery and transformation, so much so that I felt and continue to feel compelled to share the possibility of similar transformation with others. It is within this collective math-making experience that I feel most wellbeing.

This chapter sheds light on the possibilities for personal growth and wellbeing through meditative making with mathematics. I will use my research in STEAM education to illustrate how educators and others experience the melding of arts and design practices with science, technology, engineering, and maths concepts, and in so doing, achieve a sense of flow (Csikszentmihalyi, 1990). It is important to note that my aim as researcher and creative practitioner is to encourage the construction of transdisciplinary knowledge and skill in place of simply designing and exhibiting my own output. In education research contexts, the concept of 'transdisciplinarity' emerged in response to concerns about the dangers of compartmentalising areas of knowledge into siloes. The word itself appeared in a 1970 seminar on interdisciplinarities in universities sponsored by the Organisation of Economic and Development

DOI: 10.4324/9781003207863-5

(OECD) and the French Ministry of Education, held at the University of Nice. However, Bernstein (2015) places Swiss psychologist Jean Piaget at the origin of transdisciplinarity as early as 1955. The OECD seminar investigated possibilities of new syntheses of knowledge and the notion of interconnectedness. It was led by exposing theories of systems addressing human-centred preferred futures (Bernstein, 2015). Certainly, an appreciation of wellbeing in relation to humanness must be considered crucial to such futures.

While my voice assumes some authority in the context of transdisciplinarity, having developed expertise in creating innovative methods of STEAM learning, as Wagner (2012) suggests, it is tempered with

> the ability to listen well and empathically, to ask good questions, to model good values, to help an individual more fully realise his or her talents – and to create a shared vision and collective accountability for its realisation. It is the authority that empowers teams to discover better solutions to new problems.
>
> (Wagner, 2012, p. 241)

Ultimately, my sense of wellbeing relies on the challenges and frustrations felt by those alongside me in the math-making experience. Our collective experience is steeped in the myriad sensations felt during problem-solving instances and the way such emotions are levelled through collaboration. Through my education research, observing the emergence of collective pedagogical wisdom through math-making has led me to acknowledge that great ideas aren't always led from the top. Commonly, we humans work collectively and empathetically in order to experience transformation or to understand something from different perspectives. Garret (2020) says, "[I]f ignorance is empathy's poison, listening is the only known antidote" (p. 141). Therefore, listening to others and responding to their needs while they engage in challenging learning situations has increased my belief that collectively, we can achieve a sense of transformation, even for just a short time, while making with mathematics.

Transformation from individual to collective wisdom requires, as Maeda (2012) suggests, a constant dialogue based on two principles: challenge and creation. Maeda (2012) sees challenge as empowering and the world of physical creation as a pure expression of joy. Self- and collective care enacted through playful shared understandings of new knowledge or experiences defines how transformative individual thought and action is vital to increasing collective scholarly agency. Collective care requires learning about other people, their characteristics, strengths, and foibles to avoid what Garrett (2020) terms as empathy limiting. When I learn more about people through collective math-making experiences, those empathy limits crumble, and the single interest becomes the present pursuit of newness.

Such complex characteristics of the pursuit of newness in higher education experiences are akin to what I present as math-making metaphors. The beautiful paper shapes I have created through conducting workshops with peers,

Meditative math-making 55

students, friends, and participants drawn from both scholarly and general communities can only succeed when we each approach the new encounter without fear. One way of manifesting fearlessness and increasing the joy of a challenging math-making activity is to engage in the experience in the company of others rather than alone. Collectively, the encounter becomes collaborative. The joy of achievement is shared. Likewise, the possibility of wonderment is imbued with sideways collegial reassurances as an alternative to potential anxieties formed by following top-down instructions or working in isolation. I use the creation of mathematical shapes as a metaphor for challenge, community, convergence (in the context of transdisciplinarity), and joy. Hence, the framework for this chapter is imbued with what Wagner (2012) proposes are attributes of the innovator: play, curiosity, and fearlessness. Each attribute contributes to my sense of wellbeing, and this chapter is a call to action for you to perhaps indulge in the same.

Visual narrative – introducing the hyperbolic paraboloid

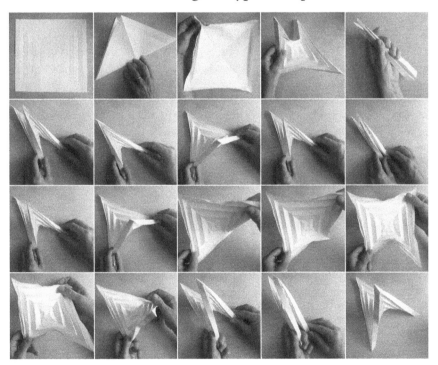

Image 4.1 Making and flexing a hyperbolic paraboloid

> Here, I introduce a shape called the hyperbolic parabola. I make these and other shapes from paper when I feel I need a little winding down from the extreme cerebral overload from work, research, and family life. More recently I have been making hyperbolic parabolas with others.

> The activity involves folding a square piece of paper into a new shape guided by alternating concentric lines, much like a paper fan. Differences between this shape and a paper fan produce intense emotional moments while making and significant joyful eruptions when making is completed. I whimsically call this process a 'flat to form' experience. It can be immersive, much like meditation. I never tire of making these shapes. Hyperbolic paraboloids are appealing, metaphoric, and ultimately biomimetic forms. They expand and contract in beautiful articulation, akin to the way we humans might breathe, calm ourselves, and appreciate things we do not understand at once but come to know over time.
>
> (Silk, 2020)

You will see there is whimsy in my visual narrative. Whimsy is what Wagner (2012) describes as the "intrinsic incentives of exploration, empowerment, and play" (p. 57), contending that the academic content of a whimsical experience must be grounded by learning in context. The point of departure for creating the elegant shape remains simply a square piece of paper, which we generally consider two-dimensional. Manipulating the paper through a series of folds in alternate directions, guided by evenly spaced concentric squares, creates a seemingly complex three-dimensional shape representing a 'hyperbolic paraboloid'. This shape illustrates the confluence of two curves: (1) the hyperbola and (2) the parabola. It also represents the mathematical union of two conic sections. The shape is recognised as both 'hyperbolic paraboloid' or 'parabolic hyperboloid' by virtue of its curved cross-sections. The representation of such unity embodies a flat-to-form experience for the maker while simultaneously introducing the idea of infinite surfaces in three dimensions. Making a hyperbolic paraboloid is a wonderfully tactile way of introducing concepts related to abstract mathematical theory, as well as concrete knowledge related to Cartesian plotting, graphing, and parametric variations in maths. The flexibility of the three-dimensional form gives rise to various metaphorical suggestions. I use the hyperbolic paraboloid in my research and practice to encourage fluid transitions between convergent and divergent thinking. I also use the shape in playful configurations related to learning about biomimicry and mechatronics. From this point on, I will refer to the shape as HP.

As a single shape, the HP holds the human properties and characteristics of *wonder*, not in the diluted sense described by Glaveanu (2020) as simply thinking about something but in the context of participating in an extraordinary experience. Constructing collective configurations of the same shape gives rise to astonishing polyhedral possibilities and experiences that, for the maker, are both intrinsically mechanical and conceptually metaphorical. To make an HP is to engage with rich tangential STEAM possibilities. To observe others making one or more HPs affords the opportunity to understand how the unique mixture of play, curiosity, fearlessness, and purpose can be unsettled by productive tension (Beckman & Ma, 2008), within which a creative encounter often produces a great degree of anxiety and agony (May, 1975). Nonetheless, the result of the math-making experience is very often momentarily, if not completely, transformative for the makers.

Literature – from fearlessness to presentness

In writing this chapter, I reviewed literature related to liminal states, (Land & Meyer, 2005) fixed and growth mindsets (Boaler & Dweck, 2016; Dweck, 2008), immersion (Csikszentmihalyi, 1990; Holdener, 2016), play, fearlessness, curiosity (Wagner, 2012), and joy in learning (Napier, 2010) through visceral experiences. Each of these states make up the relational system inherent in the action of math-making.

Fearlessness

Fear of making with mathematics might be viewed as encountering the challenge to "enlarge our thinking, our identity, our lives – the fear that lets us know we are on the brink of real learning" (Palmer, 1998, p. 39). Palmer suggests it is important to remember that fear can be healthy. "Some fears can help us survive, even learn and grow – if we know how to decode them" (Palmer, 1998, p. 39). Fear impacts a person's sense of self (Kahneman, 2011; Tait & Faulkner, 2016). Fear of failure parallels the notion of a fixed mindset (Dweck, 2008), wherein "I can't" is a perceived response based on engagement with negative suggestions, often made by the self (Maltz, 2015). Countering fear, Dweck has argued that a growth mindset would allow a person the "luxury of becoming" (Dweck, 2008, p. 25) or, in the words of Greene (in Pinar, 1998), to acknowledge that, "I am . . . not yet" (p. 81). Such a view of the self being no longer what it was before activates what May (1975) has described as "past, present and future to form a new Gestalt" (p. 93) while simultaneously, as Wagner (2012) has indicated, it is important to be having fun.

In the play, curiosity, and fearlessness arc, intrinsic motivation also includes the feeling of being lost, encased in a fear of failure (Dweck, 2008; Tait & Faulkner, 2016). Solnit (2005), in *A Field Guide to Getting Lost,* encourages us to practice awareness of this feeling in order to inspire further understanding of the role of fearlessness in self-transformation: "how do I engage this process in a way that I don't become too frightened by what it might unfold or too complacent by avoiding it?" (p. 199). *I can't, I'm lost, I don't understand* can be triggering emotional states that thrust a person out of the present, rendering them unable to persist, persevere, or problem-solve in the moment, head on (Dweck, 2008; Maeda, 2013). I find the opposite. My math-making practice forces me to stay present and encourages me to push through, thus increasing my sense of wellbeing in the moment.

Presentness

The state of 'presentness' required when constructing something with your hands underpins the literature supporting the concept of meditative math-making. Interplay between mathematical theory and the creation of physically aesthetic products weaves a subtle tapestry of knowledge and awareness enjoyed by many 'multipotentialites' (Wapnick, 2017) across a range of industry and life experiences. Wapnick (2017) sees multipotentiality denoting a person/people with endless curiosity, not broken or flaky but demonstrating "many interests and creative pursuits. And that is actually [their] biggest strength" (p. 1). Curiosity and fearlessness are revealed in the literature as human traits and characteristics that can be cultivated (Dweck, 2008; Wagner, 2012). The same can be said for mindfulness, being present, or encountering meditativeness through total absorption in a new learning activity or action.

Total absorption has been described as a state of flow by positive psychologist Csikszentmihalyi (1990) or a state of immersion, according to Holdener (2016), mathematician. Pallasmaa (2009), and Hanney (2018) have suggested transdisciplinary strategies applied to all learning and/or creative acts are greatly enhanced by both rational and non-rational elements of consciousness. Mathmaking, therefore, is reliant on giving oneself permission to play and make, to step outside a perceived comfort zone surrounded by words and equations (Craft, 2015; Maeda, 2013; Wagner, 2012). Contextually, *making* in mathmaking signifies an elaborative stage of the creative process (Gardiner, 2016), as well as a means to position the existential nature of mathematics in a dialectically emotion-charged culture of excitement *and* resistance. Both states are unequivocally felt in the present.

Literature related to fixed or growth mindsets, being stuck, or resistant, place transdisciplinarity squarely in the realm of intellectual challenge (Dweck, 2008; Ritchhart, 2015). The same challenge is perceived as neurologically charged when positioned through a lens of perseverance, haptic sensations, and embodiment (Eagleman, 2018; Tait & Faulkner, 2016). In learning through mathmaking, emotional experiences arise through transactions between mind and body, what Pallasmaa (2009) refers to as the *thinking hand*. In terms of wellbeing, such transactional relationships allow subjective and personal understandings to be felt entirely in the present, within a person's internal state. Consider the experience of joy and happiness (Burnard et al., 2018; Craft, 2015) or the state of flow (Csikszentmihalyi, 2010) or, indeed, a state of panic or anxiety (May, 1975). Such conditions are said to interrelate temporal, historical and environmental states with the objective of making the learning visible (Hanney, 2018). Previous research findings related to haptic sensations and embodiment (e.g. Maths in Motion (MiM) (Fenyvesi et al., 2020)), describe how the intelligence, thinking, and skills of the hand, taken together with intellectual challenge, form a holistic learning experience.

Connectedness

Visceral learning experiences through math-making can be viewed as holistic and connected. Studies finding interrelationships and connections between fields of knowledge and influence have often disrupted and informed life systems (Keane & Keane, 2016). In terms of STEAM learning, Keane (2019) described life systems through a lens of Wilson's (1999) Consilience Theory of how *everything connects*. However, the synthesis of learning through such cause and effect connections finds those involved in STEAM as continuously situated "on the breach" (Keane & Keane, 2016, p. 62). Analogous to the breach is the productive tension described by Beckman and Ma (2008) as being "a tension that is at once material, philosophical, historical, and institutional in its implications" (p. 9). Considering the concept of math-making as productive tension produced by compelling transdisciplinarity, Cranny-Francis (2017), in scholarly work related to creative intelligence and innovation and shifting knowledge fields, refers to this imperative as the 'wicked problem' of integration.

The 'wicked problem' of integration has spread across a multitude of domains, with some researchers defining education for the 21st century as an example of a 'wicked' problem in and of itself (Bernstein, 2015; Cranny-Francis, 2017)[1]. Educators across the globe have adopted the so-called 21st-century skills in their practice. That is, human capabilities defined as the four Cs: communication, collaboration, creativity, and critical thinking (Fadel, 2017). Emotions and empathy in particular are also considered key players in the mix (Rahm, 2016), encouraging the inclusion of forthcoming 22nd-century attributes. These are described in the literature as connection, care, community, and culture (Santone, 2019; Tomlin, 2018). Both C sets fit appropriately with the OECD Learning Compass 2030, which promotes a cycle of action, reflection and anticipation within the culture of future learning (OECD, 2019).

My creative practice leans into a culture of future learning whereby materialisation of knowledge and experience are augmented with the construction of artefacts signifying deep connectedness, co-operation, and co-creation. To dampen the flame of the aforementioned wicked problem, I align my research with others committed to valuing synergistic experiences that link learning challenges with wellbeing: Keane and Cimino (2019), McAuliffe (2016), Sousa and Pilecki (2013). Each has shown the challenge in creating a connected culture of thinking and doing as embedded in the discomfort of liminal states (Land & Meyer, 2005). The liminal in math-making can be articulated as a "troublesome and unsafe journey" (Meyer & Turner, 2006, p. 374) in which the subtle and nuanced emotions expressed while immersed in math-making actions might increase confidence and skill as a direct result of focus, absorption, and *presentness*. Each action, that is, focus, absorption, and presentness, according to McPherson and Lemon (2018) contributes to an enhanced self-perception and wellbeing.

Thresholdness

Human liminal states in relation to enhancing individual or collective wellbeing are important to consider due to their inherent quality of 'thresholdness'. Land and Meyer (2005) view threshold concepts as 'conceptual gateways' or 'portals' leading to energised and transformative thinking. What I understand of liminal states is that they are the areas *between*. Using math-making as a new way of understanding, interpreting, or viewing information presented in a situation may promote a transformed internal assessment of the *in-between* in terms of a single instance, an environment, or even a worldview. Land and Meyer (2005) suggest this may be:

- *transformative*
  (occasioning a significant shift in the perception of a matter)
- *irreversible*
  (unlikely to be forgotten or unlearned only through considerable effort)
- *integrative*
  (exposing the previously hidden interrelatedness of something)
- *troublesome*
  (that may lead to a troublesome knowledge for a variety of reasons)

How this relates to wellbeing is that positioning oneself 'on the brink' (Palmer, 1998), or poised on a threshold between knowing and not knowing (Meyer & Turner, 2006), anticipates some sort of personal journey. Math-making elicits such paths of encounter, where discomfort *and* delight both contribute to a potentially transformative, irreversible, integrative, and/or troublesome experience. In math-making, my observation is that critical liminal moments tend to be shared frequently via explosive displays of emotions. These are what Napier (2010) refers to as 'aha' moments, foregrounding the importance of playful exploration and discovery as central to the notion of the liminal.

Playfulness

Fear of failure has been suggested to be softened by play and curiosity (Tait & Faulkner, 2016; Wagner, 2012). Golden (2018) suggests humans benefit from the opportunity to understand the subtle nuances of play in terms of learning, proposing that we must give ourselves permission to play in our own world as well as the world of work. Previous research shows how playful capacity-building strategies in conjunction with harnessing the power of visual and creative arts contribute to understanding scientific concepts, including mathematics, suggesting, "without toying with possibilities, new ones cannot be opened up" (Craft, 2015, p. 54; Wade-Leeuwen, 2016). The literature proposes that the notion to be swept up in a deep state of play, immersed, engaged, oblivious to the surrounding environment, incites feelings of balance, focus, creativity, challenge, and possibility (Ackerman, 2000; Burnard et al., 2018; Craft, 2015; Holdener, 2016). Thus, finding oneself immersed in math-making may depend on maintaining curiosity for play and perseverance in playing around, complemented with acute awareness of how these states are embodied as *feelings*.

Curiousness

When acknowledged from a scientific perspective, curiosity has been positioned at the core of intrinsic learning (Feynman, 1981). Feynman (1981) notes that all kinds of questions can only *add* and not *subtract* from any given situation. Curiosity asks "why" then really "why?" (Anderson & Jefferson, 2016, p. 161). Similarly, Manguel (2015) has asked "perhaps all curiosity can be summed up in Michael de Montaigne's famous question 'Que sais-je?': What do I know?" (p. 2). The question of course is derived from the Socratic *Know thyself*, but Manguel suggests:

> It becomes not an existentialist assertion of the need to know who we are but rather a continuous state of questioning of the territory through which our mind is advancing (or has already advanced) and of the uncharted country ahead.
>
> (Manguel, 2015, p. 2)

This continuous state of questioning leads me back to the concept of multipotentiality and the endless curiosity suggested by Wapnick (2017) as our biggest strength. In relation to math-making in a STEAM context, the literature reveals critical imbricating ideas related to curiosity, perseverance, and the action of risk taking (Duckworth, 2016; Goodwin, 2012; Silk, 2020; Timm et al., 2016). The type of problem solving embedded in math-making activities is characterised by the quest for insight and understanding while simultaneously posing risk, stirring feelings of anxiety and doubt (Goodwin, 2012). Nevertheless, if curiosity can be cultivated, as Dweck (2008) and Wagner (2012) say it can, I believe *flow*, *immersion*, and *total absorption* can also be drawn into the wellbeing experience through the fearless pursuit of newness and willingness to play.

The next section of this chapter seeks to show how one's willingness to play and be curious and fearless in the context of traversing so-called disparate knowledge areas is dependent on acknowledging *felt* experiences and their impact on life-long learning and wellbeing.

Discussion

Drawn from epistemological and ontological comparisons, math-making may be, at best, embodied curiosity, enacting both algorithmic and serendipitous approaches to *knowing and being* amidst a culture that naturally thrives on play, as Ackerman (2000) suggests. Yet the teachers participating in my research agreed that they *never get to play*, specifically in a professional learning situation. My observation of many instances wherein teachers as well as academic colleagues and tertiary students are presented with the challenge of *making* showed that permitting oneself to play through math-making provided an irreversible emotional experience. Witnessing their liminal states, for me, was as significant as listening to the sound of groups of people folding paper simultaneously. The quiet shuffling audible during such concentrated activity afforded me the opportunity to not only observe a range of liminality, but to wonder if the intense neural activity was indeed becoming meditative, a state of flow, as Csikszentmihalyi (1990) suggests.

After all, the repetitive action of folding, albeit with iterative caveats embedded into the paper's surface, encouraged a situation in which the makers were undeniably situated in the present. They were playing. They were having fun. They were also wondering. Wondering related to transforming the paper on one level and self-capacity on another. Generally, the 'aha' moments of completion were met with collective emotional outbursts and a shared sense of pride, regularly voiced in terms of *I can't believe I did it, so many connections, so much we could do with this.*

Math-making experiences provide potential for 'aha' moments to transform a person's belief in their own capacity for connectedness. The shared joy I have observed in math-making collaborations has much layered significance: (1) personal, for example: *When I first tried this, I couldn't do it. You've gotta be patient . . . don't turn your back on it*; (2) professional, being *I don't want to forget about how you can use maths to make things wonderful and really entertaining to people*; (3) collaborative, such as, *It is really important to share and keep on reminding everyone that we have done it TOGETHER!*; (4) collegial, exemplified by the shift from singular to collective incentives such as *I wonder what we could do next?* According to Glaveanu (2020), wonder should be and is part of our everyday experience: "the tremendous consequences for the self, for others and society" (p. 4) are exactly the purpose of persevering in a task that sparks curiosity and encourages connected cultures of thinking and making. Watching others achieve in carefully planned math-making experiences increases *my* sense of wellbeing in that my academic pursuits have been of value to those who dare to participate.

In math-making, the maker is asked to embrace a certain level of fearlessness when diving into what Wagner (2012) calls the deep end of learning. Otherwise, there is no insight. No creative encounter. No "raised eyebrows, bright eyes, gaping mouth, and, in extreme cases, hair standing on end, or goosebumps" (Keltner & Haidt, 2003, in Glaveanu, 2020, p. 27). The purpose of this chapter, therefore, is to inspire understanding of and perhaps incite an 'aha moment' through math-making for the reader.

Your turn: the meditative math-making approach – enacting the challenge

Play is extremely important to math-making, often requiring the maker to make and fail and make again, validating Samuel Beckett's well-known adage: *fail better* (in Smith & Henrikson, 2016). In developing math-making activities, I recognised the transformational value of *effort* in risk-taking that might lead to self-discovery. My challenge to the readers now is to enact such risk-taking for yourselves. The simple rules are that 'mountain' folds are up and 'valley' folds are down.

DRAW: Use a blank sheet of paper (A4 printer paper is appropriate, although you will need to transform the rectangle into a square). Find the centre of the page and draw a small square in this location (12 mm is appropriate). Add a series of concentric squares radiating outwards with increments of 12 mm until you reach the edge of the page. Draw two diagonal lines from the corners, intersecting in the middle of the original square.

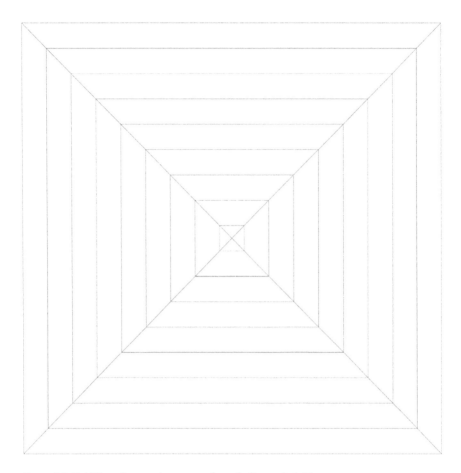

Image 4.2 Fold lines for creating a paper hyperbolic paraboloid

FOLD: Fold the diagonal lines into valleys first, dividing the paper into four quadrants. Also fold the first concentric square into valleys, being careful not to fold the paper over itself at the edges. This means that the corners of the paper will flange out like small pointed 'ears'. Fold the next concentric square in the opposite direction, into mountains. Continue to alternate the concentric square folds in the valley and mountain sequence (like a paper fan). You may feel the first of several emotions rising at this point.

FORM: As you are folding, the paper will start to curve, even through your natural desire for it to remain flat. Allow the opposing corners of the paper to lift. The final internal square will be achieved by 'controlled crushing' as you pull the opposite corners together (see Images 4.3 and 4.4). You may feel apprehensive here because you won't want to make a mistake or give up, and those two emotions will conflict with each other. Persevere; allow the paper to expose its new form and be in charge. You are the master of your materials.

Image 4.3 Opposite corners

Give your completed HP a final squeeze then spread the surfaces gently out again to reveal the double curvature inherent in the 3D shape (see Image 4.5).

How do you feel now? Frustrated? Joyful? Fearless? Curious to know more, to make more? My intention in developing this practice is to not make the experience impossible but rather, as Stinson (2013) puts it, "engender learning where risk and failure are seen as positives and important components of the learning process" (p. 19). As my visual narrative indicated, I use the hyperbolic paraboloid to represent fluid transitions between convergent and divergent thinking and to have fun (see Images 4.6, 4.7, and 4.8). Complementing such transitions is the performative embodiment aspect of HP construction whereby *playing* and *making* enhances the memorability of a learning experience.

Meditative math-making 65

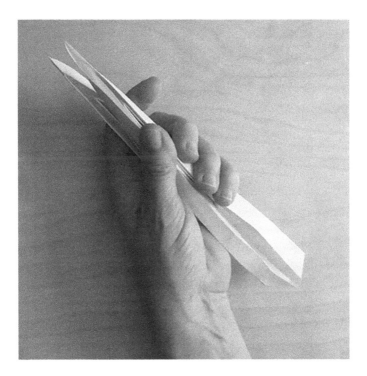

Image 4.4 HP folding completed

Image 4.5 The HP form showing the location of parabolic and hyperbolic surface curves

66 *Melissa Silk*

Image 4.6 HP embodiment

Image 4.7 Playful polyhedral construction

Image 4.8 HP-inspired story writing

Math-making might be unfamiliar meditative territory for some due to its combination of emotional, intellectual, and physical inputs. However, the pleasure of finding things out, as Feynman (1981) notes, is a rich experience. And rich experiences give us a vocabulary drawn not only from a lingual context but also from multiple forms of representation, with a variety of functional concepts. Making HPs and other mathematical paper forms affords me a dialectical framework for immersion. Math-making produces feelings of anxiety *and* calm integral to the experience of joy.

Conclusion

The pursuit of newness encountered in the shared HP-making activity recognises how we place *connection* at the heart of learning, doing, and becoming. Math-making provides a splash of playful creativity in a vast sea of transdisciplinary learning potential. The HP metaphor represents the consideration of alternative perspectives. Making one HP provides a myriad of experiential events which are individually challenging and universally essential to personal *and* collective transformation. Some theorists propose the hyperbolic paraboloid is the shape of the universe. Physically, the HP is also the shape a person makes with their hand while eating a slice of pizza (without the slice making contact with one's chin). You might ask where self-care is situated in all this?

I believe the action of mathematical paper folding offers moments of contemplation and meditation through the challenge and joy of making. It requires a person to be present. An element of self-care is almost always evident within a state of presentness. An element of self-care must always be embedded in the pursuit of newness, particularly in the face of real challenge or cognitive or emotional strain. HP making, and indeed all the math-making I do, is related to intuition, maintaining a significant link between cognitive strain *and* cognitive ease, emotions, and the action of effort while never losing sight of the complexity, beauty, and elegance of the mathematical foundation. I never tire of making these things. Math-making, for me, is meditation. Perhaps it might be the same for you?

Note

1 The term was originally identified by design theorists Horst W. J. Rittel and Melvin M. Webber (1973) and more recently popularised through human-centred designer Bruce Mau within his exploration of complexity: *Incomplete Manifesto for Growth* (Mau, 1998).

References

Ackerman, D. (2000). *Deep play*. Vintage Books.
Anderson, M., & Jefferson, M. (2016). Teaching creativity: Unlocking educational opportunity. In P. O'Connor (Ed.), *The possibilities of creativity*. Cambridge Scholars Publishing.
Beckman, K., & Ma, J. (2008). The changing face(s) of the field. In K. Beckman & J. Ma (Eds.), *Still moving: Between cinema and photography*. Duke University Press.
Bernstein, J. H. (2015). Transdisciplinarity: A review of its origins, development, and current issues. *Journal of Research Practice*, *11*(1). http://jrp.icaap.org/index.php/jrp/article/view/510
Boaler, J., & Dweck, C. (2016). *Mathematical mindsets: Unleashing students' potential through creative math, inspiring messages and innovative teaching*. Jossey-Bass.
Burnard, P., Dragovic, T., Cook, J., & Jasilek, S. (2018). Connecting arts activism, diverse creativities and embodiment through practice as research. In *Creativities in arts education, research and practice: International perspective for the future of learning and teaching* (pp. 271–290). Brill. https://doi.org/10.1163/9789004369603_017
Craft, A. (2015). *Creativity, education and society*. Institute of Education Press.
Cranny-Francis, A. (2017). *Transdisciplinarity in creative intelligence and innovation, presentation*. University of Technology Sydney.
Csikszentmihalyi, M. (1990). *Flow, the psychology of optimal experience* (2nd ed.). Harper Perennial.
Duckworth, A. (2016). *Grit: The power of passion and perseverance*. Penguin Random House.
Dweck, C. S. (2008). *Mindset: The new psychology of success*. Random House USA Inc.
Eagleman, D. (2018). *Creativity and your brain*. http://www.abc.net.au/radionational/programs/allinthemind/creativity-and-your-brain/9758846
Fadel, C. (2017). Global education: 21st century skills/interviewer: J. Earp. *Teacher Magazine*.
Fenyvesi, K., Lehto, S., Brownell, C., Nasiakou, L., Lavicza, Z., & Kosola, R. (2020). Learning mathematical concepts as a whole-body experience: Connecting multiple intelligences, creativities and embodiments within the STEAM framework. In L. C.-G. Pamela Burnard (Ed.), *Why science and art creativities matter* (pp. 301–336). Brill/Sense.

Feynman, R. (1981). *The pleasure of finding things out.* https://www.youtube.com/watch?v=ZbFM3rn4ldo
Gardiner, R. (2016). The creative hand. In P. O'Connor (Ed.), *The possibilities of creativity* (pp. 101–116). Cambridge Scholars Publishing.
Garrett, H. J. (2020). *This book will make you kinder.* Souvenir Press, an imprint of Profile Books.
Glaveanu, V. P. (2020). *Wonder: The extraordinary power of an ordinary experience.* Bloomsbury Publishing Plc.
Golden, N. A. (2018). Narrating neoliberalism: Alternative education teachers' conceptions of their changing roles. *Teaching Education, 29*(1), 1–16. https://10.1080/10476210.2017.1331213
Goodwin, N. (2012). *Developing flexible, adaptable and self- regulated students in the technology classroom.* Paper presented at the Explorations of best practice in Technology, Design & Engineering Education, Surfers Paradise, QLD.
Hanney, R. (2018). Doing, being, becoming: A historical appraisal of the modalities of project-based learning. *Teaching in Higher Education, 23*(6), 769–783. https://doi.org/10.1080/13562517.2017.1421628
Holdener, J. (2016). *Immersion in mathematics.* Paper presented at the Bridges Art Math Conference.
Kahneman, D. (2011). *Thinking fast and slow.* Penguin, Random House.
Keane, L., & Cimino, S. (2019). Design for a new generation. *The Journal of the American Institute of Architects,* 83–84.
Keane, L., & Keane, M. (2016). STEAM by design. *Design and Technology Education: An International Journal, 21*(1), 61–82.
Koestler, A. (1967). *Drinkers of infinity: Essays 1955–1967.* London: Hutchison & Co.
Land, R., & Meyer, J. (2005). Threshold concepts and troublesome knowledge (2): Epistemological considerations and a conceptual framework for teaching and learning. *Higher Education, 49*(3), 373–378. http://www.jstor.org/stable/25068074
Maeda, J. (2012). *STEM to STEAM: Art in K-12 Is key to building a strong economy.* http://www.edutopia.org/blog/stem-to-steam-strengthens-economy-john-maeda
Maeda, J. (2013). STEM + Art = STEAM. *The STEAM Journal, 1*(1). https://doi.org/10.5642/steam.201301.34
Maltz, M. (2015). *Psycho-cybernetics.* Perigee.
Manguel, A. (2015). *Curiosity.* Yale University Press.
Mau, B. (1998). *Incomplete manifesto for growth.* https://brucemaustudio.com/projects/an-incomplete-manifesto-for-growth/
May, R. (1975). *The courage to create.* W. W. Norton & Company, Inc.
McAuliffe, M. (2016). The potential benefits of divergent thinking and metacognitive skills in STEAM learning: A discussion paper. *International Journal of Innovation, Creativity and Change, 2*(3), 71–82. www.ijicc.net
McPherson, M., & Lemon, N. (2018). *It is about fun stuff! Thinking about the writing process in different ways.* Springer.
Meyer, D. K., & Turner, J. C. (2006). Re-conceptualizing emotion and motivation to learn in classroom contexts. *Educational Psychology Review, 18,* 377–390. https://doi/10.1007/s10648-006-9032-1
Napier, N. K. (2010). *Insight: Encouraging aha! moments for organisational success.* Praeger.
OECD. (2019). *OECD future of education and skills 2030: OECD learning compass 2030.* The Organisation for Economic Co-operation and Development. http://www.oecd.org/education/2030-project/teaching-and-learning/learning/skills/
Paavola, S., Lipponen, L., & Hakkarainen, K. (2004). Models of innovative knowledge communities, and three metaphors of learning. *Review of Educational Research, 74*(4), 557–576. http://journals.sagepub.com.ezproxy.lib.uts.edu.au/doi/pdf/10.3102/00346543074004557

Pallasmaa, J. (2009). *The thinking hand*. John Wiley & Sons Ltd.
Palmer, P. (1998). *The courage to teach*. Jossey-Bass Inc., Publishers.
Pinar, W. F. (1998). *The passionate mind of Maxine Greene*. Falmer Press.
Rahm, J. (2016). Stories of learning, identity, navigations and boundary crossings in STEM in non-dominant communities: New imaginaries for research and action. *Cultural Studies of Science Education*, *11*, 61–75. https://doi.org/10.1007/s11422-014-9627-7
Ritchhart, R. (2015). *Creating cultures of thinking: The 8 forces we must master to truly transform our schools*. Jossey-Bass.
Santone, S. (2019). *22nd century learning requires ancient skills*. https://www.susansantone.com/master-blog/2019/8/2/22nd-century-learning-requires-ancient-skills
Silk, M. (2020). *The value of me in STEAM* [Doctor of Philosophy, University of Technology Sydney].
Smith, S., & Henrikson, D. (2016). Fail again, fail better: Embracing failure as a paradigm for creative learning in the arts. *Art Education*, *69*(2). https://doi.org/10.1080/00043125.2016.1141644
Solnit, R. (2005). *A field guide to getting lost*. Viking Penguin.
Sousa, D. A., & Pilecki, T. (2013). *From STEM to STEAM, using brain-compatible strategies to integrate the arts*. Corwin, A Sage Company.
Stinson, M. (2013). Launching into drama as a pedagogy of hope. *The Journal of Drama and Theatre Education in Asia*, *4*(1), 13–24.
Tait, A., & Faulkner, D. (2016). *Edupreneur: Unleashing teacher-led innovation in schools*. Wiley.
Timm, J. W., Mosquera, J. J. M., & Stobäus, C. D. (2016). Profession teacher is related to lifelong [re]learning. *Creative Education*, *7*, 1765–1772. http://doi.org/10.4236/ce.2016.712180
Tomlin, D. (2018). *The 4 new 22nd century Cs for education!* http://www.amle.org/Publications/BlogABCsofMiddleLevelEducation/TabId/937/ArtMID/3115/ArticleID/793/The-4-New-22nd-Century-Cs-for-Education.aspx
Wade-Leeuwen, B. (2016). Intercultural arts-based research inquiry: First marks of the reformer's brush. *Australian Art Education*, *37*(2), 151–164. https://search.informit.com.au/fullText;dn=215073;res=AEIPT
Wagner, T. (2012). *Creating innovators – the making of young people who will change the world*. Scribner.
Wapnick, E. (2017). *How to be everything: A guide for those who (still) don't know what they want to be when they grow up*. Harper Collins.
Wilson, E. O. (1999). *Consilience, the unity of knowledge*. Vintage Books.

Section 2
Collaborative expression, embodiment, and the power of relationships

5 Stepping off the edge

Circles of connection and creativity for wellbeing in the academy

Catherine E. Hoyser

> Now is the time to know
> That all that you do is sacred. . . .
> When you can finally live
> with veracity
> And love.
> Now is the time for the world to know
> That every thought and action is sacred.
>
> (Hafiz, *The Gift*. Radinsky, Trans., 1999)

The Need for Self-Care and Balance for Wellbeing

As more tasks from upper administration crash into my email, demanding that I complete more paperwork and jump through more hoops, I know that I am not alone. Colleagues from multiple types of universities experience the same situation. Because I am a tenured, white, cisgender, full professor at a small private university in the Northeast of the USA, my position provides me with privileges and protections. Still, the institutional pressures remain regardless of one's status. Budgets and majors are being removed from programs, staff positions being eliminated, all before COVID-19 arrived to create more pressures on universities, staffs, and professors, let alone students. Often, it is hard to believe that everything I do is sacred, as Hafiz wrote. To regain that feeling of sacredness in my life, I cultivate a life of creativity and community to nurture my wellbeing.

A few years ago, feeling alienated from my institution, I realised change was crucial to preserve my wellbeing. I and other faculty attempted but failed to form a union on our campus; the reasons for that are complex, of course, but partly low morale and a sense of futility pervaded the faculty. We had successfully, in my earlier years, unified to threaten a strike that motivated the administration into creating a transparent salary rubric. Therefore, when I took a spiritual step away from the university, I had attempted to change the attitudes of administrators. Recently the university administration removed funding and the major for the gender studies program among other humanities majors

DOI: 10.4324/9781003207863-7

including the student arts journal. These cuts represent a systemic attitude of prioritising finances rather than student growth – intellectually, physically, spiritually – and wellbeing. Their policies impact many departments and professors.

Living Divided

Higher education has become increasingly a business that focuses on bottom lines and, as the offensive saying goes, "butts in seats". The needs of students receive lip service rather than practical, compassionate solutions, and faculty are replaceable cogs rather than experts who nurture future experts and community leaders. Several scholars have commented on the impact of neoliberal influence on higher education particularly (Nussbaum, 2010; Coonan, 2022, pp. 145–158; Wu, 2022). As Daphne Loads (2019) explained, "The impoverishment of academic life is, for many commentators, a result of what has come to be called the neoliberal university. This is shorthand for the accusation that the heart has been removed from higher education and replaced by the 'market', leaving no room for any other values or guiding principles" (p. 100). Furthermore, Loads continued that besides students being "commodified" as consumers, faculty suffer "intense pressure to compete for scarce resources in precarious situations" (p. 101). The result of this "crude materialism and narrow instrumentalism can lead to a profound sense of emptiness; something important is missing" (Loads, 2019, p. 101). Professors anguish over the choices administrators make as they experience more and more erosion of their time for research and writing, more stress that drains their energy from focusing on research and students, and major clashes between the institution's and professors' moral values regarding pedagogy that fosters creativity and imagination in students. Wu's (2022) detailed summary includes the impact of the hypercompetitiveness that neoliberal universities promote and the resulting depression many faculty experience.

Fostering the emotional, mental, and spiritual lives of faculty is crucial to counteract the stress of the current statistic-obsessed measure of teacher quality. I will use "faculty", "professors", and "teachers" as interchangeable terms. Like Loads (2019), Coonan (2022, pp. 145–158), and Nussbaum (2010), Sonia Nieto (2005) depicted the condition of educational institutions as embracing a corporate mindset that codifies professors and students as machine operators whose successful outcome can be measured by student test results. K–12 students have learned that tests are the only measure of learning. This perspective pushes teachers and students to devalue creativity and imagination. Without nurturing those qualities, innovations in society falter and, therefore, so do improvement and wellbeing.

Researchers have discovered the sources of teacher unhappiness. Few people, however, have inquired regarding a means of alleviating teacher burnout and distress. This teacher exhaustion and stress impact students as well. Palmer (2017) noted that education has become "more obsessed with externals, shrinking the space needed to support the inner lives of teachers and students" (p. xiii). He clarified, saying that interior work helps faculty refocus on their students and strengthen faculty so they can withstand the neoliberal perspectives that erode the profession. Institutional devaluation of faculty expertise, research, and commitment to pedagogy that engages the whole student eviscerates the intellectual, emotional, physical, and spiritual development of individuals and civil society. Spirit and heart are missing when faculty stress so much that they suffer from a cognitive and emotional dissonance between the humanising educational goals that inform their pedagogy and the soullessness of the university. This division of the self is debilitating to wellbeing.

Additionally, such tensions from the dysphoric clash between self and institution lead to a self-alienation for faculty. Palmer (2017) described this state of being as living divided. The teacher's moral values clash with the institution's, leading to a disheartening inner turmoil. The goal must be, according to Palmer (2017), "to live divided no more" by taking a spiritual leave from the university rather than physical (p. 174). Taking that spiritual leave means relinquishing being preoccupied with university politics and spending time on finding a community of people who share similar pedagogical values. The divided professor needs to "stand on their own ground" (Palmer, 2017, p. 174) and embrace the light and the dark of their self. Moreover, the professor will bring this self-knowledge to their classes.

A Fractured World

Besides the university neoliberal perspective, the education system has become one of teaching to the test rather than teaching the whole individual: physical, intellectual, and spiritual. Indeed, students have become "brains on sticks" (Lewis, 2006, p. 100). Csikszentmihalyi (2007) described the dangers of this perspective to the arts:

> When school budgets tighten and test scores wobble, more and more schools opt for dispensing with frills – usually with the arts and extracurricular activities – so as to focus instead on the so-called basics. This would not be bad if the "three Rs" were taught in ways that encouraged originality and creative thinking; unfortunately, they rarely are . . . their [students'] chance of using their minds in creative ways comes from working on the student paper, the drama club, or the orchestra. So if the next generation is to face the future with zest and self-confidence, we must educate them to be original as well as competent.
>
> (p. 11)

The impact of this removal of creative activity for students surfaces when students dismiss activities such as working on a student publication or acting in a play because they have learned that creative activity has no value for their future.

The devaluing of the creative applies to faculty who limit themselves to prescriptive lesson plans and lack the balance of creativity in their own lives. If faculty do not feed their creativity, how will they be able to develop creative classrooms that benefit their students and educate the whole person? Therefore, not only faculty suffer from a lack of flow, balance, and inventiveness, but also students. If faculty are alienated from their institution and do not seek grounding within it (or outside it) finding like-minded colleagues, and within themselves, they will not be able to teach with self-knowledge and their whole selves. Therefore, they must find alternatives that satisfy their need for moral wholeness while staying at the institution (Palmer, 2017). As Palmer (2009) explained, "The arts are a civilizing institution that can help us learn to hold tension in a way that leads to life, not death" (p. 4). Holding that tension between self and institution and within the self, feeding their imagination through the arts and using their creativity nourish faculty and leads to wellbeing. Connecting to one's creativity and achieving wellbeing are not continual states of being but processes that are ongoing.

Palmer (2017) argued that self-knowledge, for faculty, "is as crucial to good teaching as knowing my students and my subject" (p. 3). In fact, instructors need to cultivate self-knowledge to recognise "who is the self that teaches?" (p. 7). This quest for wholeness, of course, is complex as we look inside at the many aspects of our selves that equal identity. Despite my privileged status, I am a first-generation university student. This experience as well as other childhood difficulties are part of who I am when I enter a class. Cultivating holism, self-care, and wellbeing are avenues into a journey that leads to self-knowledge and healing the hollow that neoliberal institutions excavate inside faculty.

John Miller (2005) spoke of holism as a means to prevent that hollow with its dilution of creativity and self: "Holism is, literally, a search for wholeness in a culture that limits, suppresses, and denies wholeness" (p. 7). Holistic balance of mind, body, and spirit is an essential element for wellbeing. Sarah White (2008) outlined wellbeing as having control over one's decisions with a "second key quality of wellbeing . . . its holistic outlook. At a personal level it promises to connect mind, body and spirit" (p. 2). White's analysis of the complexities concluded that individual wellbeing impacts community wellbeing. Faculty wellbeing transmits itself to students, enabling students and professors as a community to pursue more holistic approaches to learning. To cope with the cognitive dissonance between self and institution, tapping into the creative self and creating a community of congruence (within or outside the institution) are steps that encourage the balance of wellbeing.

Visual Representation as Touchstone

Image 5.1 The tactile organic shapes that help centre and ground me

Hoping that my experience will inspire readers to try new creative activities, I share my process of self-care. The accompanying image of stones stacked in graduated sizes reflects the layers of community, creativity, and mindfulness that I use to care for my wellbeing. I collected them when I was at the Fine Arts Work Centre (FAWC). The tactile organic shapes help centre and ground me. It reminds me that the rushing waters of life flow around the still stone, which becomes more smooth and remains despite the water's frenzy. From day to day, the stones change their order of representation in my head. Some days, I am the top stone resting on calm, creativity, community. Other days, I am the bottom stone supporting the calm, creativity, and wellbeing of others in my collaborative community. The stones constitute a connection to the cycle of nature of which we are a small part. Whichever way I prioritise the four Cs (Catherine, calm, creativity, collaborative community), balance remains. The process is a flow of mutual relationship among people who share the same goals for the wellbeing of each other and, as a result, our students when we show up to the classroom whole with self-knowledge, wellbeing, and balance, as Palmer (2017) recommended.

Stepping Off the Edge of Safety

Allowing myself to embrace my creativity and acknowledge its importance to my wellbeing has led to wonderful collaborations that have produced new pedagogy, scholarly articles, poetry, and co-edited volumes. Thus, the path of self-care has included the bonus of satisfying creativity, productivity, and calm despite the stresses of academe. My creative pursuits and my community sustain my balance. It is not a static arrival point but a continual process of balance, imbalance, and rebalance.

Once I realised nothing would change at my university (or any other were I to try to move), I resumed meditating – who has time to meditate? I had thought – and allowed myself to take a chance on a new venture outside of my institution by attending a writing workshop at FAWC. My career had not focused on creative writing. Self-care by focusing on my creativity resulted in my finding a community of congruence, as Palmer (2017) called it. It also gave me balance, promoted my wellbeing, and, incidentally, enhanced my career. The publications that have resulted from my collaboration with others regarding a pedagogy of mindfulness and wellbeing are secondary to the creative expression, contemplative practice, and positive flow from the poetic process. Michael Franklin (2017) explained the process of art as contemplative practice and the taking of risk as essential to creativity. He stated that "what is counter to habit is good for the development of intuition; perhaps the most important ally of artistic work. There are moments when it is time to step off of the edge of safety, plunge into darker unknown spaces and take healthy risks" (p. 6). Furthermore, Franklin (2017) wrote that

> Art slows us down and wakes us up from degrees of a moral slumber. This contemplative result is accompanied by connecting our receptive and expressive channels to the vast continuum of life. The arts provide access to the majesty of landscapes, cultural trends, historical patterns, and opposing internal emotional realities.
>
> (p. viii)

Those "opposing internal emotional realities" include, of course, the conflict between our pedagogical moral values and the values of our institutions. "Stepping off the edge of safety" into an unknown space such as a creative writing class facilitated my waking up from "moral slumber". The experience taught me that nurturing my creativity and immersing myself in this new venture actually reinvigorated me as a person, writer, and professor.

In *Art as Contemplative Practice*, Franklin (2017) concluded: "studying the phenomenology of embodied experience through art and meditation awakens awareness. In essence contemplative practices are legitimate forms of interior research. Self as subject, when explored within the context of the artist/practitioner/researcher, yield disciplined standards that honour authentic artistic intentions" (p. xxix). Engaging with artistic endeavours involves the body, mind, and spirit so that self-awareness can emerge during self-expression.

Like Franklin, Audre Lorde (2007) described the process of poetry as a means of knowing the inner self's dreams and aspirations. Additionally, she argued for poetry as necessary for activism. She detailed the steps of poetic creation as:

> It forms the quality of the light within which we predicate our hopes and dreams toward survival and change, first made into language, then into idea, then into more tangible action. Poetry is the way we help give name to the nameless so it can be thought.
>
> (p. 37)

In fact, Lorde claimed that "poetry is not a luxury. It is a vital necessity of our existence" (p. 37).

Knowing oneself through embodied artistic expression coincides with Palmer's (2017) claim that to teach well, one must know oneself. My entry into the world of creative writing was a healthy risk of stepping off the edge. Incidentally, it has resulted in the contemplative mode that Franklin discussed in his study. The meditative process of creativity includes finding the centre of oneself, immersing oneself in flow, and experiencing wellbeing.

My choice to write poetry came from an interior drive to try something new and to balance my focus on students and institution with a focus on my creativity. Meditation combined with writing poetry restored a sense of myself as a whole person outside my university. The poetic process is in itself a meditative experience. In an article about the definition of poetry, poet Sarah Wardle (2015) emphasised the positive role of poetry as mindfulness:

> Poetry, I propose, has a value today both for individuals and society . . . for the way in which its positive humanism can enhance mindfulness and reinforce calm, non-aggressive rhetoric in our repertoire. Poetry helps rid us of negative thinking either by voicing it as such, . . . or by reinforcing positive messages as models. One of my favourite poems, Rilke's "Archaic Torso of Apollo" (1995, p. 67), ends: "You must change your life"; it is this aspect of poetry, . . . that I propose we should prioritize in our value judgements about it. The best poetry can instil in our hearts an open and peaceful perspective.
>
> (para. 13)

Wardle's definition of poetry as mindfulness, life changing, and corrective to being out of balance meshes with the contemplative process that I undergo when I write a poem. Even if a poem expresses negative feelings or observations, Wardle recognises the positive impact of sharing those insights.

Flow and Creativity

Research has shown that embodied creativity engages the whole person and promotes the positive state of flow. As Mihaly Csikszentmihalyi (1990) stated, flow consists of "the positive aspects of human experience – joy, creativity, the process of total involvement with life" (p. i). Being in flow is part of the intricate system of learning. The complexity of this system reflects the conditions of good teaching. The educator who teaches from a holistic philosophy arrives with the whole self – body, mind, and spirit. As cited, Palmer (2017) emphasised that a teacher needs to know their self and bring their whole self into the classroom.

Often, when I am writing, I slip into the creative flow analysed in Csikszentmihalyi's (1990) study describing the human experience of creativity. He defined flow as "the way people describe their state of mind when consciousness is harmoniously ordered, and they want to pursue whatever they are doing for its own sake" (p. 6). For a decolonising of time in academia that supplements flow, see Shahjahan (2015). Conflict and time disappear as I become absorbed in working out an idea for a poem and the best words to use. When deepest into the process, I walk around in internal debate regarding word choice for a line. It suffuses my daily activities that used to be largely rote, for example, folding laundry or taking a walk.

I write for the pleasure of the experience; I might or might not publish the writing. At this point in my career, I have the advantage that I need never publish another article, but I enjoy my process and writing so much that I would feel depleted without this outlet. Actually, during a period of believing service to my university was more important than my creativity, wellbeing, and research, I slid into a state of moral torpor. The creative process removes me from immersion in university conflicts. I can step back from the clashes and stay in balance with myself, focusing on my wellbeing and my pedagogy to empower students to learn and to use their creativity for their wellbeing. My involvement with the university has become selective now rather than fighting every battle as I did in the past. My privilege as an older faculty member protects me, I acknowledge that, but I also recognise that I could have helped myself in my earlier years by choosing judiciously the university issues I tackled.

Finding Wellbeing via Community and Creativity

On the individual level I have instituted practices of mindfulness that centre me and begin the day with calm focus. In the past, I jumped out of bed and immediately turned on my computer for email and the television for the latest news. Now, my morning starts with meditation or reading poetry or fiction, journaling, and reflecting before beginning my own writing. I give myself time by waking up earlier than usual.

Besides the daily practice that I have instituted to maintain balance, as much as possible, is the supportive community of professors from other universities in other fields than my own. When I "stepped off the edge" into the poetry writing workshop at FAWC, I unknowingly opened a new community of positive support. Part of this experience resulted from the leader of the poetry workshop, Gabrielle Calvocoressi, who definitely exemplifies Palmer's dictum that to teach well, one must arrive in class with the whole self. Calvocoressi embodied that.

In the workshop's spirit of community, we partnered to engage in a storytelling-to-poem activity that required mindful listening and creative responses to the story we were told. We transformed what we heard into poetry. We combined our stories or wrote only about our partner's story. We took no notes and listened mindfully. The prompt focused on the emotional essence. For a more precise description of this process and development of it into a multimodal arts project as well as *lectio divina,* see Hoyser (2019) and Hall et al. (2015). My partner became part of the collaborative community that developed from this working relationship. We discovered that we shared similar beliefs about pedagogy, mindfulness, and creativity as well as similar disenchantment with our institutions. Both of us were needing to "live divided no more", as Palmer (2017, p. 174) called his solution to the moral conflict between our goals and our universities' goals. As Dewey (1938) argued, the arts process provides internal and intellectual freedom. As I and Maureen developed a community of likeminded professor artists, our internal conflicts between our morals and our universities became secondary because our creative collaboration helped us step away from the cognitive and emotional dissonance that we were experiencing. The arts, indeed, gave us freedom internally and intellectually.

The creative writing workshop that I took developed into an innovative collaboration among writers and artists who teach. What began with Maureen and me extended into a domino effect of two other professors who taught at different universities in art education. I and Maureen's first project together involved the development of the original storytelling-to-poem into a song set to music, then a movie using the song and illustrated by my original photographs. We used this assignment in our classes – Maureen in graduate-level teacher training and I in undergraduate English classes. When we shared this four-step process at a conference, participants responded to the experience by telling us that they would build the assignment into a project on storytelling in multiple cultures. My "step off the edge" has led me to a collaborative community with shared values and pedagogies, continued creative poetry writing, and more scholarly presentations and articles.

An additional professor joined our community and introduced us to *lectio divina,* now a secularised version of an ancient monastic form of deep reading. This process has become part of the storytelling-to-poem conversion task. To learn more about this deep reading technique and ways to implement it, see Hoyser (2019). Moreover, I and Jane have begun collaborating in duo modalities of visual art and poetry, responding to each other's work. We have published a detailed account of this process in volume two of this series. Results from these collaborations include journal articles, conference presentations, and a co-edited volume on *lectio* and *visio divina*; achieving wellbeing through creativity, however, is the goal.

Our collaborations did not begin with academic publication in mind; they developed because we felt that our perspectives might encourage others to teach with a creative holistic, embodied, emotional, and cognitive approach. These collaborations have provided encouragement, creative outlet, and community that enable me to step back from the university. Without developing my creativity via poetry writing, I would be living in a divided state, unable to teach holistically and heart-fully. Without my community of artists and writers, my creativity and, therefore, wellbeing would suffer. Community remains even though we may be working and collaborating on creative projects with other people because we continue to communicate about our moral dilemmas regarding the university. We remind each other to focus on the important process of using our imagination and remaining true to our moral compass.

In summary, I discovered that engaging in creativity encourages healing and wellbeing. Researchers Levine (2003) and McNiff (1992) found that the arts promote wellness and restore wellbeing. Furthermore, artistic endeavours serve as catalysts for creative energy that heals the intellectual, physical, and spiritual. Developing the creative imagination can offer support when dealing with perplexing and complex problems and conflicts (Malchiodi, 2005). In fact, the poet and publisher Martha Rhodes (personal communication 9 May 2021) asserted that the process of creative writing benefits a person's health.

When I write about creative writing, I am not invoking trauma healing. Practitioners such as James Pennebaker and Joshua Smyth (2016) and Louise DeSalvo (2000), among others, have written about that topic. I am also not denying that trauma and healing may emerge during the process of immersing oneself into creative activities. The positive impact of the arts enhances personal meaning making, improvisation, creativity, and nourishment of the inner life. The personal and professional wellbeing that comes from creative endeavours and collaborative community shores up the exhausted faculty member. Eisner (2003) noted that the "actual actions of art" include "artistically rooted qualitative forms of intelligence, that are not the sole domain of artists and the fine arts, but of all professions, whether a surgeon, a cook, an engineer, or a teacher" (Eisner, p. 375). I emphasise the arts as a supplement to one's profession.

Stepping Off the Creative Edge Yourself

If I have inspired a reader to take a step off the edge into a creative activity, I suggest doing some research online for local and regional arts organisations or centres that offer workshops. Additionally, university teaching-learning centres could be a location for gathering professors together for reading groups or discussions. Many museums, senior and community centres, and universities offer lifelong learning courses.

Once, I took a Chinese watercolour class at a local senior centre. I was terrible, but I also spent the three hours in class absorbed so much that the time flew by. It was truly an experience of flow. It was also restorative emotionally and spiritually. I learned to appreciate the practice and creativity involved in painting one leaf. The other people in the class were comrades, supporting each other. My goal was the flow that cleared my head and bolstered my sense of self, not perfection. Although it is difficult to designate time for creative activity during the academic term, pursuing creativity despite the difficulty actually balances me and gives me the creative and emotional energy to be present in the classroom.

The writing workshop that I took is at a centre created specifically for the written and visual arts. It brings "students" from around the United States. Scholarships are available for Black Indigenous People of Color (BIPOC) individuals. I was surprised that most of my classmates had already published and some were professors. Nevertheless, everyone was humble and eager to learn more about their craft. Arts activities, of course, extend beyond writing poetry. While creating art, a person utilises multiple cognitive functions; connecting the body with the brain engages a cycle of creativity, somatic response, imagination, improvisation, and meaning making (Booth, 2001).

Being a Novice Again

Coincidentally, stepping off the edge of safety pushes us into beginner's mind and reminds us what our students feel when they enter a classroom (Suzuki, 2020). The ability of the educator to empathise by practicing patience with their self during their creative activity and recognising the satisfaction of transforming their spiritual moral distress into a positive spiritual separation from their institution enables the teacher to return to the classroom and apply the same self-compassion to their students. Palmer (2017) observed that educators need to recognise "the fear in the student", and "the fear within me" as a teacher (p. 48). As mentioned earlier, Palmer (2017) asserted we can separate ourselves spiritually from the institution and not physically need to leave it. The individual must find "solid ground on which to stand outside of the institution – the ground of one's own being – and from that ground is better able to resist the deformations that occur when organizational values become the landscape of one's inner life" (p. 174). If we find a collaborative community and engage our mind, body, and spirit in the flow of creativity, we can survive and thrive. We will encounter and recognise "our own being" and resist falling prey to institutional values that cause inner dissonance and crisis.

Some Parting Ideas

Recognising a need for nurturing myself, I sought positive alternatives to soothe my distress over the state of education and the impasse between my pedagogical values and the university's. I stretched myself to commit to creativity. I say "stretch" because allowing myself to focus on a realm besides my teaching and scholarship felt both precipitous and exciting. Although my scholarly research on women and history creates flow when I pursue it, my poetry process allows me to tap into my creativity with a freedom and imagination the other writing does not allow. The creative process invokes connecting the outer and the inner selves via imagination and emotion. One could say it is an intersectional coalescing of emotion, imagination, cognition, body, and spirit, engaging my whole person.

Because I have been encouraging others to try a creative activity and have been praising the impact of writing poetry on my sense of wellbeing, I insert here one of my poems. It expresses feeling alienated from my surroundings after moving from a Victorian multifamily house in Hartford, Connecticut, to a suburban apartment complex. An incident occurred that helped me recognise a metaphysical connection that counteracted the feeling of dysphoria:

> Deer Park
> And just when I thought I
> had to leave because this place
> is so boring with its beige
> wall-to-wall, swimming pool,
> garages, you leap across the grass,
> your young antlers silhouetted ghostlike
> by klieg lights, your shaggy neck hair
> dark against the toffee coat you wear after
> two years among apartments, sidewalks,
> tennis courts. Tonight, the night of the Super
> Moon, you have friends with you. When I
> cruise up the drive, my car lights fail
> to startle you. I stop to gaze as you
> graze among the gas grills.

After this encounter, I attend to the natural environment that remains rather than to the negatives of living on what once was the demesne of wildlife, and I work to preserve what remains. Miraculously, to me, I see the adaptive resilience of nature managing to survive among the built environment. If nature can survive, so can I.

Allowing my imagination to connect to the positive of what seemed morally void, the clash between my lived space and values resolved. I, and we, can distance ourselves from the moral morass of neoliberal education and nurture our wellbeing with the flow that results from creativity and community. Remembering Hafiz's words that what we do is sacred, I honour my creative self when I immerse myself in writing poetry as part of wellbeing. The contemplative flow of creativity renews my energy for living and teaching. Consequently, I feel more present with students. I am connected with my creativity, flow, and imagination despite the quashing impact of the education system. Finally, it salves the hurt and poison of the moral clash between myself and my institution (Palmer, 2017). I challenge readers to allow themselves to find flow and wellbeing. Step off the edge into creativity and community.

References

Booth, E. (2001). *The everyday work of art: Awakening the extraordinary in your daily life*. iUniverse.

Coonan, E. (2022). From survival to self-care: Performative professionalism and the self in the neoliberal university. In N. Lemon (Ed.), *Healthy relationships in higher education: Promoting wellbeing across academia* (pp. 145–158). Routledge.

Csikszentmihalyi, M. (1990). *Flow: The psychology of optimal experience*. Harper Perennial Modern Classics. https://a.co/1NBOw9f

Csikszentmihalyi, M. (2007). *Creativity: Flow and the psychology of discovery and invention*. Harper Perennial Modern Classics. https://a.co/8y23omf

Dalton, J. E., Hall, M. P., & Hoyser, C. E. (Eds.). (2019). *The whole person: Embodying teaching and learning through lectio and Visio Divina*. Rowman & Littlefield.

Dalton, J. E., & Hoyser, C. E. (2022). Creative and collaborative expression as contemplative self-care. In N. Lemon (Ed.), *Healthy relationships in higher education: Promoting wellbeing across academia* (pp. 13–26). Routledge.

DeSalvo, L. (2000). *Writing as a way of healing: How telling our stories transforms our lives*. Beacon Press.

Dewey, J. (1938). *Experience and education*. Palgrave Macmillan.

Eisner, E. (2003). Artistry in education. *Scandinavian Journal of Educational Research, 47*, 373–384. https://doi.org/10.1080/0031383032000079317

Franklin, M. (2017). *Art as contemplative practice: Expressive pathways to the SELF*. State University of New York.

Hafiz. (1999). Now is the time to know. In D. Radinsky (Trans.), *The gift* (p. 160). Penguin (Original work published ca. 1345–1390).

Hall, M. P., Hoyser, C. E., & Brault, A. (2015 [2016], November). Embodying performativity in story-to-poem conversion. *Ubiquity Journal, 3*, 43–69. http://ed-ubiquity.gsu.edu/wordpress/hall-hoyser-and-brault-3-2/

Hoyser, C. E. (2019). *Lectio Divina* and story-to-poem conversion as tools for transformative education. In J. E. Dalton, M. P. Hall, & C. E. Hoyser (Eds.), *The whole person: Embodying teaching and learning through lectio and Visio Divina* (pp. 37–48). Rowman & Littlefield.

Levine, E. (2003). *Tending the fire: Studies in art, therapy & creativity*. EGS Press.

Lewis, H. (2006). *Excellence without a soul? Does liberal education have a future?* Public Affairs.

Loads, D. (2019). The restorative power of *Lectio Divina* and the arts for university lecturers. In J. E. Dalton, M. P. Hall, & C. E. Hoyser (Eds.), *The whole person: Embodying teaching and learning through lectio and Visio Divina* (pp. 99–109). Rowman & Littlefield.

Lorde, A. (2007). *Sister outsider: Essays and speeches*. Random House (Original work published 1977).

Malchiodi, C. A. (Ed.). (2005). *Expressive therapies*. Guildford Press.

McNiff, S. (1992). *Art as medicine*. Shambhala.

Miller, J. P. (2005). Introduction: Holistic learning. In J. P. Miller, S. Karsten, D. Denton, D. Orr, & I. Coladillo Kates (Eds.), *Holistic learning and spirituality in education: Breaking new ground*. State University of New York Press.

Nieto, S. (2005). *Why we teach*. Teachers College Press.

Nussbaum, M. C. (2010). *Not for profit: Why democracy needs the humanities* (Vol. 2). Princeton University Press.

Palmer, P. J. (2009). The broken-open heart: Living with faith and hope in the tragic gap. *Weavings: A Journal of Christian Spiritual Life, 24*(2), 1–12.

Palmer, P. J. (2017). *The courage to teach: A guide for reflection and renewal* (20th Anniversary ed.). Jossey-Bass.

Pennebaker, J. W., & Smyth, J. M. (2016). *Opening up by writing it down: How expressive writing improves health and eases emotional pain* (3rd ed.). Guilford Press.

Rilke, R. M. (1995). Archaic torso of apollo. In S. Mitchell (Ed. & Trans.), *Ahead of all parting: Selected poetry* (p. 67). Modern Library (Original work published 1887).

Shahjahan, R. A. (2015). Being 'lazy' and slowing down: Toward decolonizing time, our body, and pedagogy. *Educational Philosophy and Theory: Incorporating Access*, 47(5), 488–501. https://doi.org/10.1080/00131857.2014.880645

Suzuki, S. (2020). *Zen mind, beginner's mind. Informal talks on Zen meditation and practice* (50th Anniversary ed.). Shambala.

Wardle, S. (2015). The mindfulness of poetry: Writing in practice. *The Journal of Creative Writing Research*, *1*. https://www.nawe.co.uk/DB/wip-editions/editions/writing-in-practice-vol-1.html

White, S. C. (2008). *But what is wellbeing? A framework for analysis in social and development policy and practice*. ERSC Research Group on Wellbeing in Developing Countries. Retrieved August 20, 2021, from https://people.bath.ac.uk/ecsscw/But_what_is_Wellbeing.pdf

Wu, B. (2022). Authenticity and wellbeing in neoliberal times: Imagining alternatives. In N. Lemon (Ed.), *Healthy relationships in higher education: Promoting wellbeing across academia* (pp. 197–209). Routledge.

6 Running, writing, resilience

A self-study of collaborative self-care among women faculty

Sandra L. Tarabochia, Kristy A. Brugar and Julie Ann Ward

Image 6.1 Parking lot light

> *Imagine your alarm goes off at 4:05 a.m. . . . yes, in the morning. It's dark and chilly outside and you are quietly alone as you sip coffee, stretch your legs, and lace up your running shoes. You head outside to drive to the start of your run. When you arrive, you see another car under the parking lot light, waiting. Your friend and running mate jumps out of their car, greeting the day, perhaps grumbling about the cold or the wind or the early hour. This process is consistent – the start time is always the same. The route varies only by day of the week. Your mind is free. You are ready to run.*

DOI: 10.4324/9781003207863-8

We've experienced the above scenario consistently for three years. Each time, the experience is familiar yet new. The small, repeated actions provide an opportunity to engage our minds and bodies, to set an intention for the run and day ahead. We move from the parking lot to the road; the subtle beep of trackers/watches breaks the early-morning silence; playlists are piped through earbuds, private soundtracks for a public experience. Our pace builds from a walk to a trot to a jog to a run. The course begins with a long, flat stretch of road, and as we approach the first incline, our conversation shifts from pleasantries to weightier topics. We call this our "running bubble" – a space that is both private and public but inherently safe. It is a place to take risks as we unpack personal and professional challenges or mundane experiences. These risky conversations seem easier in the darkness and in motion on the open road.

Talk and laughter (maybe some groaning) become the soundtrack as we move through the expected miles, turning left to go up the hill and right to come back down – it is easy to forget the milestones as we move over the common terrain. And yet, just as we think "everything is the same," something marks the run/journey as different from the others. It might be the overwhelming smell of a frightened skunk or a coyote bounding across our path. The unexpected moments make us pause, literally and figuratively, to appreciate the magical moments that only happen because we are out on this road, this morning. We remain present as we experience a deep state of flow (Csikszentmihalyi, 1996).

This chapter is our attempt to articulate our experiences as early-career and now midcareer faculty who have traversed many miles and many words and found running together to be a deep, dynamic, resistant act of care. Our collaborative running practice, and now collaborative writing about that practice, has become a form of mutual mentoring toward self-/other-care that counters corporatised self-care initiatives, which often blame individuals for struggles rooted in systemic injustice and structural oppression and isolate individuals from each other to perpetuate myths of success and prevent organised resistance to neoliberal notions of productivity. We believe that sharing and theorising our practice, uncovering why it has been vital for our individual and collective wellbeing, is valuable because so many faculty long for healthy, sustainable self-/other-care as we struggle to thrive in the "publish or perish" climate of higher education, intensified by a growing neoliberal agenda that promotes austerity and individualism.

Although cross-disciplinary scholarship offers best practices for successful academic publishing (Boice, 1990; Ezer, 2016; Sword, 2017; Tulley, 2018), we know little about the lived experience of faculty writers and the strategies used to survive and transform oppressive systems and structures of academia (Tarabochia, 2020). As Sandy has argued elsewhere (Tarabochia, 2020, 2021), research and support for faculty writers too often emphasises strategies for increasing productivity rather than building a healthy, sustainable writing life. By exploring the link between running and self-/other-care in the academy, we attempt to humanise faculty development, attending to holistic wellbeing through the embodied activity of running with others.

This chapter is a manifestation of our critical collective inquiry to understand how and why collaborative running became a safe, brave space (Arao & Clemens, 2013; Boomstram, 1998) for us, a space in which we've felt emboldened to be "vulnerable and exposed" (p. 407). In reflecting on how that space cultivated (and was cultivated by) mutual mentoring toward self-/other-care, we extrapolate insights that might be useful to others – faculty writers (at various institutions navigating their own career ladders) and those who mentor, support and evaluate them – whether or not running is a shared passion. We emphasise the importance of acts that go beyond the act of running: time to reflect; time to share dreams, fears, passions, worries; time to be in relationships in a culture that privileges isolation and competition; as well as the freedom and encouragement to examine unquestioned systems that often disproportionately dismiss and undervalue the work of women. These opportunities to critique messaging about wellbeing in academia promote the authentic, relational work scholars need to navigate academic spaces.

As we critically consider why mutual mentoring through collaborative running has been meaningful for us, we are mindful of our positionalities. We are (now) tenured faculty members who must publish at a research university. We are straight, cisgender, temporarily able-bodied white women. We are writers. We are runners. We acknowledge the privilege inherent in our experience of running and training for sanctioned races, in our careers as professors who write (among other things) for a living. We do not assume running is an activity available or enticing to all bodies. At the same time, we sense that unpacking what collaborative running has done for us might open possibilities for others to imagine collaborative engagements that might achieve similar ends given their own unique circumstances.

We each joined our university as assistant professors at different times, in three different disciplines: education; English; and modern language, literature and linguistics. We happened to meet in a faculty writing group in 2016 and discovered a common interest in running for health and pleasure. Since then, we have collectively completed local 5K races, run half-marathons at home and across the country, published two books and many articles; we have all earned tenure.

In May 2019, we registered for the Dallas Marathon, scheduled for December that year. The marathon would be Kristy's 11th, Sandy's 1st and Julie's 2nd. As we headed into the fall semester, preparing our course syllabi and wrapping up summer writing projects, we committed to a rigorous 16-week training program. In what follows, we share our individual and collaborative critical reflections on our preparation for, experience of and reflections since that race, proposing that the process allowed us to become more attuned to our body/mind/emotion centres (Welling, 2014). The work of a tenure/tenure-track faculty is not a sprint; it is a marathon. It requires a plan, long-term commitment, willingness to be vulnerable and challenged, attention to a variety of visible and invisible expectations and the support of those closest to us. Training for the marathon made us realise attunement to body/mind/emotion centres was not only important for the race but a key to navigating academic expectations and prioritising wellbeing and self-care.

Training and Preparation (or a Conceptual Framework)

Two concepts have been central to our understanding of collaborative running as a sustained and dynamic source of self-/other-care. First, physical feminism (Velija et al., 2013; McCaughey, 1997; Faulkner, 2018), a concept rooted in women's practices of martial arts and self-defense, theorises physical empowerment through gendered embodiment. Physical feminism is a process through which women develop physical and mental strength along with a "feminist consciousness" through which to critique cultural norms that position women as weak (Velija et al., 2013, p. 538). In the process of conditioning and inhabiting our bodies in previously unimagined ways, women reconceive of who we are and strengthen the relationship among body, mind and spirit (McCaughey, 1997, pp. 204–205). Physical feminism need not reinforce ableist assumptions about bodies and what they can do. Sandra Faulkner's work on running as an act of physical feminism seeks to "challenge and resist normative running bodies, typical femininity and staid expectations"; as women, she says, we "run toward and run away from expectations, relationships, and ways of being" (Faulkner, 2018, p. 114). As Faulkner points out, it is important "to attend to and connect women's actual experiences in their bodies with the political project of deconstructing the mind–body split" (p. 114). As we share our experiences in our running bodies, our goal is to honour the role of all bodies in meaning making, to theorise how embodied experience of all kinds "entails power and resistance" (p. 114). For us, integrating running and writing generally, and training for and completing the Dallas Marathon in particular, invited us to condition and inhabit our bodies in new ways, a process through which we were able to re/conceive of our strengths, not only the physical strengths of our particular bodies but the vital body/mind/spirit connection that sustains a "feminist consciousness" on the road and in the academy. We invite those whose physical bodies and/or personal inclinations reject or resist the activity of running to imagine more relevant embodied activities that involve collaboration and mind/body attunement (i.e., dancing, creating art, making or listening to music, etc.).

Complimenting physical feminism is Cheryl Glenn's notion of rhetorical feminism – a set of tactics, anchored in hope, for disidentifying with and resisting hegemonic ideologies (e.g., those promoted by academic discourse and practice) by actively "negotiat[ing] cross-boundary misunderstandings and reconciliations" and "energizing" feminist teaching, research and leadership (Glenn, 2018, p. 4). Particularly, our long conversations while running – often in the dark, always while in motion – became opportunities for mutual mentoring, an aspect of rhetorical feminism, which departs from masculinist models by investing in reciprocal relationships in which all parties develop personally and professionally through engagement, information sharing and community building (Boomstram, 1998; Glenn, 2018). As opposed to one-directional advice giving, partners in mutual mentoring honour the "mystery" in one another, remaining open and responsive to different approaches and pathways to success (Hinsdale, 2015). The "running bubble" we step into each time we lace up our shoes is a space in which we honour the "power of dialogue, silence, and listening to enhance" our interactions (Glenn, 2018, p. 150). The vulnerability of pushing our physical limits supports a "mutually trusting relationship" (ethos), encourages attunement to "authentic emotional connection" (pathos) and establishes a shared source of reasoning (logos) rooted in experience (Glenn, 2018, pp. 150–151). Collaborative running upholds mutual mentoring as a consistent practice of participatory self-care and collective wellbeing as well as a site for cultivating transformative imagination and enacting meaningful change in our personal and professional lives. These concepts illuminate intersections among our experiences as women runners and writers/professors. As we move through this chapter, we identify and unpack these pivotal points physically and intellectually along the journey of a marathon and academic career.

The Race

Our visual narrative unfolds across images anchored by the Dallas BMW Marathon course map (see Image 6.2). Each image represents a memory from our training for and running of the marathon and corresponds to key aspects of collaborative running as a practice that supports our wellbeing as writers and as women in the academy. These images serve as a catalyst to explore extended examples from different perspectives the body/mind/emotion connection so often dismissed in academic culture that privileges productivity and the life of the mind.

The Start/Finish Line: Reflecting on Beginnings and Endings

We bounce excitedly in the chilly morning, two bobbing heads in a sea of runners funneled into the "B" corral. Music blasts, bodies stretch, adjusting bibs, retying shoes, syncing watches. We feed on the energy pulsing through the corral and the crowd gathered to see us off. We are still for the National Anthem, and then a gun blast, fireworks, the race has begun! We feel hopeful, carried by adrenaline, unable to imagine the visceral challenges, physical, mental, emotional, spiritual, the race will bring. For now, we are compelled by the promise of the unrun road. And again, as we near the finish line, a voice booms through a microphone, the strong bass and inspirational song lyrics return, finish times are announced, and the PR bell rings out. Sweet adrenaline again carries the pain of our aching bodies, accomplishment gleams on the horizon as mind and spirit ride the wave of certainty to the end, the medal, snacks, photos, smiles, and sighs.

92   *Sandra L. Tarabochia et al.*

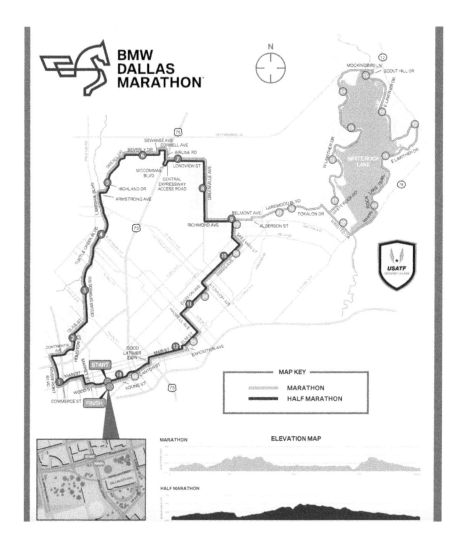

Image 6.2 Map

The start/finish line on a race route conjures the idea of beginnings and endings and the lived experience of mind/body/spirit these times/spaces invite. Reflecting on beginnings and endings through the lens of physical feminism surfaces questions about how the starting line and finish line – in terms of road races and academic research projects – can foster disembodied experiences.

Beginnings and endings are public times and spaces, moments when we size up competition, find our place within existing scholarship, identify an audience, find a publisher, play to the crowd.

Running, writing, resilience 93

Image 6.3 Kristy and Sandy just before running the Dallas Marathon

Starting races and writing projects forces us to question belonging: Can I hang with the runners I see around me, or will I be left in the dust? How do I fit into this conversation in the field? Do I have anything to say? These moments demand a conscious "opting in": Am I ready to run this race? Do I want to be part of this institution, this journal publication, this scholarly conversation? It can be easy to forget our own agency and efficacy in the process of race training and the grind of academic life. Beginnings and endings remind us.

At the same time, reflecting on beginnings and endings reveals the constructedness of these moments. Adrenaline-infused celebrations accompany them so they stand out, root down into our memories. While that serves a purpose, it feels important to remember the markers are arbitrary, a human construct. The processes are always underway. Both writing and running are iterative and ongoing. The start of a race is also the end of a training cycle, and the start of a new manuscript marks the end of a research project, which hopefully is generative to the next inquiry. Our experiences of these moments together as runners and researchers and now our experience co-writing about our mutual activity have crystallised for us the reciprocal relationship between accomplishing goals and setting new ones – on the road and along our career paths.

Mile 5: Listening to the Body

Image 6.4 Bicycle

> *The crash was inadvertently caused by a prior accident – the week before, I had accidentally cut my index finger while slicing some bread. It was a bad cut and, a doctor later told me, should have been stitched up, but I had only bandaged it. When I ran it would throb and bleed, so it interrupted my training in that way. I wore a cumbersome bandage on my left hand, which made cycling a little bit awkward. One day, riding home from work, I wanted to adjust the rearview mirror on my left handlebar. Because of the bandage, I had to reach across with my right hand, which caused me to turn the handlebars all the way to the left. I crashed, out of the blue, riding slowly on an empty, flat street. My pants ripped and my knee swelled up – my training plan was, once again, interrupted.*

Mile 5 is the first mental and physical hurdle as runners settle into a long run and the commitment it invites. This is a point of checking in, taking stock. We identify a mangled bicycle with this milestone to honour the unexpected/unanticipated challenges that emerge along a seemingly clear footpath, project plan, or career trajectory. Julie experienced a painful bike

Running, writing, resilience 95

crash about one-quarter of the way through our marathon training program. This coincided with submitting her materials for tenure, and she was feeling distracted and anxious, a mind/body location she associates with the crash.

Writing projects and career trajectories can work this way too. What we imagine when we write a grant proposal, book prospectus or article abstract is not necessarily the reality we find as we sink into the project. Whereas at the beginning (of a run or a project) our intentions are hypothetical, the real and metaphorical mile 5 demands careful listening to the body/mind/spirit "in situ" – in the moment – in order to determine the next right step. The crash unexpectedly thwarted Julie's training program, and it was the second "accident" to do so in a short period of time. Her body disrupted the plan her mind so carefully constructed. Julie chose to listen.

> *What still surprises me is the clarity I had about the reasons for both the knife and the biking accidents – I knew that I was distracted and anxious about my tenure application. I was on the cusp of the biggest moment of my career so far and felt that I was teetering on an enormous edge. Though I was aware of this and took steps to care for myself (eating healthily, trying to maintain a sleep routine, exercising, socializing, seeing a therapist and a life coach), my body was experiencing the anxiety on its own terms. I knew, in my mind, what was happening with my body and my sentimental world and couldn't do a thing about it.*

Often, we hear that running relieves stress. As Edwards articulates, "It's empowering to know that we can combat the negative impacts of stress on our brains just by getting out and running" (referencing Miller et al., 2018, of which Edwards is a research team member). But running did not combat Julie's stress and anxiety – she "couldn't do a thing about" what was happening in her "body and sentimental world." Instead, her body told her to stop moving, stop running. Colleagues have shared similar experiences of waking up in the night sweating, heart racing, crying jags, weight gain or loss, excessive substance use. These experiences don't make it into tenure dossiers. The bike crash crystalises the ways in which individual and collective wellbeing often entails resisting an academic culture that relies on conceptual hierarchies that privilege the mind and rational thought over the body and emotions. Because we'd been running and training together, Kristy and Sandy were able to support Julie's move to listen to her body and encourage the rest and recovery she needed.

We locate the crash at mile 5 to highlight that moment of pause, the call to listen. It reminds us that physical feminism isn't only about conditioning strong bodies. Collaborative running nurtures and sustains the "feminist consciousness" Julie demonstrated that drove her to honour the messages of her mind/body/spirit as a foundation for institutional critique. Moreover, Julie's experience illustrates the role of rhetorical feminism in mutual mentoring. Instead

96 *Sandra L. Tarabochia et al.*

of signalling weakness or the need for advice, Julie's vulnerability enriched her ethos in our group, reiterated the need for emotional attunement in the face of oppressive institutional demands and reinforced lived experience as a source of reasoning.

Mile 8: Regeneration

Image 6.5 Prairie Fire

> *We were excited to race as training had been going well. As part of our marathon journey, we decided to run a half-marathon race, the Prairie Fire in Wichita, Kansas, to celebrate the midway mark of our training. The morning was colder than our training runs had been by about 20 degrees, but with the crowds and camaraderie, the cold was easily forgotten. As the race started, it was easy to move quickly, maybe too quickly, with the enthusiasm of the race and the pent-up energy to begin. Kristy, alone, moved through the first 10K faster than recent training runs and a bit faster than the intended pace for this run. While she felt strong, this race plan (or rather abandonment of her race plan) was short-sighted; she did not approach this as a training run. At mile 8, Kristy, an experienced marathon runner, was escorted from the course due to an Achilles injury. She faced a tough decision at that moment, to continue the race, run through the pain, or admit she was injured*

and leave the race in hopes of recouping for the full marathon, which was less than two months away.

An image of a prairie fire at mile 8 links the natural burning of prairie grasses to the body's need to rest, lie dormant and regenerate. It is a pause in nature and, as we see it, a pause for runners and writers. Kristy's decision to leave the course was certainly about care but also an opportunity to reset her intention – a new beginning as a prairie fire often is for the land. Kristy had two intentions associated with the half-marathon: to complete a planned training run with a much-needed change of scenery and to spend time with friends enjoying the act of running. The second intention was most important to acknowledge – it was Kristy's purpose for training and running the Dallas Marathon. As with Julie's bike crash, Kristy's injury invited us to contemplate the reasons we push our bodies as we train and race and to remember the role of intentionality in the pursuit of wellbeing.

Kristy related her injury in the Prairie Fire to her struggle with a manuscript. Kristy was writing about teachers she cared about, whose stories she felt passionately needed to be told. Yet when the article was rejected for a third time, she decided to abandon the piece. This was a tough decision to make – she felt as if she was letting down those teachers by not continuing to pursue publication. To let the piece go, she drew on a similar faith that carried her off the Prairie Fire course. The manuscript had been a learning experience. It was important for her to recognise the value of these experiences and to believe there would be other opportunities and move on.

An aspect of mutual mentoring, infused with physical and rhetorical feminism, is openness to different pathways to success. Kristy's injury and the manuscript rejections were not part of her plans – to run a celebratory half-marathon as part of rigorous marathon training and to publish a piece of her dissertation she cared deeply about. In both cases, she'd invested a great deal of time and energy, so letting go could easily feel like failure. Instead, physical feminism encourages re/consideration of our strengths. In this case, Kristy's strength was in acknowledging tough breaks and forging new paths forward. She could leave the race knowing when she healed, Sandy would be waiting for her, happy to shift their training schedule to account for wounded body and spirit and build strength again. Similarly, attunement to her emotional connection to the manuscript gave Kristy faith that perhaps she'd return to it someday or find other ways to honour those teachers and their stories in her future work. Collaborative running as a site for mutual mentorship built the foundation for Kristy to handle each of these setbacks, like the burning of prairie grasses, as natural moments of necessary destruction in the long-term health and evolution of her running and writing career.

98 Sandra L. Tarabochia et al.

Miles 13–20: A Leap of Imagination

Image 6.6 Skunk

> The crowd of runners at the start has thinned out, as has the groups of family and friends lining the streets and cheering on the participants. We are directed to a lake in Dallas and instructed to "take a lap" (a 10-mile lap!). The run changes from a public event among thousands of friends to a seemingly private experience. As we transition to the isolation of the lake, we hear the birds chirp and the rustling of leaves, reminding us of the wildlife we'd spotted during training runs in our small college town. From snakes and skunks to coyotes and foxes, these creatures indicate the necessary leap of imagination that spurs us on when we are farthest from home.

As we consider the metaphor of the marathon, miles 13 through 20 are pivotal. These miles in the Dallas Marathon allowed us to refocus from the larger event to our individual minds and bodies running next to one another, like they had been on so many training runs before. Mentally, we realised we'd completed 13, 14, 18 miles many times before. The act of running was not new; however, in that moment, it looked and felt very different. Recreational runners must acknowledge that completing a full marathon means more than "running a half-marathon twice"; miles 13–20 require perseverance and a willingness to see things differently or for the first time. The magic of the wilderness cultivates this necessary shift in perception – to truly acknowledge the newness of what can appear to be commonplace.

We see a parallel between these conspicuously private middle miles of a marathon and our experience transitioning to associate professors post tenure. For us, the time was marked by initial relief (we made it!) quickly followed by anxious uncertainty, "What do we do now? Something new? Or the same thing again?" Becoming an associate professor is a moment of reckoning, ushering in a series of questions and concerns that are often only voiced in one's head. We wondered how, as associate professors and emerging lifelong runners, we could develop the ability to breathe physically and intellectually, to use the space in front of us – practices that seemed so different from checking off training days or publications. Being able to connect with others, experiencing mutual mentoring, in ways that are safe and brave have been essential as we sort through identity-making questions at mid-career.

Mile 16: (Re)gaining Equilibrium

Image 6.7 Bridge

> We are over halfway through the race course, making consistent progress, when it happens. Our feet move from the solid flat of concrete to a softer surface carpeting a short footbridge. Presumably built to give in response to wind, weight, and the cadence of many other runners, the bridge seems to move as we jog across. We are getting tired, starting to feel the miles and the unanticipated effects of the Texas sun, unseasonably hot in late December. Is the ground really moving under our feet? Are we woozier from the heat and the miles than we thought? Can we trust our minds and bodies and the road beneath to carry us forward?

A feeling of disequilibrium is often experienced by distance runners and women in academia as friends and family deem us "crazy," (ableist language that troubles us on many levels) for writing books and for running marathons. Each of us has had the experience of hearing colleagues marvel at the time we spend running –

> How do you find the time? I could never train for a marathon with my busy life!
> You *ran* to your son's soccer practice today? How far is this from your house?
> You did it in the morning, in the cold, just in time for kickoff?

We hear similar sentiments related to our scholarly work, most often from people outside academia, but sometimes from academic colleagues working under different evaluation criteria:

> You are writing/wrote a *book*?
> You published eight articles last year? That's crazy! How is that possible?

And when people realise we are reaching for and achieving ambitious running *and* publishing goals, the incredulity doubles.

> You must be superhuman!
> I could never do that!
> I am a real person who likes to eat and sleep and do frivolous things.

These reactions negatively impact our wellbeing. We can start to question our decisions and our perceptions of reality, much like we did crossing the wobbly bridge mid-marathon. Am I spending my time wisely? Is this a realistic thing to do? Can I really reach such ambitious goals? The doubt can be disorienting, distracting, counterproductive and isolating. The need to hide aspects of ourselves and our lives for fear others will perceive us to be bragging or assume we look down on those who make different choices is stifling. The wobbly bridge just past mid-marathon represents the loneliness of downplaying or doubting ambitious running and writing goals for fear of drawing attention, being misunderstood, dismissed as unrealistic.

Here, collaborative running as a means of cultivating mutual self-care is key. The processes we engage in as academics and distance runners are often misunderstood even by those intimately involved and invested in our success on the road and along our career trajectories. However, pursuing both activities simultaneously and alongside one another has given us the perspective and the words to critically interrogate comments from others and to validate one another's ambitions and commitments. We are not "crazy." We are engaged in dynamic activities and a reciprocal relationship to which we can bring our full selves.

The role of rhetorical and physical feminism in this process is clear. Training and racing together, a form of physical feminism, is a process through which we've developed physical and mental strength, a "feminist consciousness" that reveals how gaslighting can be gendered. Each comment we hear about our "crazy" endeavours is weighted differently because we are women runners, pushing our physical limits, and ambitious women scholars striving in the sexist, misogynistic academy. Processing these experiences in relation to each other allows us to see their connectedness and counter with critique of cultural norms that position us as weak. Likewise, we see how collaborative running as mutual mentorship toward self-/other-care creates space for rhetorical feminism. Just as we looked to each other for confirmation of the wobbly bridge, we look to each other to confirm our experience of the realities of the academy and of a running world that can be unfriendly toward aging women. Through dialogue, testimony, silence, and resistance, we remind each other of the systemic roots of our reaction to the wobbly bridges we face as runners and scholars.

Sunset: Ending to Begin Again

Image 6.8 Sunset

"Sandy and Kristy, we have been waiting for you!" blared over the loudspeaker in Dallas as we crossed the finish line, completing the 26.2 mile race. There were smiles, hugs, recognition of the challenge, pride in the accomplishment. We slowed our pace as we walked toward our loved ones and wondered, "what's the next race?" In many ways, this is similar to our faculty inner voices curious about the next research project, book or article. The end is an opportunity to reflect on an experience, appreciate the process, revel in the achievement before the process begins again.

Collaborative Self-Care and Mind/Body/Spirit Attunement

Toor (2014) and Murakami (2009) testify to the "incredible intersection" of running and writing. For us, the activities interlock in ways that usefully dismantle binaries that keep women faculty from living our fullest lives. Insights gleaned from our self-study of this phenomenon suggest that other embodied activities could function similarly to cultivate the attunement we describe. Thus, we offer the following suggestions for pursuing collaborative self-care in higher education:

1. *Integrate embodied activities that traverse traditionally distinct domains* (Toor, 2014; Murakami, 2009). We show how intentionally integrating running and writing creates an opportunity to "acknowledge and honor the information gathered" and "work toward harmonising the three centres [body, mind and spirit] into one intention" (Welling, 2014, p. 70). These are places in which flow (Csikszentmihalyi, 1996) can and does occur. Collaborative self-care emerges from shared activities that draw attention to and traverse these centres, resisting false binaries established through cultural norms. This may occur as one practices yoga or recreationally reads. Each activity provides space before proceeding in ways that directly or indirectly inform future actions.
2. *Lean in to relational vulnerability* (Bracke, 2016; Jordan, 2004). Our weekly runs create "sacred bubbles" to vent, lament, experiment and try on new roles or perspectives. We commiserate about tough feedback (or outright rejection) from reviewers, outline articles and conceptualise scholarly arguments during long runs without fear of judgement or repercussion. Traversing neighbourhood streets in the wee hours of the morning, we can be vulnerable with each other as we navigate conflict, make leadership decisions and consider career opportunities. The ability to admit fear of failing, injury, illness and temporary inability to run (or to write!) is vital as we think about the distances (physically and intellectually) we strive to cover. In a neoliberal culture that rejects vulnerability as antithetical to resilience (Bracke, 2016), women professors need space, forged through running or otherwise, to be vulnerable, to cultivate "relational resilience" rooted in mutuality and connection (Jordan, 2004).

In this piece, we share our experiences; they are unique to us. We do not offer them as a model, a series of steps or an example for others to follow or even adapt. Instead, we surface a path to wellbeing that goes beyond the corporate slogans that identify self-care as an individual responsibility. Pushing back, we celebrate the value of relationality and resistance to holistic, sustainable wellbeing.

Acknowledgements

Images in this chapter are acknowledged as: Image 6.1 – sunnydot3 accessed from https://www.needpix.com/photo/916527/; Image 6.2 – BMW Dallas Marathon; Image 6.3 – Sandra L. Tarabochia; Image 6.4 – Kristy A. Brugar; Image 6.5 – U.S. Fish and Wildlife Service; Image 6.6 – Jean Beaufort has released this "Skunk" image under Public Domain license; Image 6.7 – Brian Frazer (awesomebundy) has released this "Wobbly Bridge" image under Public Domain license; and Image 6.8 – Kristy Brugar.

References

Arao, B., & Clemens, K. (2013). From safe space to brave space: A new way to frame dialogue around diversity and social justice. In L. M. Landreman (Ed.), *The art of effective facilitation: Reflections from social justice educators* (pp. 135–150). Stylus.

Boice, R. (1990). *Professors as writers: A self-help guide to productive writing*. New Forums Press, Inc.

Boomstram, R. (1998). "Safe spaces": Reflections on educational metaphor. *Journal of Curriculum Studies, 30*(4), 397–408.

Bracke, S. (2016). Bouncing back: Vulnerability and resistance in times of resilience. In J. Butler, Z. Gambetti, & L. Sabsay (Eds.), *Vulnerability in resistance* (pp. 52–75). Duke University Press. https://doi.org/10.1215/9780822373490-004

Csikszentmihalyi, M. (1996). *Creativity: Flow and the psychology of discovery and invention*. Harper Perennial.

Ezer, H. (2016). *Sense and sensitivity: The identity of the scholar-writer in academia* (Vol. 6). Sense Publishers. doi:10.1007/978-94-6300-241-7

Faulkner, S. (2018). *Real women run: Running as feminist embodiment*. Routledge.

Glenn, C. (2018). *Rhetorical feminism and this thing called hope*. Southern Illinois University Press.

Hinsdale, M. (2015). *Mutuality, mystery, and mentorship in higher education*. Sense Publishers.

Jordan, J. V. (2004). Relational resilience. In J. V. Jordan, M. Walker, & L. M. Hartling (Eds.), *The complexity of connection: Writings from the stone center's Jean Baker Miller training institute* (pp. 28–46). Guilford Press.

McCaughey, M. (1997). *Real knockouts: The physical feminism of women's self-defence*. New York City Press.

Miller, R. M., Marriott, D., Trotter, J., Hammond, T., Lyman, D., Call, T., Walker, B., Christensen, N., Haynie, D., Badura, Z., Homan, M., & Edwards, J. G. (2018). Running exercise mitigates the negative consequences of chronic stress on dorsal hippocampal long-term potentiation in male mice. *Neurobiology of Learning and Memory, 149*(28), 28–38. https://doi.org/10.1016/j.nlm.2018.01.008

Murakami, H. (2009). *What I talk about when I talk about running*. Vintage International.

Sword, H. (2017). *Air & light & time & space: How successful academics write*. Harvard University Press. https://doi.org/10.4159/9780674977617

Tarabochia, S. L. (2020). Self-authorship and faculty writers' trajectories of becoming. *Composition Studies, 48*(1), 16–33.

Tarabochia, S. L. (2021). From resilience to resistance: Repurposing faculty writers' survival strategies. *Peitho, 23*(3).

Toor, R. (2014, June 23). What running and writing have in common. *Chronicle of Higher Education*. https://www.chronicle.com/article/What-WritingRunning-Have/147193

Tulley, C. (2018). *How writing faculty write: Strategies for process, product, and productivity*. Utah State University Press.

Velija, P., Mierzwinski, M., & Fortune, L. (2013). "It made me feel powerful": Women's gendered embodiment and physical empowerment in the martial arts. *Leisure Studies, 32*(5), 524–541.

Welling, T. (2014). *Writing wild: Forming a creative partnership with nature*. New World Library.

7 Making mindful moments

Made artefacts as a form of data visualisation to monitor and respond to self-care and wellbeing

Sharon McDonough and Narelle Lemon

Introduction

The act of knitting has long been regarded as a relaxing leisure pursuit, but there is also a body of literature identifying the positive impact of knitting and other handcrafts on wellbeing (see, for example, Burns & Van Der Meer, 2020; Burt & Atkinson, 2012; Court, 2020; Riley et al., 2013). In recent years, fibre arts and crafts, including knitting, have undergone a resurgence (Riley et al., 2013; Robertson & Vinebaum, 2016), with Davidson and Tahsin (2018) arguing that engaging in making enables self-expression. In this chapter we draw on narratives to examine the ways a knitting project has supported our wellbeing and provided opportunities to represent our experiences in a tangible and creative way.

The image that we have included shows a knitted scarf that Sharon is making as a record of the meetings she has via the Teams Platform. As noted in the caption of the image each row and colour indicates the number of meetings that she has on a given day. Narelle is also making a similar product, but instead of a scarf it is a blanket recording any virtual meetings no matter what the platform, and we use these both as a form of mindful making, but also as a way of monitoring our work practices and self-care/wellbeing needs. We outline the genesis of this making project in the Context and Literature section of the chapter.

Context and literature

The advent of the global COVID-19 pandemic across the globe in 2020 has changed the way that we all live and work, and like many others, those working in higher education have faced the challenge of remote teaching and working for periods of time during the pandemic. This has added to the already intensified workload of academics in higher education contexts, as we now find ourselves tethered to our screens for hours on end – having meetings, classes, virtual afternoon teas, all the moments of our working days shifting to be in the online, virtual space. As makers and crafters, the act of knitting or crocheting is one that we have used to enable us to reconnect with our hands and bodies after being absorbed in the cognitive work of academia. In the following section of the chapter, we each provide a narrative that describes how we turned to a particular form of making – a data visualisation knitted object.

DOI: 10.4324/9781003207863-9

Image 7.1 and *7.2* Photo of Sharon's data visualisation scarf and a snapshot of the meeting logs that forms the pattern for the scarf (on the left), with each colour representing the different number of meetings held on a day. Narelle's blanket and virtual meeting log (on the right) represents the total number of hours per day in virtual meetings.

Knitting: wellbeing, public spaces, and data visualisation

As noted in the introduction, there is a body of literature examining the role that knitting and making might have on wellbeing and social connection. Riley et al. (2013) argue that knitting has been considered a "taken-for-granted domestic pursuit" (p. 50), but the resurgence of interest in the practice has seen a growing appreciation and understanding of both the skill and creativity it enables, along with the benefits for mental health and wellbeing. Both the cognitive and creative skills that kitting requires and the physical, repetitive act of the process itself are indicated as positively supporting wellbeing. Knitters describe the social benefits (Court, 2020) and the creative and meditative, flow-like effects that occur through the process of engaging in knitting (Lampitt Adey, 2018; Riley et al., 2013).

Over the last few years there has been an emergence of knitted objects as a form of data visualisation – most commonly shared in popular media in the form of temperature/climate scarves, where each row and colour indicates a pattern of the changing climate. Others have represented train delays, population trends, working hours, or baby sleeping patterns. In each of these knitted objects, making becomes the medium for visualising data and representing the experience of the world. Fibre artist Rickie van Berkum describes that she "draws insights from peer-reviewed publications, teasing out trends in the data and translating them into wearable art" (Fleerackers, 2019). It is in the translation of the data into the knitted object a shift occurs too between the individual and the collective, the personal and the public. Daher (2020) writes that "unlike graphs depicting climate change data, temperature blankets and scarves offer a tangible representation of the global phenomenon – and add a personal touch to a technical subject". This personal touch marks a shift in the way that objects are used and the audiences that they are intended for. Robertson and Vinebaum (2016) contend that the "substantial shift in site from private space to public space, away from the domestic sphere and into public sites" (p. 5) is one of the most significant developments in contemporary fibre art. This shift from knitting as a private, individual, domestic practice to one that occurs in the public space and in collective ways is reflected in both face-to-face and online communities. This shift into a public space is not only about the practice of knitting itself but also the design and focus of the types of pieces being created, with "artists using skill instruction to foster dialogue and discussion across socio-economic and cultural differences" (Robertson & Vinebaum, 2016, p. 8). The use of data visualisation to inform the design of knitted objects can therefore function as a way of moving the private sphere into the public domain (for example, through sharing visual representations of work, sleep, etc.). It also provides the opportunity for knitted objects to highlight social justice, environmental, and other issues. In acknowledging these potentials, however, we need to note our privilege in being able to work with fibre and knitting in this way. As Court (2020) notes, to engage in the practice and process of knitting as a leisure or art-making pursuit one needs to "have surplus time, or control over one's working patterns, and surplus income to participate in the community" (p. 283). Similarly, Robertson and Vinebaum (2016) argue that in collective, participatory projects attention needs to be paid to ensure that they are more "than feel good opportunities" (p. 9) which still hide issues of "exploitation, access and privilege" (p. 9). We acknowledge these issues in the fibre arts and knitting world and acknowledge that as working, white academics we have access to the surplus income and privileges that enable us to engage in knitting as a leisure and art-making pursuit.

In the narratives that follow, we each individually highlight how we have used knitting and data visualisation as a strategy for supporting our wellbeing before connecting the threads of our narratives and providing strategies for others.

Sharon's narrative

In early 2021 as I commenced a new year in higher education, and one grounded in the uncertainty of the continuing pandemic, I saw a tweet from Alex Holmes (@aomholmes), who was creating a data visualisation knitted scarf of their number of Zoom meetings. I'd been interested in the idea of data visualisation knitted or crocheted objects for some time, and this seemed like a great way to track my own experience of working in online spaces due to the pandemic and period lockdowns. I am always keen to start a new crafting/making project! As a part-time staff member, I was particularly interested in using the scarf to keep a record of my work practices and how many meetings I was participating in during the days I don't work. One of the things I'd started to notice was that with the geographic boundaries between home and work dissolving due to the pandemic, it was logistically easier to dial into meetings on days I didn't work – but I was worried early on how that might impact my wellbeing and my self-care.

I chose colours for my scarf based on what yarn I had in my already burgeoning yarn collection rather than buying anything new. I decided upon the following key for the pattern in terms of colours and what they represented:

- Dark maroon/claret: 0 meetings
- Dark purple: 1–2 meetings
- Light purple/lavender: 3–4 meetings
- Black: 5 + meetings

In order to create my pattern, I made a grid of each day of the week and would log how many meetings I was participating in throughout the week. As a part-time staff member, I only work two days a week, and these two days are not consecutive, so in theory, there should always be rows of dark maroon/claret between every other row. By creating a pattern that required one row per day I was also figuring that it would provide me with the opportunity to participate in some mindful making each day.

I'd been following along with a hashtag called #10minsofmaking and thought that might be a good way to find at least 10 minutes each day to engage in some making. As the year progressed, I discovered that finding 10 minutes a day or doing one row a day was not as easy as I had anticipated.

In May I shared an image of my data viz scarf on Twitter and Instagram, commenting that I had fallen behind in doing my scarf each day (Image 7.3). Sharing images of my making and crafting had been something I'd started to engage in as the pandemic shifted some of my face-to-face crafting groups into virtual spaces (McDonough, 2020). When I began catching up and knitting rows, I began to get a stark visual representation of my patterns of overwork as a part-time staff member. Where I had commented that there should have been rows of dark maroon/claret to signify no meetings between my two workdays, I was finding instead that I had working weeks filled with meetings. I made a mental note to begin to track my meeting participation more carefully and to not just dial in every time there was a meeting that I was invited to.

Again, I fell behind in my scarf, and when I once again caught up, the same pattern was emerging: my scarf was littered with colours that showed I was still working on days for which I was not paid. While everyone knows that academic work balloons out beyond the boundaries of the working week, as a part-time employee I had to begin to think about 'how much overwork is too much when you are part-time?'

Making mindful moments 109

Image 7.3 #10minsofmaking

While I was seeing the dialling into meetings to stay connected with projects, colleagues, and the faculty in which I work, the visual of my scarf began to tell a different story- one of unpaid labour and the donating of my time to the institution. I started to become conscious of the fact that each time I chose to dial into a meeting on a non-workday, I was choosing to set something in my personal life aside – my family, my own time to relax, my self-care, and my wellbeing – I was choosing to privilege work over those things. This wasn't something I had consciously considered prior to making the scarf. I enjoy my work, and some meetings hadn't felt like work. That combined with the normalisation of overwork within the academy had been something I had internalised, and it was only through the process of making that I was able to identify this. I found myself getting my scarf out and showing colleagues and using it to get them to visually see and understand that my part-time load was blurring across into the rest of the week. This was particularly useful for colleagues who would invite me to meetings saying that they knew it wasn't my workday, but perhaps I could join in. Each individual meeting invitation began to add up to me working 5 days a week. Sharing my scarf and process on social media also created opportunities with colleagues.

Image 7.4 Mindfully reflecting on patterns of work

As I write this, I continue with the making of my scarf. Each time I pick the scarf up and look at the pattern I am provided with an opportunity to stop and mindfully reflect on my patterns of work (Image 7.4). This enables me to connect to my own self-care and wellbeing and to privilege them rather than the work itself. Picking up the scarf also enables me to connect back to the joy of making, to the ways that I can get lost in the flow and rhythm of the knitting itself and of experiencing the pleasure that comes from watching my scarf grow.

Narelle's narrative: mindful making project

Something intrigued me about mixing my long-term mindful moment making projects (McPherson & Lemon, 2018) with my day job. If the pandemic has taught us anything, finding new ways of working is a must. Also, what has been revealed is that self-care requires our attention. The shift to working digitally, remotely, and in our personal spaces has been exhausting. It continues to be so. Ways to relax, to stop are required. Thus, to be able to knit data and observe the cultural practice of what was becoming a pandemic norm, that is spending

Making mindful moments 111

a significant number of hours meeting with others via virtual video conferencing utilising the platforms such as What's App, Zoom, or Microsoft Teams, seemed fitting. I was intrigued about what might be possible. I was not exactly sure of how the project would progress but all I knew at the time of beginning in January 2021 was that I was fascinated with this visual representation, was excited about a long-term mindful making project, and I was looking forward to visualising work patterns during a pandemic (with the intention that there would be less hours spent this way and we could hopefully document a shift back to being in the office or at least talking to people in real life). I had also purchased some wool online in 2020. I fell for the classic 'what appears online is not usually what it is like in real life' colour mistake. I thought I was ordering two shades of pink and two shades of grey. Instead, I received cream, tan, and two shades of blue. Not a colour palette I would normally engage with personally. So this project was also a way to work with this wool rather than have it sit in a basket unloved.

Image 7.5 I began knitting a scarf . . .

I began knitting a scarf in late January. I was on leave for the first 17 days, beginning the year as I wished to continue; more breaks and mindful moments to listen to my body. Dedicating the back of my notebook for recording hours, I created a plan for tracking hours, translate to my four-colour code, with space to tick off the line once knitted. I celebrated on Instagram to document the process. However, after a month being visually represented, I didn't like what I was

112 Sharon McDonough and Narelle Lemon

Image 7.6 Growing slowly

Image 7.7 Sparking a conversation

Making mindful moments 113

Image 7.8 Representing growth

making. It wasn't appealing. Perhaps it was the colours in partnership with the shape. It just wasn't working for me. My mindful making dataviz project sat for months. Untouched. Every time I looked at it did not bring me any joy. This is interesting as I am representing hours spent on virtual meeting platforms, and it was becoming increasingly obvious to me pandemic lockdowns and restriction in movement would be accompanying us more regularly than we all wanted in Melbourne. Perhaps my mindful making was hitting a raw nerve. A tension was being evidenced. If I was going to represent working hours, I didn't want this to be just a scarf, I wanted this to be a piece of work more significant that could be hung on a wall or draped over a lounge suite that sparked conversation.

So in May I decided to start again. I experimented with adding two stitches each second row. The effect would be the piece that not only grows in length but also width, representing the growth of the pandemic, but also growth in shifts of ways we are working in higher education.

I slowly knitted each row. Mainly on weekends with the radio or sport playing on television in the background. Usually, my partner would be beside me. Many times, he asked, "Tell me again what you are knitting?" "Ah, living art", he would say. "You are making an installation". And indeed, he may be right. A representation of living through the pandemic. Representing working hours. As I was knitting, I was working with different colours, noticing the data growing. Each time I knitted a collection of Zoom days in a cluster, representing my sitting time making a change of stitch, moving between moss stitch and single rib.

114 *Sharon McDonough and Narelle Lemon*

Image 7.9 My data dump

My dataviz mindful making project sits on the end of the couch. I engage with it each day. Looking at it. Calling it my data dump. The piece is now becoming large and it sits in different ways, drawing attention to different moments in time. A flare out, a pile or ripples. The weight of the piece is becoming evident now, and in June I moved from needles to circular needles with a stopper on the end. The width is expanding, as are the hours clicking in and out between meetings. I'm searching for ways to knit more dark blue that are not weekends of staycations (holidays booked but cancelled due to lockdowns . . . I'm at three and counting already by mid-June 2021). The dark blue represents downtime but also deep-thinking time. The deep thinking that has escaped me since March 2020 began as personal and professional spaces blurred with working at home. I miss deep thinking time. Instead, I am accompanied by a COVID hangover, forever tired and with foggy brain. Time blurs.

In early August I completed knitting the first six months of 2021. From January to June, I have 81 days dark blue (staycation leave and weekend time accounting for the majority of these 0-Zoom days); 36 baby-blue days of 1–2 hours; and 45 days of cream of 3- to 5-hour days on Zoom. There is more tan than I would like to see: 19 working days of more than 6 hours of being on Zoom. Those are super-long days, usually 12 hours, sometimes more hours in a day spent working. Not only do you meet, click in and out of meeting links, usually back-to-back, but you have to prepare, then there are action items while still managing all other tasks. It's a juggle of being

Making mindful moments 115

Image 7.10 Being present with the representation

Image 7.11 Recording hours to make the colour pattern

present in meetings but also taking advantage of meetings while being on screen . . . I type my notes from meetings now, just having to fix up spelling mistakes after. Everything has become digitised for work. Archives, shared documents for projects, project management, research, writing, planning, tracking, etc. There is an efficiency, a fascination in ways to be productive from a working smart perspective, but . . . so much screen time. I miss the days of cafe meetings, in-person conversations, bouncing off the energy from each other; no screens.

Mid-August I am back in a staycation. I'm exhausted. But this gives me a chance to knit for pleasure. This was my intention for this dataviz project. An excuse to connect with the clicking of needles, being present with making a stitch, watching the rows grow, and just stopping and being with making. I've noticed my ticking off on paper of the rows I have completed is as therapeutic as the making itself. There is a slowing down, a mindful appreciation of the day recorded.

Discussion: knitting as a relaxing leisure pursuit or mindful act of wellbeing

In this section we knit together the threads that we have identified in our narratives and what these highlight for us in relation to knitting as both a leisure pursuit and a mindful way to support wellbeing.

Designing, representing, and understanding the process of making

In sharing our narratives, we have discovered that we have each adopted different design techniques and processes in making our knitted works. These differences were related to the ways we were coding our data to represent it in the pattern. Sharing these processes highlights the creative and cognitive work involved in the process of making knitted objects and of using data to inform the pattern design. Court (2020) describes social knitting as the "practice of knitting which has a social element either through attending a knitting group or through participating in online communities" (p. 283), and in sharing our narratives with each other and our making through social media, we are participating in a form of social knitting that enables us to connect with others. The act of the making itself provided us with the opportunity to be mindfully present and to focus on the act of making. Riley et al. (2013) argue that the repetitive and rhythmic nature of knitting can "free up thinking and promote reflection" (p. 55), and our narratives highlight the ways the act of making enabled us to reflect on our working lives.

New ways of being an academic

Through the design and production of our pieces we have been able to reflect on the new ways of being an academic that the pandemic has required of us. Rather than meeting colleagues and students face to face or attending conferences in person, we find ourselves engaged in a virtual click in and click out as we interact with our colleagues. Our calendars fill with meetings, often without spaces between them, and in these spaces, we are finding that the connection and relationships we have with others are different.

Working hours

Collecting data of the hours we spend working lends itself to reflective and metacognitive thinking about the place of work, how much time is blurred between personal and professional during the pandemic, and enabled each of us to realise the ways in which we were overworking and jeopardising our self-care and wellbeing. The process of making the pieces provided a tangible and visual representation of our working life that enabled us to make change. They are a visual reminder of the need to stop working and to spend time doing things for ourselves and our wellbeing. As with some of the data visualisation objects mentioned, our knitted pieces representing our working hours move our own individualised practice into the public space and open an opportunity to engage others in dialogue about ways to monitor our working hours and to interrupt habituated practices. Robertson and Vinebaum (2016) argue that "textiles are embedded with social meanings" (p. 7) and that "public, collective types of making have a performative bent" (p. 5), with our data visualisation pieces forming to publicly share and explore patterns of work.

Creating your own data visualisation: some guiding points

Through the sharing of our narratives, we have highlighted how the construction of data visualisation pieces has enabled us to pay conscious attention to our self-care and wellbeing. Apart from the reflection that the piece enables, the process of making also provides an embodied connection and returns us from the cognitive to our hands. For those who wish to embark on a similar process, we offer the following suggestions.

1. Decide what you would like to track – is it hours of meetings/meetings/amount of meetings/time of commute/some other measure?
2. Consider are you recording work hours only or is personal also included (we tracked work hours only)?
3. Think about how you will record this to create your pattern.
4. Choose colours to represent your pattern.
5. Decide on your mode of making, i.e., knitting/crochet.
6. Consider how to make a pattern.
7. Decide if you'd like to share the process on social media to encourage dialogue with others.
8. Plan for an approach for how the making will be a part of your self-care (such as a mindful making project) or a representation or perhaps both.

Conclusion

In this chapter we have highlighted how drawing upon a leisure activity of knitting has provided us with the opportunity to engage in an embodied reflective practice and to visually represent patterns of our work. In a time of intensification and immersion in virtual and digital spaces, designing and making knitted representations of our work enable us to engage in a mindful, embodied practice that moves us from our head to our hands. It also offers us the ability to be more mindful in the ways we approach our work, promoting us to take action to support our wellbeing. We invite others to experiment with the strategies we have shared in this chapter and to also consider sharing their pieces with others as a way of creating a community that considers the potential of mindful making to support wellbeing.

References

Burns, P., & Van Der Meer, R. (2020). Happy hookers: Findings from an international study exploring the effects of crocheting on wellbeing. *Perspectives in Public Health, 141*(3), 149–157.

Burt, E. L., & Atkinson, J. (2012). The relationship between quilting and wellbeing. *Journal of Public Health, 34*(1), 54–59. https://doi.org/10.1093/pubmed/fdr041

Court, K. (2020). Knitting two together (K2tog), "If you meet another knitter you always have a friend". *Textile, 18*(3), 278–291. https://doi.org/10.1080/14759756.2019.1690838

Daher, N. (2020, February 19). How knitting enthusiasts are using their craft to visualize climate change. *Smithsonian Magazine*. https://www.smithsonianmag.com/smart-news/knitting-enthusiasts-are-using-their-craft-visualize-climate-change-180974231/

Davidson, R., & Tahsin, A. (2018). *Craftfulness*. Quercus.

Fleerackers, A. (2019, November 23). Knitting together the data: Interview with fibre artist Rickie van Berkum. *Nightingale*. https://medium.com/nightingale/knitting-together-the-data-d5f44e350f7d

Lampitt Adey, K. (2018). Understanding why women knit: Finding creativity and "flow". *Textile, 16*(1), 84–97. https://doi.org/10.1080/14759756.2017.1362748

McDonough, S. (2020). Endings and beginnings: Reflections on crafting and mothering. *Textile, 19*(2), 183–186. https://doi.org/10.1080/14759756.2020.1833408

McPherson, M., & Lemon, N. (2018). It's about fun stuff! Thinking about the writing process in different ways. In N. Lemon & S. McDonough (Eds.), *Mindfulness in the academy: Practices and perspectives from scholars* (pp. 113–127). Springer.

Riley, J., Corkhill, B., & Morris, C. (2013). The benefits of knitting for personal and social wellbeing in adulthood: Findings from an international survey. *British Journal of Occupational Therapy, 76*(2), 50–57.

Robertson, K., & Vinebaum, L. (2016). Crafting community. *Textile, 14*(1), 2–13. https://doi.org/10.1080/14759756.2016.1084794

Section 3
Creative practice as interruption

8 Using arts-based and feminist methodologies to slow the wear and tear/s of academic work/life

Alison L. Black

Introduction

This chapter is concerned with the impact of the neoliberal university on experiences of wellness in academic work/life. It highlights how arts-based and feminist methodologies can help us explore the distress of toxic workplaces and attend to slowing down. Such slowing down is needed to ascertain and interrupt the psychosocial and bodily harm academic culture inflicts. Our stories of crisis matter. Through writing and sharing them we create a feminist record and archive that enables us to better recognise, contest, and resist the neoliberal injuries and conditions we have encountered and are living/working through. This chapter is an invitation to readers to consider the damaging impact of their own institutions and to commit to working collectively in a 'feminist snap' of revolt, resistance, and reimagining.

The neoliberal university is toxic

The impact of neoliberal agendas and pervasive corporatised and economic representations of the academy, where universities recommend and reward positivist illusions of meritocracy and productivity over messy, embodied, rich, and complex experiences of being human, has been the subject of much research (Bottrell & Manathunga, 2019; Gill, 2010; Gregg, 2018; Hartman & Darab, 2012; Taylor & Lahad, 2018), including my own (Black, 2018; Black et al., 2019; Henderson et al., 2019). Gill and Donaghue (2016, p. 91), describe the impact individualistic, ruthless and competitive neoliberalism is performing on academics as a "deep crisis", and a "psychosocial and somatic catastrophe" in terms of how it is manifesting – with increased and chronic stress, exhaustion, and escalating rates of depression and illness leaving academics (and students) "stretched to breaking point".

Self-care strategies are clearly important so academics (and students) do not break. However, a focus on the intensification/extensification of academic work must continue – it must not be glossed over. The contemporary university with its increasing surveillance and audit culture is relying on individuals to be highly productive and responsible amidst "institutional and gendered

DOI: 10.4324/9781003207863-11

practices and dynamics", causing "cumulative harm and hurt" (Taylor et al., 2020, p. 8). We must not "reproduce the psychic landscape of neoliberalism" by repeating or succumbing to the myth that "responding to the growing crisis" requires "increasing work on the self" (Gill & Donaghue, 2016, p. 98). Turning away from structural/social/political interventions to frameworks of individualism – where the "coping" response to neoliberal agendas focuses on greater self-awareness/self-management/self-discipline/self-belief or self-care – is dangerous. Clear goals, choice in approach, taking a break, making and movement, and other mindful acts might engage us in the workplace, but ultimately they will not save us from the "harsh psychic consequences of the always-on, constantly striving, contemporary academic culture" (Gill & Donaghue, 2016, p. 98). Adding personal wellbeing and self-care practices as remedies for stress and overwhelm in an "otherwise untouched system" is highly problematic and potentially "silencing and paralysing" (Gill & Donaghue, 2016, p. 96). Alarming levels of "stress, unhappiness and overwork" are "structural consequences of a system placing intolerable demands upon its staff" (Gill & Donaghue, 2016, p. 97).

One way to ensure we do not obscure the systematic nature of this crisis and catastrophe and leave toxic power relations unchallenged is to find channels of expression to make visible our "hidden injuries" (Gill, 2010, p. 39), our stress and distress, the detrimental effects of excessive overwork, and the fear and shame that neoliberal processes are provoking in us. Offering vulnerable stories and representations of scholarly life are ways of ensuring history and context are not erased by a climate of continuously raised expectations of achievement. This is more than sharing strategies for self-care or coping. Rather, it involves a shedding of light on the psychosocial experiences of academic life/work in order to encourage interrogation, collective analysis, a politics of resistance, and a reimagining of universities (Gill & Donaghue, 2016; Black & Dwyer, 2021). Sharing "our grim tales" in which we speak of the "everyday humiliations, damages and hurts that attend our lives in neoliberal institutions" does "important feminist work" and enables "a move beyond the individual" by "surfacing the injurious relations and institutional conditions that prevail", and, inviting "collaborative work" as a means through which to "contest these conditions" (Taylor et al., 2020, p. 8).

A glimpse of my scholarly life

Across my academic career of more than 25 years, the neo-liberal academy has compelled me to compete and compare, to work on my own, to overwork, and to count narrowly. At various times, neoliberal ideologies have crept into my mind/writing/body, breaking me down. The academy's "finite games" of winners and losers, the demands to prove I am a "credible academic", the narrow counting and the changing and hardening rules of entry have kept me running on the production treadmill, frequently distracting me from what matters most (Harré et al., 2017, pp. 5, 9).

Harré et al.'s (2017, p. 5) metaphor of "the university as an infinite game" and their call to keep "the infinite game alive" as a "much needed form of academic activism" has been a great source of encouragement. For many years, I have been trying to create and hold spaces from which to dream new and infinite stories for myself, for women, and for the academy. I have been feeling my way gently: dreaming, visioning, yearning, writing, researching, and creating collective spaces for slow scholarship and stories of lived lives. Alison Mountz and colleagues call for slow scholarship focused on "cultivating caring academic cultures and processes" (Mountz et al., 2015, p. 1238). They remind us that how we work and interact with one another creates spaces and possibilities for "community", "solidarity", and "resistance" (Mountz et al., 2015, p. 1249). They instil a sense of hope that we can shift the culture with a focus on kindness and friendship, quality and depth, reflection and relationship. They encourage me to count differently, to do academia differently, to do less, to not-do. Such deeply ethical ways of working, relating, and imagining require different ways of working; they take a special kind of time and effort – embodied, contemplative, present (Shahjahan, 2015). Ethics of care and caring, ethics of rest and renewal, they require us to play "the long game", a game "as long as an academic life, perhaps" (Harré et al., 2017, p. 12). And so, a long game is also a slow game of nudging the university toward cultural shifts that nourish and support. This quest is not easy or assured. It is tiring, and it sometimes feels hopeless. The intensified deadline-driven agendas of the neoliberal university challenge our ability to think and engage in care-full and contemplative inquiry (Shahjahan, 2015). The academy's individualistic and competitive games make it hard to build communities of collaboration, kindness, and care. Its patriarchal practices rarely include or honour the lived experiences of women; and reimagining broader conceptions of and for an academic life requires continued faith and energy.

As part of our "long game", this year my colleague Rachael Dwyer and I published an edited collection *Reimagining the Academy: ShiFting Towards Kindness, Connection, and an Ethics of Care*. Forty-four authors from around the globe explored their lived experiences and provided evocative conceptual content that responded to the symbolic nature of transformation in the academy. They engaged in feminist writing to shed light on their experiences and considered what it means to build caring, compassionate academic communities. Their writing offers landmarks for how we might collectively and actively build a culture of kinder possibilities.

In my early thinking about "transformation", I played with ways of 'MAKING shiFt HAPPEN' in the academy, identifying meaningful phrases and feminist methodologies and intentions (hence the capitalised F in shiFt) (see Black & Dwyer, 2021) that captured my longings to 'do academia differently', phrases that felt spacious and offered me life-giving alternatives and options. In too many institutions, in my institution, women are an underused undervalued knowledge resource. Their precarious juggling of family/carer/career responsibilities at the expense of their own wellbeing and advancement is rarely acknowledged. My own personal/professional juggle infuses my current thoughts and feelings and causes me to wonder whether transformative shiFt in the academy is even possible. But if it is, I keep thinking about what it might involve:

shiFt

1. *a new beginning*
2. *to create, to transform, to transport, to delight*
3. *to take care of oneself and others, to flourish, and engage in slow scholarship*
4. *promoting ideas, sharing stories, finding connection, collaboration, and friendship*
5. *creating meaning together, supporting and celebrating each other, lifting each other up*
6. *like [the pleasure of wearing] a loose-fitting garment – finding liberating and enabling ways to wear an academic life*
7. *activating personal and professional alchemy, kindness, movement, and change in the academy.*

Reviewing these phrases, I feel the tension of attending to "grim tales" and injuries while hoping for structural/social/political change (Taylor et al., 2020, p. 2). Like Mountz et al. (2015), Henderson et al. (2016) urge academics to develop a desire for generating "new ways of thinking, acting, feeling and seeing . . . embracing our failure and wounds . . . [in order to] find joy and friendship in our work" (Henderson et al., 2016, p. 16). So perhaps the tension is required.

This chapter, then, offers a space and place to embrace my failures and wounds. Because somewhere in the recent past, I lost my way. I misguidedly found myself seeking recognition (through promotion) for the contribution I had made. I was duped by the "productivity imperative", in which I thought I could "prove my value" through responsible, autonomous, continuous and "extensive investments in work" (Lamberg, 2021, p. 466).

In the years leading up to submitting my application to associate professor, I engaged in extreme efforting, evidencing, and overwork, becoming a player in the university's finite career games (Harré et al., 2017). I took on more responsibility than I had time or energy for. The documentation of citation scores, impact factors/fractures, h-indexes, Higher Education Academy case studies, student evaluations, grant writing, and more, to show and prove my knowledge and value was deadening. Alas! The violent verdict from the university was "not good enough", "not successful", "you don't belong". It wounded me, deeply, and sent me spiralling into darkness. I had to find ways to live with it, knowing there would be more to live with.

Two years on, coinciding with the writing of this chapter, I attend again the promotion information sessions to hear how expectations are communicated. The trauma of career games and not-enough-ness resurfaces. I listen and sense the feelings of depletion, disillusionment, and emptiness stirring again, rising like bile in my throat. It is clear the "qualculations" (Callon & Law, 2005,

Arts-based and feminist methodologies 125

p. 718) that measure my value have multiplied and intensified. The goal posts, shifted again, are highly monetised and quantitative and dismiss my contribution, knowledge, and expertise. The unique obstacles of my gendered experience and discipline area and the impact of pandemics, restructures, and rolling redundancies within and beyond our institution are ignored. We are told that many people have actually been able to increase their research outputs during lockdown.

It will be years before my circumstances change and my dollar metrics rise to the new numbers they demand; years before I can reapply with any hope of success. The weight and the pressure of this most measured, monitored and surveilled profession (Burrows, 2012) bears down on me. I have been bearing this pressure for a long time – a too-long history of pressure, damage, and "taking it" (Ahmed, 2017a, p. 189).

As I sit with this remembered and reactivated pain, it is hard to write this chapter. I find myself wasting hours staring blankly at the screen, shifting words around, unable to write. Stuck. Paralysed. How is the sense of loss and not-enough-ness still so acute? How can it be lurking, taunting, still? It seems I have not recovered from this "not being seen", the injustice of the decision from the promotion committee that still, after decades of performing and efforting in the academy (albeit interrupted due to carer responsibilities and mothering), I am still "not up to scratch". I console myself with the fact seven other professors read my application prior to submission, told me I had met the standard, affirmed I had prepared a bulletproof, well-evidenced case.

UGGGH! I am so tired of this game! I am so sick of "not mattering" (Taylor et al., 2020, p. 2). The elitist, exclusionary university has f*cked me over. I feel the fury, the injustice, the deadening sensations of overwork. I feel grief in heart and mind and body. I haven't sat with this debilitating exhaustion for a while. I have been too busy.

Since COVID-19 I haven't stopped. I have worked harder than ever through this global pandemic of death, fear, and uncertainty. I have worked harder than ever through national and local job loss and highly publicised precarity; through institutional restructures and horrendous belt-tightening initiatives; through administrative overload; new workload formulas; new "research active" definitions; new academic standards; and through union meetings contesting all the former. These new auditing processes and benchmarks during a year where our psyches are already fully impacted feel caustic and corrosive. Yet, on I have worked, pushing through these processes full of risk, through endless emails and back-to-back Zoom meetings, engaging in ongoing pastoral care of students under stress; through delayed practicum placements and updated handbooks, through changes to learning management systems and course offerings and an avalanche of minutia and detail requiring immediate attention and action by close of business, thanks (of course, no one actually said thanks)! I have pushed on through family stress and sickness; through my own anxiety and sense of overwhelm; through heart monitoring and cardiologist visits; through the onset and symptoms of menopause; through my fears of blood clots and my not-quite-right blood test results; through fires and evacuations; through lockdowns and panic buying; through request after request, expectation after expectation, demand after demand.

My academic work/life has had no balance. Little has been meaningful or slow. Zooming into the promotion panel presentations for this year, I can't bear to turn my camera on. Or perhaps "not showing my face" is an act of resistance. I listen to the arrogance of this old white man who is making all the rules, telling us who "qualifies". "We want sustained performance, more than doing your job, five years of working at the standard you are applying for", "ensure you apply at the crescendo", "know in the end it's only the dollars that count!" His privilege, his passive-aggressive and disrespectful tone as he describes to hopeful, deserving applicants his unachievable views on all that must be evidenced despite all we have collectively experienced this past year, is astonishing and revealing. My exhaustion and rebellion move and shiFt within me. I feel a "crisp, sharp, cracking . . ." (Ahmed, 2017a, p. 188).

The wear and tear/s of trying times

I have been trying to do academia differently (since I had to move from a regional area so my kids could go to high school, and securing employment required accepting a lower-paid position and title than the one I'd held for six years previous. It was hard going "down" the ladder, and it has impacted my 'career').

I have been trying to do academia differently (since they then created an "unadvertised" position for the "male applicant" who had applied for the job I got but who was "not successful", giving him the higher pay and title they said they couldn't give to me).

I have been trying to do academia differently (since the workplace bullies broke me, and HR, instead of helping me, got me to sign a statement outlining I would not sue).

I have been trying to do academia differently (since my workload reached toxic and unsustainable levels but the demands to do more were repeated, repeated, repeated, repeated).

I have been trying to do academia differently (since my emotional collapse).

I have been trying to do academia differently (since my father died unexpectedly).

I have been trying to do academia differently (since my husband had a heart attack).

I have been trying to do academia differently (since my year on antidepressants).

I have been trying to do academia differently (since I have been the sole breadwinner).

I have been trying to do academia differently (since I applied for seven grants and none got up).

I have been trying to do academia differently (since it became impossible to do the work demanded of me in a normal working week, and I found myself working extremely long days and across my weekends again and again and again).

I have been trying to do academia differently (since my son left home for the city).

I have been trying to do academia differently (*since my friend and colleague Rosemary died. Mourning her disappearance, I became aware of my own*).

I have been trying to do academia differently (*since I, and four education colleagues, were unsuccessful in promotion; yeah, that part in the procedures about taking into account the features of our field and discipline is total bullsh*t*).

I have been trying to do academia differently (*since climate-change threats and frightening fires saw us having to evacuate twice*).

I have been trying to do academia differently (*since being "officially" in menopause*).

I have been trying to do academia differently (*since COVID-19 changed all our lives*).

I have been trying to do academia differently (*since I saw my cardiologist and he said a future heart valve replacement is in store*).

I have been trying to do academia differently (*since I turned 53 – my mum died at 63, two years after her open-heart surgery for a valve replacement which then left her in a nursing home; life suddenly feels short, precious*).

I have been trying to do academia differently (*since my daughter experienced a rough patch in her final year of school – 2020 was a helluva year for our young people*).

I have been trying to do academia differently (*since she left home too, and I have an "empty nest"*).

I have been trying to do academia differently (*since lockdowns have further blurred the boundaries between work and home life, keeping up with endless email has become impossible, and Sunday mornings often look and feel the same as Monday mornings*).

I have been trying to do academia differently (*since the writing of this chapter and attending to the damage and the brokenness*).

> *(I have been **trying, trying, trying**) trying to choose my own path. To find some balance.*
>
> *(I have been **trying, trying, trying**) trying to create a kinder academy. To make space for stories of experience. To make space for research that listens. For slow scholarship.*
>
> *(I have been **trying, trying, trying**) trying to show how creative and contemplative methodologies capture the living of a life. Help us feel. Help us connect and understand. Change us. Might help us change the culture.*
>
> *(I have been **trying, trying, trying**) trying to create spaces for collective authorship, for women in academia to know they are seen, heard, and are enough.*
>
> *(I have been **trying, trying, trying**) trying to advocate, to help, to mentor.*
>
> *(I have been **trying, trying, trying**) trying to push back against the patriarchy and value many ways of knowing.*
>
> *(I have been **trying, trying, trying**) but this machine is relentless. Greedy. Unseeing. Cruel.*
>
> *(I have been **trying, trying, trying**) but I find myself crying, crying, crying. Will I survive this academic life?*

I need to make space, to slow down, to catch my breath. I am injured. Stretched. Broken. Torn. Snapped in two.
Time to make space.
Time to slow down for more than just a moment.
Time to breathe. To gulp in clean air. Time to walk toward a different life.
Ah, the fragrance of spacious, slow, lazy time wafts in my direction.
Freedom, joy, authenticity, wellbeing call out my name. The institutional walls muffle their sounds. I try to walk towards them, but I cannot see or hear them. They are not here in the academy.
Instead, I hear the **SNAP**.

Self-care, self-soothing and SNAP!

I employ an enormous number of self-care and self-soothing strategies in order to negotiate the harsh psychic consequences of academic culture: slow morning cups of green tea with a "no screens" rule; hopeful quotes scattered around my home/office: "it is not the critic who counts", "we rise by lifting others", "say NO", self-care checklists, and more; working from places other than my desk; calendar reminders to stop work at 5 (too often ignored); weekend "out of office" messages; shaking on the vibrodisc; sitting on my shakti mat; using and diffusing essential oils; sitting in silence; priming my intuition with oracle cards and affirmations; facilitating sleep with a set bedtime; yoga nidra; prayer; guided meditations; Netflix bingeing; creative writing; Nia dancing; beach walking; weekend slumping; Jin Shin; EFT tapping; Eden energy exercises; swinging smovey rings; making vision boards; tracking moon/body cycles; hopeful online courses; motivational books/blogs/podcasts; diarising "untouchable days" and buffers between meetings; turning off app notifications; not watching the news; staying off social media; keeping a gratitude journal; writing morning pages; only working with people I like on projects I like; decorating my planner; planning for the week ahead; monthly visits to my psychologist; and on and on it goes . . . This mass of strategies and mindful acts is never enough. Nothing from this long and varied list has saved me from the psychic landscape of neoliberalism. Where would I be without them? I am not sure, but I know I need them all. For the finite games of the academy disorient me still. Slow mornings and cups of green tea (and all of these acts of self-care) offer moments of support. They help me feel more myself – less brittle, less worried, less tense, less overwhelmed, less prone to falling completely apart. But they are not a solution to the structural problems of neoliberal values, unachievable expectations, and never-ending workloads (Gregg, 2018). Using self-care and self-soothing tools to maintain our sanity or our "integrity", trying to "stay true" to who we are, trying to "not let work colonise [our] values" (Lamberg, 2021, p. 466), they are worthy goals. But we will continue to know injury while being forced to comply with the constant demands and expectations to manage and transform ourselves into better economic subjects

(Banet-Weiser, 2018). I recognise how I have mistakenly taken on an "ethos of aspiration", thinking my personal character, my resilience, my wellness could be "a key instrument" to help me navigate my work (Lamberg, 2021, p. 466).

As I review all I have enacted over the last five years – my deliberate, activist, heartful strategies, my acts of self-care, my dedication and contribution – I see how much I have been hoodwinked. Academia is a damaging, discouraging place, a place of too many grim tales (Taylor et al., 2020).

I am injured. Stretched. S – t – r – e – t – c – h – e – d to capacity. The "catastrophic" rating/radar in the finite game of comparison and winners and losers is glaringly and dangerously red. I am exhausted, defeated, despondent. I have given all I can give. I cannot work any harder than I have. Yet this work is "disputed", "denigrated", "or simply ignored" (Taylor et al., 2020, p. 2). Across the years, with every email, every hour, every relationship, I have been asked by the academy to give more. And I have given it. My body has been screaming at me for months, pain shooting and settling around my upper body making me worry. Yet I have pushed on. Believing it was my responsibility. The obedient academic. The good worker. The ideal subject. Always.

When I stop and pause, I recognise I am broken. These "cumulative damages" have changed "my sense of self as an academic" (Taylor et al., 2020, p. 2). My heart is broken. My body broken. My spirit broken. So many injuries. So much structural inequality. So much wear and tear/s. The grief leaks out of me.

Sara Ahmed (2017a, 2017b, 2017c) speaks of "Feminist Snap", describing a full range of potential meanings (see 2017a, pp. 187–212). Exploring what it means to "snap" she writes of pressure, breaking points, frustration, pain, feeling weary and teary. She writes of tension and spinning and revolution. She speaks to me. She says "snap" can come from "sap" – from being tired out and depleted. Perhaps I am snapping?

Just like a twig. Her metaphor resonates and tells me of my life/work:

> And when I think of snap, I think of a twig. When a twig snaps, we hear the sound of it breaking. We can hear the suddenness of a break. We might assume, on the basis of what we hear, that the snap is a starting point. A snap sounds like the start of something, a transformation of something; it is how a twig might end up broken in two pieces. A snap might even seem like a violent moment; the unbecoming of something. But a snap would only be the beginning insofar as we did not notice the pressure on the twig. If pressure is an action, snap is a reaction. Pressure is hard to notice unless you are under that pressure. Snap is only the start of something because of what we do not notice. Can we redescribe the world from the twig's point of view, that is, from the point of view of those who are under pressure? . . .
>
> . . . If the twig was a stronger twig, if the twig was more resilient, it would take more pressure before it snapped. We can see how resilience is a technology of will, or even functions as a command: be willing to bear more; be stronger so you can bear more. We can understand too how

130 Alison L. Black

resilience becomes a deeply conservative technique, one especially well suited to governance: you encourage bodies to strengthen so they will not succumb to pressure; so they can keep taking it; so they can take more of it. Resilience is the requirement to take more pressure; such that the pressure can be gradually increased . . .

. . . When you don't take it, when you can't take any more of it, what happens?

(Ahmed, 2017a, pp. 188–189)

Image 8.1 Exploring feminist snap

> *My visual narrative of "feminist snap" asks me to pay attention to the wear and tear/s of academic life/work, to my innermost feelings of "sap and snap" (Ahmed, 2017b). "Sap and snap" – noticing the pressure, the stretching, the breaking, the damage. Snap – as crisis – a finite games danger rating –* ***WARNING! WARNING! CATASTROPHIC!*** *Snap – as interrupting the production, snapping when the effort to do what I have been doing is too much to sustain, snapping and releasing the pressure. Snap – as a feminist pedagogy of slowing down, learning to hear exhaustion, when it is all too much. Listening to the sounds of wearing and tearing, to what this academic life/work is costing me. A feminist snap – sharing grim tales, snapping damaging bonds to production, promotion, and finite games. Using stories as starting points for*

> unbecoming academic, for counting what counts to me. Snap – a way of saying NO MORE. Snap – as moments of clarity, pain, fatigue, and breaking points. Snap – as a way of holding on. Snap – as an opening, a new way of proceeding – refusal, revolution, seeing through the daze/haze of neoliberal production and surveillance. Snap – playing the long game, the infinite game. Snap – refusing to experience myself in the terms used to dismiss me. Snap – as a feminist support system where I can shelter, find ways to keep going, keep shiFting the pressure and the weight. Snap – as a feminist pedagogy of collectively breaking things up, revolting, causing mayhem, shattering the pieces, getting through to others, working/living/writing/counting differently. Snap – as a feminist communication system, the creating of feminist records, an archive, recording what we do not get over, what is not over, what will never be over (Ahmed, 2017a).

Channels of expression and interruption

Creative expression and feminist writing are important. They are channels (I have used, am using now) to interrupt the never-ending production demanded by the academic machine. Such writing is a way to include our embodied vulnerable selves, our hearts-spirits-minds-bodies-stories, enhancing "our quality of life and work" (Shahjahan, 2015, p. 499).

Contemplative, arts-based and feminist methodologies can look like poetry, memoir, photography, walking, metaphor, art, and more. They offer ways to make personal and collective meaning and create spaces to explore the texture and history of experience and of current academic life/work. These creative interruptions are more than just writing or working differently. Slowing down, writing this chapter, has helped me to hear the "snap", the bodily impact and breaking points. It has helped me hear the gradual sapping of energy, wear and tear/s, the frustration, and the whisper of resistance. Sharing, expressing, and representing my stories of experience has interrupted the distress, providing a way "to recognise the pressures and strains, and resources and resiliencies, required to (continue to) 'be' academics in the present moment" (Taylor et al., 2020, p. 2).

> To hear snap, one must thus slow down; we also listen for the slower times of wearing and tearing, of making do; we listen for the sounds of the costs of becoming attuned to the requirements of an existing system. To hear snap, to give that moment a history, we might have to learn to hear the sound of not snapping. Perhaps we are learning to hear exhaustion, the gradual sapping of energy when you have to struggle to exist in a world that negates your existence. Eventually something gives.
>
> (Ahmed, 2017b, Snap the bond section, para. 8)

Creative channels of expression offer ways to slow down and listen. They offer ways to resist and engage in "feminist snap" (Ahmed, 2017a, p. 187). With my creative and poetic writing and arts making I am challenging the "rules of emotional expression [that] are part of the discourse that upholds certain hierarchies and practices"; I am pushing back, expressing what I cannot express verbally but what "seeps out in tears" (Taylor et al., 2020, p. 7). Through my expressive writing I am "snapping", playing with snap as a feminist pedagogy, and determining "I will not reproduce a world I cannot bear" (Ahmed, 2017a, p. 199).

Creating space is "about meaning, and it is about how we come to matter – to ourselves, to others" (Taylor et al., 2020, p. 7). Through the space and expression of this chapter I have had an opportunity to consider whether I will continue to experience myself in the terms used to dismiss me (Ahmed, 2017a). Through this writing I have (re)discovered I want my bond with the finite games to snap. I am exhausted by this bond. I am so tired of being weighed down. I am tired of being tired. I don't want to keep on holding on to what diminishes me. I am snapping "not only at what is in front" of me but at "what is behind me" as well – I am snapping at this long "history" of "exhaustion", "endurance", and "struggle to exist in a world that negates [my] existence" (Ahmed, 2017b, Snap the bond section, para. 8).

This space and this expression help me see that my "lack of fit" in the academy is not a form of failure (Shahjahan, 2015, p. 491). My "private hurts" are "patterned throughout the academy" (Taylor et al., 2020, p. 4). These channels of expression have offered me a lifeline and encouragement to keep walking towards *my* definition of a valuable academic life (Manathunga et al., 2020). They are creating a scene of feminist instruction, helping me see "it is too much" (alas) "after it is too much" (Ahmed, 2017a, p. 198).

This is why our stories matter, why our expression matters. They are a "feminist pedagogy" and a "feminist record", a way of "recording what we do not get over, what is not over" (Ahmed, 2017a, p. 198). Telling our stories can be instructive, "a way of saying no", a way of giving our grief/fury/frustration/pain/exhaustion "somewhere to go" (Ahmed, 2017a, p. 198). What is expressed/shared is no longer contained, no longer pushed down or away, no longer internalised or individualised. Writing our lives offers clarity and direction.

Through writing this chapter I have connected again with a politics of resistance and protest. I recognise the efforting I have been engaging in is too much to sustain. I don't want to continue down this path of "slow death" (Berlant, 2007, p. 754). I have been holding on to a hope that has already broken, investing myself in "aspirational labour" (Lamberg, 2021, p. 47). With this chapter I am "snapping". I am refusing to continue.

For Ahmed (2017b), her snap, and her feminist protest, was resigning from her academic position as a professor without having another academic post to go to. She believes "if a resignation is to become a protest it needs to become public" (Ahmed, 2017b, Snap as feminist work section, para. 11). Perhaps one needs a certain level of experience, privilege, security, and material resources to make one's protest public? Public protest certainly feels risky. But what will happen *without* refusal and resistance?

This chapter is my tipping point. It is my "making public", my act of "feminist protest". My writing has become data collection, a way of releasing the pressure, a place for deciding my own fate. It feels simultaneously dangerous and necessary. It is my "feminist vigil to stay awake . . . to mark or to mourn, to make a protest, to pray, to count [my] losses" (Ahmed, 2017b, After snap section, para. 11).

Resigning from my job, however, is not an option. Unlike Ahmed, I do not have the necessary material resources; I am the sole provider for my family financially. The now-precarious culture of academia in Australia, where 40,000 university jobs were lost in recent months and more budget cuts and job losses are flagged, means such an action would be foolish. Job security is no longer a given, and like the new waves of COVID outbreaks, so too come new waves of redundancies. So perhaps our privilege and position determine our various capacities to resign or refuse. And influence our choices? Resigning passively to one's fate? Or enacting acts of "snapping" and "keeping open the question of how to live" (Ahmed, 2017a, p. 197).

Refusal and feminist protest can be acts of pushing back, acts of snapping bonds, acts of claiming freedom and rebooting. We can refuse to neglect our stories of experience. We can protest with our writing. We can create a feminist record. And the "riskier it is to snap, the more inventive we might have to become" (Ahmed, 2017b, After snap section, para. 13).

I have decided to resign in a way that feels doable and right for me, a necessary and nourishing gesture of refusal. With this chapter I make public my decision to resign in feminist protest from any further striving to progress my career. Not getting promoted has an emotional cost and a financial cost, but "cruel nourishment", "soul killing", and "slow death" have undeniable costs too (Berlant, 2007, p. 780). Years of being overburdened, overworked, and deadened by the finite games have not served me. My dedicated actions over decades in the academy have not accomplished anything. I have tried and failed to get through. Instead of choosing ongoing efforting in this space and history of slow death, I am choosing life, I am choosing health, I am choosing balance, I am choosing another way.

I am choosing to define and decide my own life/work. For I simply cannot continue as I have been. My protest will see me doing "just enough of what is expected" so that I can live and work in the academy in ways that are meaningful and life-giving for me and for others. There is still much I love about my academic life. This decision will support these things that I love. Working with an ethics of care and rest, creating feminist support systems and shelters, spaces to listen, to go, and keep going – this will be my contribution.

Conclusion

This chapter has offered glimpses of grim academic tales across a long, interrupted, undervalued career. It has offered vulnerable stories which shed light on distressing psychosocial experiences.

There is great value in communicating our stories of experiences – for ourselves and for others – and something subversive about women academics slowing down, giving time to writing/speaking of themselves and their stories, creating an archive of current academic life, revealing injustices and injuries, connecting to each other, to the infinite game (Manathunga et al., 2020; Gill & Donaghue, 2016; Henderson et al., 2019). Such channels of expression interrupt the injurious care-lessness and individualising nature of neo-liberalist and masculinist regimes where numbers, dollars, weightings, and production are valued over lives, bodies, and names. Sharing the damage and the stress, sharing "the sap and the snap" is important feminist work. It is work that commands collective analysis and attention. It summons us to engage in collaboration and to work together to recognise, contest, and resist the neoliberal conditions and crises we have experienced, suffer, and face.

Snap – the end. Snap – begin again.

Snap that moment when the pressure has built up and tipped over, is revolting, a revolt against what we are asked to put up with. Snap here is not only about individual action, those moments when she does not take it anymore, when she reacts to what she has previously endured, though it includes those moments. A movement is necessary so a moment can happen, a moment when the violence comes out; spills out. A movement is necessary. Snap makes what is necessary possible.

(Ahmed, 2017c, See how she spins; out of control section, para. 4)

References

Ahmed, S. (2017a). *Living a feminist life*. Duke University Press.

Ahmed, S. (2017b). *Snap! Feminist moments, feminist movements*. Lecture given May 11, as part of the Launch Swedish edition of Living a Feminist Life; Posted on May 21, by feminist killjoys blog. https://feministkilljoys.com/2017/05/21/snap/

Ahmed, S. (2017c, September 4). Snap as revolutionary time. *Los Angeles Review of Books (LARB) Quarterly Journal, 15,* Revolution. https://lareviewofbooks.org/article/snap-revolutionary-time/

Banet-Weiser, S. (2018). *Empowered: Popular feminism and popular misogyny*. Duke University Press.

Berlant, L. (2007). Slow death: Sovereignty, obesity, lateral agency. *Critical Inquiry, 35*(4), 754–780.

Black, A. L. (2018). Responding to longings for slow scholarship: Writing ourselves into being. In A. L. Black & S. Garvis (Eds.), *Women activating agency in academia: Metaphors, manifestos and memoir*. Routledge.

Black, A. L, Crimmins, G., & Henderson, L. (2019). Positioning ourselves in our academic lives: Exploring personal/professional identities, voice and agency. *Discourse: Studies in the Cultural Politics of Education*. Article first published online: November 3, 2017. http://www.tandfonline.com/doi/full/10.1080/01596306.2017.1398135

Black, A. L., & Dwyer, R. (2021). *Reimagining the academy: Shifting towards kindness, connection, and an ethics of care*. Palgrave Macmillan.

Bottrell, D., & Manathunga, C. (2019). *Resisting neoliberalism in higher education volume 1: Seeing through the cracks*. Palgrave Macmillan.

Burrows, R. (2012). Living with the h-index? Metric assemblages in the contemporary academy. *The Sociological Review, 60*, 355–372.

Callon, M., & Law, J. (2005).On qualculation, agency and otherness. *Environment and Planning: Society and Space, 23*, 717–733.

Gill, R. (2010). Breaking the silence: The hidden injuries of the neoliberal university. In R. Flood & R. Gill (Eds.), *Secrecy and silence in the research process: Feminist reflections*. Routledge.

Gill, R., & Donaghue, N. (2016). Resilience, apps and reluctant individualism: Technologies of self in the neoliberal academy. *Women's Studies International Forum, 54*, 9 1–99. https://doi.org/10.1016/j.wsif.2015.06.016

Gregg, M. (2018). *Counterproductive: Time management in the knowledge economy*. Duke University Press.

Hartman, Y., & Darab, S. (2012). A call for slow scholarship: A case study on the intensification of academic life and its implications for policy. *Review of Education, Pedagogy, and Cultural Studies, 34*(1–2), 49–60.

Harré, N., Grant, B. M., Locke, K., & Sturm, S. (2017). The university as an infinite game [online]. *Australian Universities' Review, 59*(2), 5–13. https://files.eric.ed.gov/fulltext/EJ1157040.pdf

Henderson, L., Black, A., Crimmins, G., & Jones, J. K. (2019). Civic engagement as empowerment: Sharing our names and remembering our her-stories: Resisting Ofuniversity. In G. Crimmins (Ed.), *Strategies for resisting sexism in the academy: Higher education, gender and intersectionality* (Chapter 16, pp. 287–304). Palgrave Studies in Gender and Education.

Henderson, L., Honan, E., & Loch, S. (2016). The production of the academicwritingmachine. *Reconceptualizing Educational Research Methodology, 7*(2). https://doi.org/10.7577/rerm.1838

Lamberg, E. (2021). Ambivalent aspirations: Young women negotiating postfeminist subjectivity in media work. *European Journal of Cultural Studies, 24*(2), 464–481.

Manathunga, C., Black, A. L., & Davidow, S. (2020). Walking: Towards a valuable academic life. *Discourse: Studies in the Cultural Politics of Educa tion*. https://doi.org/10.1080/01596306.2020.1827222

Mountz, A., Bonds, A., Mansfield, B., Loyd, J., Hyndman, J., Walton-Roberts, M., Basu, R., Whitson, R., Hawkins, R., Hamilton, T., & Curran, W. (2015). For slow scholarship: A feminist politics of resistance through collective action in the neoliberal university. *ACME: An International Journal for Critical Geographies, 14*(4), 1235– 1259. https://www.acme-journal.org/index.php/acme/article/view/1058

Shahjahan, R. A. (2015). Being "lazy" and slowing down: Toward decolonizing time, our body, and pedagogy. *Educational Philosophy and Theory, 47*(5), 488–501.

Taylor, C. A., Gannon, S., Adams, G., Donaghue, H., Hannam-Swain, S., Harris-Evans, J., Healey, J., & Moore, P. (2020). Grim tales: Meetings, matterings and moments of silencing and frustration in everyday academic life. *International Journal of Educational Research*, *99*, 101513.

Taylor, Y., & Lahad, K. (Eds.). (2018). *Feeling academic in the neoliberal university: Feminist flights, fights and failures*. Palgrave Macmillan.

9 Playing with pictures to make sense and interrupt the hurly-burly university game

Mark Selkrig

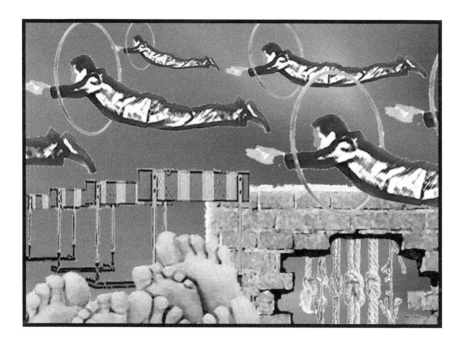

Image 9.1 Photographic collage: Community engagement is . . .

> *Central in my well-be(com)ing is a need to create and manipulate images to make sense, reflect and represent the strange game of working in academia. This photographic collage that I produced contains fragments of animate and inanimate objects to create a dynamic, almost whimsical and humorous spectacle. Although with closer investigation of each component in the collage a potentially more disturbing, satirical or allegorical story is revealed. It is one of several visual representations I present in this chapter to explore how my image-making and presenting these images become a type of activism while also serving as therapeutic tools to think, comment and respond to my work world.*

DOI: 10.4324/9781003207863-12

138 *Mark Selkrig*

Introduction

Many would remember that even prior to COVID-19 the field of higher education was in the throes of massive changes, due in part to the creeping pervasiveness of neo-liberal ideology and discourse. As such, the spirit and nature of the work we do as academics has shifted. Despite the turmoil, institutions spruik a rhetoric of care and concern, although those of us involved in the academic game experience a machine-like operation that can dehumanise and contribute to an enduring sense of precarity and insecurity. I produced the photographic collage presented here as my initial visual narrative during a research project in which I was a chief investigator. The aim of that project, which I will discuss further later in the chapter, was to engage colleagues in multimodal ways to capture their individual 'small stories' about working in a rapidly and ever-changing higher education sector. It is a sector in which academics' voices can be silent or silenced, and the visual and textual representations of university life are often manicured and sanitised for an external market.

In this chapter, I explore opportunities for using the ambiguity inherent in visual representations and images to make visible the absurdities that contribute to the current era of emotional insecurity existing inside universities and to potentially assist in "breaking taboos about scholars expressing pain and vulnerability" (Smith & Ulus, 2019, p. 846) as a result of working in higher education. In the first instance I offer a context and some theoretical perspectives of how I see the nature of my working life and circumstance. I then explore how particular views about art have shaped my approaches to reflect not only on the cognitive domain but also the emotional energy that has become a regular feature of our work as academics. Drawing on my collage and visual materials from other projects, I then consider how foregrounding the emotional energy (cathexis) that academics invest in their work offers an aesthetic mode of interruption to the dominant managerial discourses that have colonised higher education. In tandem I reflect on how I worked alone and with colleagues to generate images and text to 'make sense' of our circumstance. I do not view wellbeing as something static that we have as individuals, and I articulate how making and presenting these works became sites or events to engage in dialogue and make tangible what Küpers (2005) describes as "well-be(com)ing" – that is, possibilities that are always emerging through complex relational and interrelated interactions.

The messy field of university work in a supercomplex epoch

Despite the turmoil that persists, universities have tried to manage and control their business through various policies and frameworks to portray a sense of stability and authority. Although Barnett (2000a), well before the impacts of the global pandemic, identified that universities were operating in an era in which "contestability, challengeability, uncertainty, and unpredictability" (Barnett, 2000b, p. 415) were common features. This set of notions marks out the conceptual geography of "supercomplexity" (Barnett, 2000a) as a time of fragility, where nothing can be taken for granted, and an age of conceptual and emotional insecurity amongst academics who work in these institutions. Furthermore, Barcan (2013) describes universities as a "fractured and palimpsestic work world" in which three different types of institutions simultaneously coexist: "a scholarly community, a bureaucracy and a corporation" (p. 69). Each institution has its own demands, expectations, values, rhythms and senses of time and purpose.

When the demands, values and rhythms are combined with the supercomplexities of our post pandemic world which are even more precarious and where emotional insecurity proliferates, the notion of self-care for me remains problematic. We are seeing a discourse surface in which individuals have the agency to determine and manage their own "wellbeing" although this perspective negates or simplifies the responsibilities of the organisation and the hurly-burly of the contexts in which academics are situated. It is little wonder therefore that academics experience deep emotional insecurity, and for me, it is paramount to explore "how the neoliberal academy – disembodied in its assumptions, yet violent in it consequences – affects academics' well-being" (Smith & Ulus, 2019, p. 841).

Bourdieu's (1977) concepts related to practice theory have offered me a way to consider the strange and murky field of the neoliberal academy. For Bourdieu, the social world is a system of relatively autonomous fields, that exist in relationship to one another. Like other fields, the world of academia has dynamic boundaries (Bourdieu & Wacquant, 1992) and a 'doxa', a set of behaviours, rules and fundamental principles which agents in a field view as inherently true (Webb et al., 2002), internalise and reproduce. The concept of the field for Bourdieu and Wacquant (1992, p. 98) can be compared to a 'game'. Agents or players make an investment or have a stake in the game. The players engage in competition to advance their position in the field through increasing the levels of capital they possess or through changing the rules of the game (Bourdieu & Wacquant, 1992). Due to the high-stakes nature of the game, symbolic violence, which involves subtle forms of hierarchised power that influence human relationships, "is exercised upon a social agent with his or her complicity" (p. 167) can also prevail. In looking back at my initial visual narrative above, you as a reader or viewer may see some of the images that infer or represent that violence, which can be "a gentle violence, imperceptible and invisible, even to its victims" (Bourdieu, 2001, p. 1).

Carnival, liminality and spaces of resistance

By viewing the field of academia as a game, in which symbolic violence can manifest, the continual shifts, absurdities and tensions have also created

140 *Mark Selkrig*

a fragile work environment. It has also generated opportunities for cracks or fissures to appear. Within these fissures, circumstances become ambiguous, and during these liminal periods, "persons slip through [or] elude the network of classifications that normally locates states and positions in cultural space. They are neither here nor there [they are] betwixt and between" (Turner, 1969, p. 96). The idea of slipping through or eluding 'network classification' appeals. It reminds me of the carnivalesque cultures and practices described by Bakhtin (1984a, 1984b) that are developed to reflect a tone of anti-authoritarianism and become unique times when members of society who are usually powerless could interact or speak back to the powerful. The concept of 'carnival' described by Bakhtin "invoke an exciting prospect of disruption; the disruption of established hierarchies and social systems" (Cooper & Condie, 2016, p. 29). What resonates for me with Bakhtin's ideas is where laughter and openness during carnivalesque practices lead to types of communication and an "atmosphere of freedom, frankness and familiarity" (Bakhtin, 1984b, pp. 15–16). Similarly, carnival can offer "a place for working out, in a concretely sensuous, half-real and half-play-acted form, a new mode of interrelationship between individuals" (Bakhtin, 1984a, p. 123), and as such, a "characteristic of Bakhtin's carnival is a world turned 'upside down' or 'inside out', where life becomes unpredictable" (Mclean & Wallace, 2013, p. 1520). I have attempted to engage the carnivalesque as a type of activism, allowing the absurd and ridiculous to surface as a way for truth to speak back to power through humour.

Within the academy, numerous academics have lived experiences and felt the consequences of participating in explicit or open acts of resistance. For example, when strong collective action is not forthcoming, protests or objections are seen as individual actions, and individuals can undergo "victimization and retaliation" by university management (Anderson, 2008, p. 259). It becomes easy to target these individuals as difficult and "individually deviant" (Clegg, 1994, p. 291). Anderson (2008) argues micro acts of covert resistance, such as feigned ignorance and foot dragging, can work, although other examples of micro resistance that can be effective occur when creativity and humour are employed. These acts are more difficult to trace and are open to various interpretations, and as I have argued with colleagues elsewhere (Manathunga et al., 2017), arts-related approaches and practices fit nicely as a type of microresistance to speak back, stay sane and safe and make sense of existing in the corporate managed university.

Meaning making through art practices

My focus in this chapter is to discuss how arts making and representing aspects of academic work has been crucial for my self-care (whatever that means). From my perspective, coming to academia via a visual art background, art or image making has been an inherent way for me to make meaning. It has allowed me to: present ideas that are hard to put into words and force myself and others to pay attention to things in new ways (Weber, 2008); discuss sensitive topics through intermediary materials more easily (Prosser, 2011); and enhance embodied and empathic understandings of phenomena (Cousin, 2009; Weber, 2008). Similarly, Maxine Greene's activist ideas about art have resonated for me since I encountered her work several years ago. Greene (1995) insists that the arts are crucial in promoting wide-awakeness and aesthetic experiences, as art can bring people into touch with themselves, permit confrontation with the world and allow us to access multiple perspectives. Biesta's (2017) arguments about how the arts allow us to be in an ongoing exploration of what it means to be *in* the world also resonate for me and echo Greene's views. Art can also serve various functions in the political, educational, spiritual, social and individual domains. Kelly (2003) outlines the notions of identity, dilemmas, courage, alternatives, action, hope and communication as ways to consider the functions of art. de Botton and Armstrong (2013) also advance a view that art is a "tool", and "like other tools, art has the power to extend our capacities beyond those that nature has originally endowed us with" (de Botton & Armstrong, 2013, p. 5). Art therefore is a therapeutic tool assisting us to explore our human weakness, frailties and ordinary dilemmas, and these various tools can be helpful in thinking about my art/image making to engage in dialogue with the world.

In my doctoral work I used the arts to make sense of complex ideas (Selkrig, 2012a). The figures represented in Image 9.2 became sculptures that were

Image 9.2 Renderings for sculptures made to reflect my doctoral journey

presented in a public exhibition (Selkrig, 2010, 2012b). They represented not only the cognitive overload and exhaustion but also the messy and emotional roller coaster of undertaking doctoral studies. These sculptures, with their carnivalesque, half-real and half-play-acted forms adopted titles such as *I don't know any more*, *I had it then lost it*, and *Climbing the wrong greasy pole*. Upon reflection and in writing this chapter, they were precursors for my continuous need to make and represent the academic world.

My own art making became the space for me to engage in a dialogue, to remain wide awake, to clarify and live with my uncertainty. My work became a series of surfaces to construct, place and arrange my thoughts. The works, as Pasztory (2005) claims, allowed me to work out ideas and think with objects.

Collage and poster to re/present academic work

In relocating to another university and becoming firmly ensconced in the academy, the carnivalesque game of higher education became even more familiar while also disturbingly highlighting the quirks and symbolic violence that permeates these institutions. In this new location, my capacity to make sculptures became difficult, and by walking the streets of the inner suburbs of Melbourne, I started to refamiliarise myself with the power of posters as an accessible medium. I was reminded of Barbra Kruger's (1989) feminist print *Your body is a battle ground*; the confrontational and explicit posters by Australian artist David McDiarmid (1991) during the HIV epidemic to challenge gay communities' perspectives about safe sex. And more recently, artworks were suddenly appearing on facades of buildings and laneways near where I lived by 'poster boy' Peter Drew (2016). His posters, using an image and limited text, confronts and challenges our perspective about Australian identity.

In blending aspects of collage with making posters I wanted to explore playful ways to offer a concrete representation of a sensory or embodied response in which single or lineal thoughts "[give] way to relations of juxtaposition and difference" (Rainey, 1998, p. 124) and fragments work together or in opposition to produce new connections and ideas. I was also drawn to the ideas of Butler-Kisber (2010), who outlines how with written text, authors usually work from ideas to feelings (head to heart), whereas with collage, the opposite can occur. If you're gluing or joining fragments together they are 'stuck' and cannot be altered, although collage can create an experience that permits a re-seeing, relocating, where the tacit might bubble to the surface. There is also the mischievous aspect in knowing; the allegorical relational qualities allow for many interpretations which can occur over time or at the same time (Butler-Kisber, 2010), the collage or artwork acts as a mediating object. I was reminded of a diagram (see Figure 9.1) I was introduced to while undertaking my teacher education degree

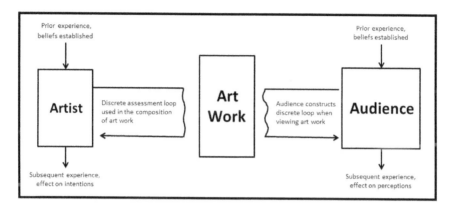

Figure 9.1 Traditional relationship between artist and audience by Willats (1976)

many years ago, where Willats (1976) outlines at a very rudimentary level how we engage with an artwork or image. This engagement by the artist as well as the audience/viewer will depend on facets such as our respective biographies, contexts, lifeworlds and a particular moment in time. Therefore, when we engage with the work, we do not really know about the artist/maker by looking at the artwork, and there are countless ways of interpreting the image.

Being reminded that artworks are always ambiguous, have multiple interpretations, and viewers never really know the artist's intention helped me consider and think about how I might deflect potential reaction or symbolic violence that I could be exposed to if certain players of the academic game or university management decided to retaliate or target me as being difficult. These ambiguities would act as a protective mechanism for me in speaking back and putting perspectives out there.

Having offered some insight about how I see my work contexts and some underpinnings of why I engage in aesthetic modes of interruption to make sense, I want to share some particular events in which this meaning making occurred. In the next sections, I turn to ways that colleagues and I attempted to explore, address and represent the challenges and concerns facing those who work in universities, to let voices and experiences be heard and provide opportunities to bring the emotional or affective aspects to the fore. I focus on three events: one in which I worked alone; another in which I worked with colleagues to engage the visual to counter some of the cleansed, polished narratives that are conveyed to the outside world about university life; and the final event, which emerged as a response to lockdown during the pandemic as a strategy to 'stay the distance' and shift the viewer's gaze from me during the onslaught of Zoom.

Event 1: passageway provocations

As an arts educator this event 'morphed' from a class with post-graduate art pre-service teachers about providing clarity with instructions for an art activity. It involved working as a group to construct a poster of 36 individual parts to make the whole image by Seurat (1884–1886) and placing the finished work in a very bland mundane passageway of the education building at the university where I was working. There was a high level of foot traffic – both staff and students – that passed this spot every day, and the image generated quite a level of interest! After a few months and several 'faculty issues' and 'outside issues' later, I commenced a project of presenting a visual reflection/prompt that I would replace semi-regularly at the end of the same passageway. I was aware of my own volatile context and increasingly toxic workplace setting and needed to find a safe way to convey or present messages. I found some playfulness in using existing public works of art that would be familiar to most people and juxtaposing these with snippets of song lyrics that were also familiar works in the public domain. I wasn't sure if I was appropriating, plagiarising, breaking copyright or something else, but it offered a way to stay safe.

This sporadic project ran for 2 or more years with positive feedback from colleagues. The posters became a way to brighten a dark space, consider the events going on – internally and in the outside world, where there were many parallels – and being discussed in the corridor. The images would simply appear, and most staff were not aware who was posting them. Some examples of these posters are presented in Image 9.3: works by Drysdale (c1945) and Arthur Streeton (1889) were combined with lyrics by Debra Harry (Blondie) (1979) and Bruegel's (1559) imagery with song lines from Talking Heads (1981) and Géricault's (1818–19) image of *The Raft of the Medusa* juxtaposed with words from a Glen Campbell (1970) song.

But perhaps unsurprisingly, alongside the jovial corridor conversations prompted by the posters, I was being watched. A change of faculty management occurred that also coincided with a massive redundancy program. Opportunities for staff to meet in groups to discuss and converse became non-existent. It became a time of 'terror'. At that time, I created a poster based on the album cover of the '80s band New Order and the lyrics for a track from the album (bottom left image in Image 9.3), and, as usual, placed the poster on the corridor wall early one morning. The next day, I received a phone call from the university's People and Culture Department indicating someone had filed a complaint and the work needed to be removed immediately. I was working off campus for a few days, and the following email was forwarded to me.

Hi Mark,

Thanks for taking the time to discuss the artwork display in Building C this morning. As I mentioned, this piece has caused offence and as such I have removed it from the workplace. I understand that you regularly display artwork and on the whole this is much appreciated and well received, however in this instance has not hit the mark.

I have taken pictures for you as mentioned (enclosed) and have the artwork at P&C (K3) when you are ready to collect it.

Playing with pictures 145

Image 9.3 Four examples of the passageway posters

I was never told officially who made the complaint, but several colleagues were able to provide clues. I was also never sure what to read into the email from P&C and how serious they felt the issue was, but they were obliged to act. From my perspective, the poster was commenting on the recent election of Trump and the first round of White House sackings and fake news discourse that was emerging. I can only surmise someone in faculty management took the poster more personally in the way they had interpreted the message. In making these works and being asked – or questioned – by others, I would frequently refer to the lines by Francis Urquhart in the original British version of the television series *House of Cards* (1990), where he would state, "You might very well think that; I couldn't possibly comment". While I became a little more cautious because of the complaint, I persisted in putting posters in the passageway for some time, and they all remained until I left the institution. The incident signposted for me that it was dangerous times where knowledge workers can be shut down or silenced by more privileged or powerful voices in the institution.

Event 2: postcard project

Through talking with a group of colleagues about the symbolic violence that was prevalent in our workplace at the time, it prompted us to undertake a research project to hear and see what other academics were experiencing. Our

146 *Mark Selkrig*

aim was to consider the 'small' narratives that individuals produce to the meta-narratives about academic work promoted at a faculty and university level to gain insights into what it means to be an academic in the current higher education climate.

This series of works emerged when 22 academics, or approximately one-quarter of the faculty's teaching and research academics, elected to be involved. Participants were asked via email to send a return email that included an image and a short text of less than 30 words in the style of a traditional postcard in response to separate prompts: 'Teaching is . . .', 'Research is . . .' and 'Community engagement is . . .'. Each prompt was sent separately to participants at intervals of 3 to 4 weeks. (You may recall at the start of this chapter; I introduced my collage and text that I provided for the 'Community engagement is . . .' prompt.) The postcard format was chosen to generate a "juxtaposition of words and images" that might produce new meanings (Leavy, 2015, p. 235). We then included all responses in a series of three posters, each being A1 in size (see Image 9.4), which meant there was less likelihood – even though their responses were anonymised – being targeted because of their responses. Participants were less vulnerable and safer amongst others, yet their diverse perspectives were captured.

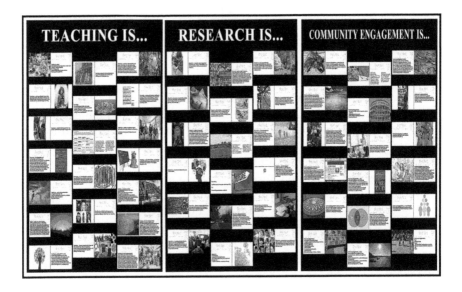

Image 9.4 Posters that resulted from the postcard project

These collective views became easy to display and provided significant impact and numerous conversation starters in various locations around the campus and beyond. The posters were powerful in depicting the maze-like pathways and often messy journeys that academics take in the work. Similarly, the notion of cathexis, the investment of mental *and* emotional energy and passion

(Neumann, 2009), was foregrounded where academics talked about research as a journey, rather than outputs, and the passion that comes with teaching. The posters also captured the ways in which symbolic violence, through subtle forms of power, impacts the well-be(com)ing of academics.

Event 3: lockdown Zoom backdrops

The final project I discuss here emerged during the second COVID-19 lockdown in Melbourne, where I live (which ended up lasting for over 230 days). Based on my previous work as a health educator, I was mindful of the potential dilemmas and stressful conditions that would surface for many (including myself) during this uncertain and very bizarre time. There was also a stark realisation that my world of working in higher education would consist of perpetual Zoom meetings for months, and my presence in the world would be via a Zoom square inside a series of other Zoom squares on a screen. Rather than rely on virtual backgrounds, I embarked on a project to print large (A0-size) black-and-white images that were in some way personable, such as old maps of my neighbourhood, favourite artworks, distant family members or places I had been. The images in the posters that I mounted on cupboard doors behind my home office chair also remained ambiguous with potential levels of symbolic meaning related to the frailties of remembering, hope, sorrow, rebalancing, self-understanding, growth and appreciation that de Botton and Armstrong (2013) suggest that art helps us with.

My reason for this project was multiple. I wanted to avoid the temptation of quirky virtual backgrounds that would blur or morph me into the image depending on my movements. My aim was to establish a point of interest or focus that deflected the viewer's gaze from me while I was trapped inside Zoom. I also wanted to ensure that whatever I did would involve some embodied, physical mark making by me. By relying on 'good old-fashioned' paper-based images, I had the opportunity of transforming these backdrops, progressively colouring them by hand over a period of weeks using various drawing implements. My strategy of replacing the posters on a semi-regular basis and gradually colouring them became a type of ritual for me to get through the long lockdown. At times I would shut my camera in a Zoom meeting, and while still listening and contributing to the conversation via my headset, I could swing my chair around and work on the image with my pencils. My poster and colouring ritual developed a bit of a Zoom following as colleagues would tell me how they looked forward to our meetings to see how the colour was appearing in a poster or what the 'newest' image was. My aim had worked in a way that Willats's (1976) diagram (see Figure 9.1) suggests: the gaze was on the artwork and not me, the maker. Likewise, colleagues and other visitors who could see my Zoom backgrounds were becoming comfortable enough to make suggestions or interpret the imagery in ways that I had not considered, with these contributions depending on the various biographies of those in the Zoom room. The lockdown backdrops also acted as a catalyst for my Zoom visitors to engage in 'other' conversations, providing a means by which others could talk to me about how they were coping with life during lockdown. The images also prompted unexpected conversations about the absurdity we were all grappling with during this liminal period in every aspect of our lives. It also concentrated our common gaze on how our work in the academy had become even more carnivalesque.

My Zoom colleagues could relate to the posters I displayed (see Image 9.5) of works by David Shirgley (2021) and his cheeky, bold statements that accompanied his drawings such as: *We hate meetings*; *Sorry I fell asleep whilst you were talking* and *Weak messages create bad situations*. Likewise, when the gloominess of Dürer's (1514) engraving *Melencolia* became more animated and finer detail more pronounced through colour, I was able to converse with others about the power of symbols and how we manage sadness. The mask-wearing adaptation of da Vinci's (1503) *Mona Lisa* provoked some debate (as this was before masks became a necessity in the city where I live). Colleagues wanted to know if I was referring to the virus or about me being restricted in talking about aspects of university work. On another occasion, for example, Zoom visitors would ask whether the juxtaposition of a trees print alongside a mushroom poster (in Image 9.5) reflected the circumstances of my work at a given time. I would be asked, "Are you feeling like a mushroom or pine tree today, Mark?"

Image 9.5 Collage of various Zoom backgrounds

Although I had my own self-care reasons for the paper Zoom background, I was intrigued how posters took on a role or purpose of their own; they, like other events described in this chapter, became mediating objects to reflect or prompt discussion about not only my but others' changing circumstances. These Zoom backgrounds offered a way to move beyond the rational cognitive reactions; instead they encouraged playful and imaginative responses that gave us permission to consider the emotional dimensions that are crucial for us in staying well.

Drawing some thoughts together: why don't you have a go?

Crafting this chapter has forced me to develop a more articulated and nuanced narrative as to why the creation or manipulation of objects and images is a crucial aspect for me to make meaning of the volatile and impersonal worlds that institutions are becoming. Through thinking with images, I could reflect on an academic game in which policy is not necessarily practised, and knowledge and understandings are seen for economic gain and commodification. A game in which those working in these environments (academics) can find themselves brutalised, victimised and de-humanised and at times deemed not to be trusted and their voices and concerns negated or shut down. By sharing my images and encouraging others to engage, it became apparent that this type of art making, in which meanings can be ambiguous, is a subversive (but safe) vehicle to irritate, speak back to power and comment on flawed systems and overwhelming situations. Making or producing images offers a way to represent the embodied, affective, emotional aspects of those involved in knowledge generation and dissemination. The images also offer a way to engage in dialogue with the world (Biesta, 2017) and arouse the desire to be in and with the world – not just with ourselves.

In placing these images in the public domain, both my own and those made by my colleagues as in the Postcards Project, there is also a chance that behaviours, rules and fundamental principles, or what Bourdieu and Wacquant (1992) refer to as 'doxa', that we as academics view as inherently true can be disrupted and questioned. It offers possibilities and questions if we need to stay trapped in the current game. Perhaps it may help to advance ideas about de-centring the notion of wellbeing by thinking in terms "of dynamic relationalities where instead practices of well-be(com)ing are continually changing and created as a result of being practised" (Küpers, 2005, p. 228).

The events described here have also reinforced the need to remain 'wide awake', as Maxine Greene asserts, it involves being curious, often furious, to take risks, see things that you probably would not want to see, and it needs

> to be expressed in intentional action of some kind. The one who drifts, who believes that nothing matters outside of his or her own self-preservation, can hardly be considered to be free.
>
> (Greene, 1978, p. 153)

I concur with Smith and Ulus (2019) where they draw on the ideas of Contu (2018) and how we need to 'walk the talk' to consider how our academic praxis and critical discussions of the current higher education game can offer alternatives. I also wonder, having now read this, if you have considered the images you would create and share with others to reflect your experience of being a player in the higher education game? Take a risk; give it a go!

References

Anderson, G. (2008). Mapping academic resistance in the managerial university. *Organization, 15*(2), 251–270.

Bakhtin, M. M. (1984a [1963]). *Problems of Dostoevsky's poetics* (C. Emerson, Trans.). University of Minnesota Press.

Bakhtin, M. M. (1984b [1965]). *Rabelais and his world* (H. Iswolsky, Trans., 2nd ed.). Indiana University Press.

Barcan, R. (2013). *Academic life and labour in the new university. Hope and other choices*. Routledge.

Barnett, R. (2000a). *Realizing the university in an age of supercomplexity*. Society for Research into Higher Education & Open University Press. http://0-search.ebscohost.com.library.vu.edu.au/login.aspx?direct=true&db=cat02404a&AN=vic.b1380959&site=eds-live

Barnett, R. (2000b). University knowledge in an age of supercomplexity. *Higher Education, 40*, 409–422. http://0-search.ebscohost.com.library.vu.edu.au/login.aspx?direct=true&db=edsjsr&AN=edsjsr.3448008&site=eds-live

Biesta, G. (2017). *Let art teach*. ArtEZ Press.

Bourdieu, P. (1977). *Outline of a theory of practice* (R. Nice, Trans.). Cambridge University Press.

Bourdieu, P. (2001). *Masculine domination*. Stanford University Press.

Bourdieu, P., & Wacquant, L. J. D. (1992). *An invitation to reflexive sociology*. University of Chicago Press.

Bruegel, P. (1559). *The fight between carnival and lent*. Kunsthistorisches Museum. https://www.khm.at/objektdb/detail/320/?offset=27&lv=list

Butler-Kisber, L. (2010). *Qualitative inquiry: Thematic, narrative and arts-informed perspectives*. Sage.

Campbell, G. (1970). *Try a little kindness* [song]. Capitol.

Clegg, S. P. (1994). Power relations and the constitution of the resistant subject. In J. Jermier, D. Knights, & W. Nord (Eds.), *Resistance and power in organisations* (pp. 274–325). Routledge.

Contu, A. (2018). ". . . The point is to change it" – yes, but in what direction and how? Intellectual activism as a way of "walking the talk" of critical work in business schools. *Organization, 25*(2), 282–293. https://doi.org/10.1177/1350508417740589

Cooper, A. M., & Condie, J. (2016). Bakhtin, digital scholarship and new publishing practices as carnival. *Journal of Applied Social Theory, 1*(1), 26–43.

Cousin, G. (2009). *Researching learning in higher education*. Routledge.

da Vinci, L. (1503). *Mona Lisa* [Painting]. Louvre Museum. https://collections.louvre.fr/en/ark:/53355/cl010062370

de Botton, A., & Armstrong, J. (2013). *Art as therapy*. Phaidon.

Drew, P. (2016). *Monga Khan* [Poster]. https://www.peterdrewarts.com/monga-khan-aussie-posters

Drysdale, R. (c1945). *The drover's wife* [Painting]. National Gallery of Australia. https://artsearch.nga.gov.au/detail.cfm?irn=76616

Dürer, A. (1514). *Melencolia I* [Engraving]. National Gallery of Victoria. https://www.ngv.vic.gov.au/albrecht-durer-melencolia-i-1514/

Géricault, T. (1818–19). *The raft of the medusa* [Painting]. Louvre Museum. https://collections.louvre.fr/en/ark:/53355/cl010064841

Greene, M. (1978). *Landscapes of learning*. Teachers College Press.

Greene, M. (1995). *Releasing the imagination: Essays on education, the arts, and social change*. Jossey-Bass.

Harry, D. (1979). *Dreaming* [song]. Chrysalis.

Kelly, W. (2003). *Art and humanist ideals: Contemporary perspectives*. Palgrave Macmillan.

Kruger, B. (1989). *Untitled (your body is a battleground* [photographic silkscreen]. The Broad. https://www.thebroad.org/art/barbara-kruger/untitled-your-body-battleground

Küpers, W. (2005). Phenomenology and integral pheno-practice of embodied well-be(com)ing in organisations. *Culture and Organization, 11*(3), 221–232. https://doi.org/10.1080/14759550500204142

Leavy, P. (2015). *Method meets art: Arts-based research practice* (2nd ed.). Guildford Press.

Manathunga, C., Selkrig, M., Sadler, K., & Keamy, K. (2017). Rendering the paradoxes and pleasures of academic life: Using images, poetry and drama to speak back to the measured university. *Higher Education Research & Development, 36*(3), 526–540. https://doi.org/10.1080/07294360.2017.1289157

McDiarmid, D. (1991). *Up and down* [Gouache on paper]. Heide Museum of Modern Art. https://collection.heide.com.au/objects/971

Mclean, P. B., & Wallace, D. (2013). Blogging the unspeakable: Racial politics, Bakhtin, and the carnivalesque. *International Journal of Communication, 7*, 1518–1537.

Neumann, A. (2009). Protecting the passion of scholars in times of change. *Change: The Magazine of Higher Learning, 41*(2), 10–15. https://doi.org/10.3200/CHNG.41.2.10-15

Pasztory, E. (2005). *Thinking with things: Toward a new vision of art*. University of Texas Press.

Prosser, J. (2011). Visual methodology: Toward a more seeing research. In N. Denzin & Y. Lincoln (Eds.), *The Sage handbook of qualitative research* (pp. 479–496). Sage.

Rainey, L. (1998). Taking dictation: Collage, poetics, pathology and politics. *Modernism/Modernity, 5*(2), 123–153.

Riddington, K. (1990). *House of cards* [TV series]. BBC.

Selkrig, M. (2010, May 28–June 19). *Caprichos* [Series of fifteen sculptures exhibited as part of the exhibition entitled *Rustic Antics* at Artspace Gallery, Wodonga]. Artspace Wodonga.

Selkrig, M. (2012a). Becoming a bricoleur: Constructing sculptures to explore complex and troublesome dimensions in educational research. *International Journal of Research & Method in Education*, 1–14. https://doi.org/10.1080/1743727x.2012.742051

Selkrig, M. (2012b). *Mapping the in-betweens*. La Trobe University, La Trobe University Visual Arts Centre.

Seurat, G. (1884–1886). *A Sunday afternoon on the Island of La Grande Jatte* [Painting]. Art Institute of Chicago. https://www.artic.edu/artworks/27992/a-sunday-on-la-grande-jatte-1884

Shirgley, D. (2021). *David Shirgley: Drawing and painting*. Retrieved June 4, from http://davidshrigley.com/category/drawing-painting/

Smith, C., & Ulus, E. (2019). Who cares for academics? We need to talk about emotional well-being including what we avoid and intellectualize through macro-discourses. *Organization, 27*(6), 840–857. https://doi.org/10.1177/1350508419867201

Streeton, A. (1889). *Golden summer* [Painting]. National Gallery of Australia. https://cs.nga.gov.au/detail.cfm?IRN=61325

Talking Heads. (1981). *Once in a lifetime* [song]. Sire.

Turner, V. W. (1969). *The ritual process: Structure and anti-structure*. Aldine.
Webb, J., Schirato, T., & Danaher, G. (2002). *Understanding Bourdieu*. Sage.
Weber, S. (2008). Visual images in research. In J. G. Knowles & A. L. Cole (Eds.), *Handbook of the arts in qualitative research* (pp. 41–53). Sage.
Willats, S. (1976). Artwork as social model. *Studio International, 191*(980), 100–106.

10 Self-care in the time of crisis

An *a/r/tographic* conversation to explore self-care as academics that took an unexpected turn

Nicole Brunker and Robyn Gibson

In 2019, we were inspired to develop a project exploring how we self-care in academia. The plan was to compose a weekly reflection and attach a black-and-white photograph reflecting on our self-care, which we would send to each other with the intention of growing our self-care. We proposed to commence in semester 1 2020, a time that was to mark substantial change for us both. We had no inkling at the time just how significant this project would be for us as we confronted the global pandemic and our different experiences of 'lockdown'. The following is an *a/r/tographic* journey through snippets of our weekly reflections and the subsequent meta-reflection on our self-care practices that raises questions about the possibilities and potentialities of and for self-care.

Through engaging in the living inquiry of *a/r/tography*, our process was an act of self-care in and of itself. Central to this sharing was recognition of self-care as a multifaceted, fluctuating, and evolving practice, contextually based within the demands of academia. The essential need for self-care is not only about self but also an opportunity to disrupt contextual practices that may challenge our wellbeing and/or ability to self-care.

A/r/tography is a relational, aesthetic inquiry, a "coming together of . . . image and word . . . wherein the two complement, extend, refute and/or subvert one another . . . (a) contiguous interaction" (Springgay et al., 2005, p. 900). Through engaging in *a/r/tographic* conversation, we share not only our experience of self-care but also the pressures that increase the need for self-care, those that potentially inhibit self-care, and the ways in which our increased responsibility for self-care may maintain and enable harmful practices.

A/r/tography takes a rhizomatic form (Deleuze & Guattari, 1987). Rhizomes depict the contiguity of academia and self-care, the touchings and not touchings and thus the space for otherness. Through the entangled spread and assemblage "rhizomes activate the in-between" (Irwin & Springgay, 2017, p. 163). It is in these 'in-betweens' that space exists for transformations in the way of Heideggerian 'throws' which provoke and rupture accepted understanding and build new perceptions (Siegesmund, 2012). As such, "the in-between disrupts dualisms" (Irwin & Springgay, 2017, p. 163).

The contiguity of *a/r/tography* mirrors the contiguity of academia – it is the ever changing, multi-faceted context and activity that touch and don't touch;

DOI: 10.4324/9781003207863-13

overlap and continually shift that enables further contiguity: space for damage, harm, toxicity, as well as space for self-care. Enacting self-care requires awareness of the pressures touching upon it and space to inquire: "a willingness to allow for discomfort, frayed edges, and holes" (Springgay et al., 2005, p. 901). As academics at very different points in our careers, we offer each other and readers a 'throw' in which to disrupt accepted and imposed understandings and practices through which other dualisms may be explored: institutional pressure and individual self-care; to care or not to care; the toxic and the healthy.

Starting the Semester With Hope

Change was the theme we held dear as we entered 2020. Robyn, an experienced academic, was to embark on-long overdue study leave at the same time as becoming an 'empty-nester', living alone for the first time in more than two decades. Nikki, moving from early- to mid-career academic, was preparing her son to start high school after home educating almost 4 years, as a full-time working solo parent. 2020 was to be our year to finish-up lingering projects, submit the multiple half-completed articles and develop clear research programs to move forward, while also finding time to consider ourselves and how we wanted to move forward as people.

As we looked upon the journey ahead, we were both aware of the need for more self-care in our lives without quite being able to give definition or direction, knowing our shared experience of being too busy to self-care adequately. We were all too well-aware that:

> (I)t is no longer a (thinly veiled) secret that in contemporary universities many scholars, both junior and senior, are struggling – struggling to manage their workloads; struggling to keep up with insistent institution demands to produce more, better, faster; struggling to reconcile professional demands with family responsibilities and personal interests; and struggling to maintain their physical and psychological health and emotional wellbeing.
>
> (Pereira, 2016, p. 100)

The contemporary managerialist agenda of universities, driven by neoliberalism, has resulted in increases in generic work-related stressors as well as those specific to academia (Kinman, 2014). Increased workloads have seen academics working hours equivalent to a seven-day working week (Gill, 2017). The unbounded and portable nature of academic work often leads to work colonising other parts of our lives (Kinman, 2014), jeopardising the individual pursuit of work–life balance. Self-care is often touted as the alleviant to stress and preventor of burnout (Posluns & Gall, 2020). But how?

> *Amidst what is unquestionably the busiest start to the academic year I have ever experienced, I have the treat of working from home. Working from home is often*

Self-care in the time of crisis 155

Image 10.1 'Sitting in the bush that surrounds us'

not a treat, rather a time to intensify the juggle of work, family, life. Today though my house is empty. . . . Academia has flexibility built into every angle of our work. I have made best possible use of that flexibility, often to the detriment of my self-care. 'Working from home' can equal childcare, and other family and life responsibilities, then working til the small hours of the morning, working all weekend. Today though working from home has been true balance . . . I actually took a lunch break, which I never do at work, and while I didn't use it to eat, the reality of cleaning the bathroom, loads of washing and general cleaning enabled me to smile in the lightness that comes from a tidy home . . . taking moments in between to take in the environment around our home. . . . Sitting in the bush that surrounds us, listening to the trickle of the water through the creek I am reminded why it is that I endure the commute to work each day. Even if only for the odd day like today. Self-care is not regular in my life, it is far from a priority, in fact I have to stop to think what it actually is that I could do to care for myself. This image holds for me a reminder of how brief moments may be renewing, recognition that I may take working from home as a treat and acknowledgement that my move towards self-care may take small steps.

(Nikki, 27/2/20)

This is my last day in my office before I commence study leave. This door has opened and closed so many times over the past few months that it seems strange to consider life away from 'the busyness'. My challenge now is to slow down; "to live one day at a time" (Cameron, 2009) and to find depth within the small things. I'm not sure that this is possible given my obsession with finding something to do even when nothing needs to be done! But I welcome the next few months as an opportunity to refocus both on my work and myself. Who will take care of me, if not me? And so, the journey begins. . . .

(Robyn, 28/2/20)

We were aware of how our personalities and life circumstances impacted the nature of self-care. Crucial to these initial reflections was the incoming freedom within our lives. Freedom enabling autonomy is well recognised as crucial for self-care and wellbeing (Winefield et al., 2014). The letting go of external demands offered both space and time. This was our first reminder that work can be a form of self-care, carving personal identity and self-worth. We were not running away from work to value ourselves; rather we were seeking greater opportunity to run into our work, recognising the importance of slow scholarship (Mountz et al., 2015), stepping off the production treadmill academia has become and enjoying ourselves within our work.

Slowing down, hmmmm perhaps it is just that, reducing the speed at which we feel compelled to act. And maybe it is the shift in activity that will shift the speed. I look forward to looking out the window of the chaos to see how you shift gears and how I may take a little into how I juggle the manic nature of academia.

(Nikki, 1/3/20)

A week has passed with a conscious decision to change the pace of life; to afford myself the luxury of time to think, reflect and at times, refocus. "To enjoy just being somewhere, rather than rushing from somewhere, to somewhere" (Potter, 2010). Not feeling guilty about a morning coffee and reading for pleasure amid the craziness of the world as we know it. I recognise this as a gift not offered to all, so I grasp it with both hands and take a slow step forward.

(Robyn, 6/3/20)

Opportunities opened for us to self-care, which ultimately meant doing things for ourselves. Self-care is "the ability to refill and refuel oneself in healthy ways" (Gentry, 2002, p. 48), including "engagement in behaviours that maintain and promote physical and emotional wellbeing" (Myers et al., 2012, p. 56, as cited in Posluns & Gall, 2020, p. 4). Absent from self-care is work, separated from life in pursuit of balance. The self is compartmentalised in the workplace, life to be resumed outside of work hours. The crossover of work and life raised the time-weary trope of guilt and pushback.

Image 10.2 'To afford myself the luxury of time'

> *A day in hospital this week had me label self-care as a nuisance. . . . My imposed self-care meant some challenging questions (Bosanquet, 2019): is this really important? Does this really need my attention? Weighing up priorities, measuring out where time and attention would be devoted.*
>
> (Nikki, 6/3/20)

Flexibility is a hallmark of work–life balance. Once inherent to academia, flexibility has been eroded or overloaded, so that what remains may simply enable academics to "work longer and harder" (Kinman, 2014, p. 239). All the while, the historic stress-free life of academia remains pervasive in society's view, the "poisonous myth that" academics "are time-rich and leisured" (Gill, 2017, p. 6).

158 *Nicole Brunker and Robyn Gibson*

Image 10.3 'I'm far from alone in this experience'

> *Academia is a foreign land to my family and friends outside of work. One that they fill with ill-placed assumptions and judgement. Adding the concept of 'self-care' to this picture means 'giving in' to the beliefs that surround me of having an easy, effectively part-time job that lets me explore my passion rather than actually 'work'. After all I don't teach all day every day; perhaps a bit of writing, but hey that's not work, that's what I like doing; reading? 'oh, please!'; while the full magnitude of academic work is missed entirely. I am far from alone in this experience and far from the extremes this schism of cultures may evoke. It is however a crucial point of understanding reluctance to self-care, even a learned ignorance to the need or activity of self-care when self-care is viewed as indulgence, even laziness and self-absorption highlighting the individual focus and limiting its benefits.*
>
> (Nikki, 8/5/20)

Kinman (2014) suggested "(A)ssumptions about the inherent flexibility of academic work may mean that universities have made little effort to develop work–life balance interventions beyond basic compliance with legislation" (p. 230). This in turn fuels individualist requirements for self-care. Individualism is central to neoliberalism from which the managerialist culture of academia has sprung (Budak, 2017; Rogers, 2012). Responses to stress take "a resolute focus on individual psychological functioning . . . with courses, training sessions, yoga, meditation, events on time management", subsequently "instilling the idea that it is our *relation*[1] to work that needs to be changed, rather than the nature of working conditions themselves" (Gill, 2017, p. 12).

Recognition had long ago dawned for us that self-care is our personal responsibility, although being a personal responsibility as well as having personal consequence for not meeting that responsibility saw us push that aside. Self-care was prioritised below the many, often conflicting external demands of work and life. We fell into the view of self-care as a luxury, something that takes us away from what is really needed. Justification was sought, and again we found ourselves looking back upon ourselves.

> *Measurement and evaluation have become ubiquitous to our work lives to the point that we view ourselves through the metrics of student evaluations, publication outputs, grant successes. Where "is the metric for self-care?" (O'Dwyer et al., 2018, p. 243). . . . Of course, there are no metrics for self-care, for it is the ultimate individual pursuit.*
>
> (Nikki, 6/3/20)

The intertwined nature of our work and lives leads to our life being viewed through the same lens imposed upon our work, feeling the pressure to live the "affectively thin and relentlessly diagnostic lives" due to the "steady poisoning and paralysing effects of managerialism" (Collini, 2012, n.p., as cited in Black et al., 2017, p. 138). When do our lives lead our work? When would our lives be the priority and pushback on the external demands? All too soon, to our surprise!

Crisis, Fear, Uncertainty, and Isolation

2020 began with an ever-increasing sense of international panic. Before we knew it, we were looking at working remotely, seeking ways to maintain social and intellectual connection. Already removed from university campus life, Robyn watched the escalating panic fuelled by fear that our very wellbeing was under threat both directly and indirectly as the counter-measures initially looked harsher than what we were fleeing.

> *Each day brings further concerns about our own wellbeing, that of family and friends and the planet itself! So, we take those sprinklings of joy where and when we can find them . . . it gives me hope that perhaps we will all be OK; that we can turn things around if we just care a little more.*

Image 10.4 'I yearn for the warm embrace'

> In such unprecedented times, let's consider our own wellbeing and that of others as a priority? While we remain 'connected' via technological devices, I yearn for the warm embrace of a loved one.
> From isolation without end
> Prolong'd; nor knew although not less
> Alone than thou, their loneliness
>
> (Martin Arnold, Isolation: To Marguerite, 1897)

> Feeling isolated although not self-isolating. I need to practice what I preach and enjoy the sunshine!
>
> (Robyn, 20/3/20)

Nikki was knee deep in the overnight switch to emergency remote learning that saw the already-strained academic workload become all-consuming. This project provided a much-needed impetus to consider self-care.

> Self-care has been written on the top of my to do list every day this week. I even have an alarm set to alert me to think about self-care, prompt me to do something to

self-care. . . . A gentle prod, a push to make time to at least write, and self-care has now extended beyond reminders to connection, thank-you!

(Nikki, 21/3/20)

Amidst this dizzying new world order, our shared need for action reflected the different demands of our contexts.

This morning I bought an exercise bike online! Thinking that if I have to 'bunker down' for the next, however long, then I could at least exercise. Exercise especially walking has been my saving grace through some emotional periods in my life. Walking long distances such as the Camino de Santiago has become a meditation; a living in the moment experience that I cherish. I definitely believe that there is a connection between walking, thinking and creativity. . . . So, while an exercise bike isn't any substitute for walking across Spain, I relented and bought one!

(Robyn, 27/3/20)

Image 10.5 'In being prepared I was proactive'

Baden-Powell bestowed the motto of "be prepared" upon all scouts with the intention of being prepared in mind "having thought out beforehand any accident or situation that might occur, so that you know the right thing to do at the right moment, and are willing to do it" as well as being "Prepared in Body by making yourself strong and active and able to do the right thing at the right moment, and do it" (Baden-Powell, 1908, p. 48). So, feeling a bit like a mother squirrel preparing for hibernation I prepared us for the ensuing winter of working and schooling from home. It was an act of practicality. It was also an act of fortitude, and resilience; taking action, being productive to counter the overwhelming lack of control and uncertainty that is facing us all. In being prepared I was proactive in my self-care. Doing something physical allowed me to expend some energy in a manner that also let me express anger and aggression; loudly voicing my torment upon the wood I was carting and stacking. It also focussed my thinking to the future. Not far into the future though enough to ease some concerns, knowing that we will be well set up to stay warm through our winter of discontent.

(Nikki, 27/3/20)

We thus opened ourselves to the possibilities for and of self-care.

We began this arts-based research project using a/r/tography to unravel aspects of our artist/researcher/educator lives as we reflected deeply on that liminal space between work and home; that sliver of time that we call 'self-care.' Springgay et al. (2005) suggest that in using a/r/tography we are moving "toward an understanding of interdisciplinarity not as a patchwork of different disciplines and methodologies but as a loss, a shift, or a rupture where in absence, new courses of action unfold" (p. 897). I think more than anything else, I like many, feel this sense of perpetual loss. A loss of freedom, a loss of connection, a loss of normality, a loss of me! What can I do to recapture, reinvent, reinvigorate in these days of solitude? So I draw on one of a/r/tographies' six renderings: openings. I will open myself up to my creative spirit and acknowledge that "creativity occurs in the moment" (Cameron, 2009, p. 12). I will look at my 'creative' sign decorated by yours truly . . . and realise that by encouraging something to grow, to read for pleasure, to walk in the sunshine, I am encouraging my creative self and in doing so opening myself up to the possibilities that tomorrow holds.

(Robyn, 17/4/20)

The commitment of a weekly post planted a seed to consider self-care. A conscious reflection on moments throughout our days to photograph and share, reflecting further on how, why a thought of self-care had been triggered. Rhizomes sprouting, spreading, reaching back and forth between us. We started with ideas of what we would do, even taking photos before we began our project, planning what we might do. We were seeking order, control, knowledge of what lay ahead. This time of worldwide uncertainty gave an opportunity to sit in the unknown and see the rhizomes rather than try to propagate or bonsai. We took on Deleuze and Guattari's (1987) guidance to "(a)lways follow the rhizomes by rupture; lengthen, prolong, and relay the line of flight; make it wary, until you have produced the most abstract and tortuous of lines of in dimensions and broken directions" (p. 11).

Image 10.6 'Self-care came from the universe today'

Self-care came from the universe today; the uplifting sound, smell and feel of the rain teeming down outside my office window, enlivening the bush that surrounds us and intensifying the rush of the creek. The wisdom of an academic experienced in working through catastrophes (Ahmad, 2020) helped me see that the past couple of weeks have been an acclimatisation phase. It has been a phase that I tried to intellectually reason my way through. I was prepared in so many ways. I was tackling the challenges head on. It was exhausting and difficult at times, yet I was moving, I was in a state of constant action. This week the reality hit me. . . . My confidence in being able to hold us together through this chaos was being eroded and the tears flowed in my inability to set things right. Just as I began to feel truly incapable, the universe joined me in tears and took them away. I have been reminded of the need to self-care by others, today it was the world stopping me with a gentle reminder that I am part of something so much bigger, so beautiful and so incredibly resilient. Just as Ahmad (2020) gave me understanding of my initial response to the crisis, the rain shifted my perspective to remind me that while so much is changing and so much is uncertain, so much more remains unchanged in reassuring patterns of uncertainty.

(Nikki, 1/4/20)

Opening ourselves to the spaces for self-care took many forms. The previous liminal positioning of self-care was shifting, no longer satisfied with relegation to the spaces between, self-care began to set the agenda. Our lives were taking priority.

Image 10.7 'Embrace the chaos'

This week I have attempted to embrace the chaos, to 'let it be[2]'. Thank you Paul McCartney, not my favourite Beatle though key to my psyche this week which is definitely not the frightening Disney anthem 'let it go[3]'! I am attempting to sit with things and allow things to sit. From the washing up that waits to be completed once a day rather than three times, to my son devouring hours of screen time. I am embracing the chaos in whatever form it comes. Leaving work to make sure I walk every day, luxuriating in the abandonment of one screen for the next as I sink into movies of an evening. Key to my shift this week has been recognising that self-care does not need to be an addition to my week rather it can be a way of prioritising what is important, letting go (no Disney no!) of what is not important – at least what can wait. Most crucially it means questioning my own need for . . . not perfection so much, as high expectations. It has been about making choices such as spending time in a part of the garden that I really enjoy, to weed, plant and just be, while ignoring the ever-increasing jungle of the grass. While my distaste for Disney princesses averts me from taking on 'let it go' as my theme song, I am also aware that my high expectations tend towards the maladaptive perfectionism in the self-criticality I impose on myself when I do not meet my own expectations (Moate

et al., 2016). It is a life's journey to let go, for now I am finding ways to let my self-criticism be and allow myself to care for myself through not doing, rather being.
(Nikki, 24/4/20)

Space opened for self-care to take form beyond survival, beyond the individualist, psychological drive (Gill, 2017) and capitalist push of luxury. Our lives opened space for us to contemplate, to reflect, and opened memories as a form of self-care.

Image 10.8 'Hold tight to the memories'

Contemplating our current surreal world, I have spent a great deal of this week thinking about how we look after ourselves and those we love in times of distress and upset. Our lives are broken and it seems that our way back is through remembering. In Touching eternity, Tom Barone (2001) said that "memory is the glue that holds meaning together, that allows a life story to be fashioned and related" (p. 165). I should know, I wrote a book about The memory of clothes (2015) and through that heartfelt exercise realized that memories enable us to capture moments in time – some sad, others joyous; some confusing yet always there, waiting to draw you back. So I set aside time this week to look at old photographs and read travel journals and remember that those special people and faraway places are still with me and someday those precious memories will become a reality once more. Hold tight to those memories!

(Robyn, 24/4/20)

Memories were sought, memories were shared and memories were triggered. Our reflection in writing and image prompted each other's reflection and thus self-care. The rhizomes grew, sending tendrils to appear in places and shapes that took us by surprise.

Image 10.9 'Bittersweet memories of my mother'

You have derailed me! When I started reading your reflective thoughts this week, I was taken aback that you still have both parents alive and even though your father had an undignified fall, he is still with you! So, bittersweet memories of my own mother started flooding back. It's been fifteen years but I still miss her dreadfully. She was the impetus for The memory of clothes *(Gibson, 2015).*

I had not realized that those feelings of loss were still so close to the surface. Thoughts of spending Mother's Day alone without my own mother or son were enough to pry them open? So, my image this week is a photo of my mother taken on her wedding day and with it I ponder the self-care of mothers like us. "A child's first teacher is its mother" (Peng Liyuan, 2014). Do we worry about ourselves when we have children? We are like birds feeding our young rather than ourselves. They always come first and we often eke out an existence in the little bit of time/space that is left. And as academics that time/space is consumed by the not-so-silent pressures to 'succeed.' Publish or perish became the mantra! How is that possible when you are juggling a dozen essential tasks and feeling as though none of them is at a standard that you are truly happy with?

(Robyn, 8/5/20)

As rhizomes flourished with the unexpected forms and spaces for self-care, we also opened to our self-care not being enough, focussing not just on life after COVID but also our lives before.

Life Pushing Back on Work

Academia is ripe for "blurring the lines between personal and professional identity" (Shaw & Ward, 2014, n.p., as cited in Wilcox & Schroeder, 2017, p. 81), leading to constant decisions for academics "about when, and how, to create boundaries between work and personal life" (Wilcox & Schroeder, 2017, p. 81). Technology has contributed significantly to this blurring of boundaries, "making it difficult to disconnect from the demands of the academy" (Wilcox & Schroeder, 2017, p. 82). COVID-19 brought rapid escalation of this dilemma as lockdown forced us all to work from home. Boundaries became essential for self-care.

I'm done. I need a break. I have worked from home some part of every week for the past fifteen years. I have juggled the advantage of academic flexibility to my own expense. It has not been uncommon for me to work til 5am only for the alarm to go off at 6am. Laptop in the kitchen to make the best use of moments. Longing for time to binge upon. Now that I am working from home solely it has become 24/7. I am more organised, not dealing constantly with the half-finished bits hanging between work and home offices, the mess from flying out one door to get to the other. But. There is no leaving. It never ends. It is always there. Every part of work is now in my home . . . Today, I am done . . . I need to close the door on my office and not open it again until next week.

(Nikki, 9/4/20)

Being unbounded (Kinman, 2014) academia requires our individual decisions to determine when our work is finished, when to knock off for the day.

I need boundaries and I find that working from home has blurred those even further. I know that as academics we don't work from 9–5 but I find that I'm reading 'work-related' stuff while eating dinner, checking and responding to emails before

Image 10.10 'I'm done. I need a break'

> *I go to bed, etc. At least when I had an office, a lot of that stayed there! My trip home . . . was the demarcation line!*
>
> (Robyn, 10/4/20)

Boundaries became integral to self-care yet insufficient when the culture within which we exist is supportive of advantage in minimal boundaries. Our new reality shone attention on many of the inequities in our world. In academia a significant inequity impacting on self-care and wellbeing is gender, especially mothering (Dugan & Barnes-Farrell, 2020). An inequity that is not resolved through boundaries, through separation of work and life.

> *COVID has sent everything askew. We have been told 2020 is to be the year of no disadvantage, well for students at least (USyd, 2020) – what about academics? The disadvantage is already all too visible for many groups, and like many areas, in academia it is the mothers paying the greatest cost (Kitchener, 2020). . . . As I cancelled*

a meeting to be with my son (when he needed me) I felt the resentment creep in. Not resentment for my son, rather resentment that while with him I continually drifted to 'what I should be doing'. With evidence suggesting self-isolation has resulted in male academics submitting more articles, while the number from women has dropped substantially (Kitchener, 2020), I wondered how many men knew that type of resentment.
(Nikki, 2/5/20)

Connection was key to our self-care, moving beyond self-care to caring and being cared for.

Image 10.11 'This week is reflective of the Tree of Yggdrasill'

Long before the popular Viking television series, I was drawn to Norse mythology. Its temperamental Gods, Bifrost, the rainbow bridge that connects Asgard to Midgard and the ultimate rebirth of the world Ragnarok.

"If the Norns determine the weirds of men, then they apportion exceeding unevenly, seeing that some have a pleasant and luxurious life, but others have little worldly goods or fame; some have long life, others short"
(Sturluson, 1995, p. 18).

> . . . academia doesn't work in favour of women especially those parenting alone. While men climb the ladder to advancement (often using female colleagues as the rungs on that ladder), it's the hard-working women who keep the wheels turning. And turn they do! Often to their own detriment.
>
> So, self-care for us means turning to others and asking for support. . . .
>
> To that end, my image this week is reflective of the Tree of Yggdrasill – a mighty ash which is timeless and has no origin. It is under this tree that the norns sit and spin our fates. Skuld is waiting for you Nikki to become what you know you will be!
>
> (Robyn, 3/5/20)

COVID-19 brought us all an experience of social isolation that challenged connection.

> I have come to detest my life in front of a screen. If this is 'the brave new world' then please make it stop because I want to get off! "There is a difference between solitude and isolation. One is connected and one isn't. Solitude replenishes; isolation diminishes" (Henry Cloud, 2015). I wake to a day like the one previously. I write on a screen; I watch news reports on a screen; I talk to friends and family on a screen. If this continues will I resort to reading books on a screen? Where is the human interaction that we all crave? I can feel winter nipping and with it comes the realisation that this feeling of uncertainty will drag on. What damage will it cause in its wake? I'm fearful . . . "for many a long day loneliness will sit over our roofs with brooding wings" (Bram Stoker, Dracula, 1897, p. 200).
>
> (Robyn, 10/4/20)

Our building connection amidst our struggle for connection in the ways in which we are familiar and reliant brought new questions. Central was whether self-care is ever really possible.

> The most significant thing that has hit me is the problematic nature of self-care, that it is an inherently individual responsibility, one that is essential to deal with the trials and tribulations of our society and in being an individual act it is removed from social responsibility. The crux of what we have been doing has been the sharing, the collaboration that has been the impetus and motivation to self-care. I am also struck by our aloneness and do people alone self-care? Is self-care actually even possible, or does it require the care of someone else to help us feel valued enough to believe we deserve to self-care? . . . is that the key to self-care in higher education, the need to collaborate?
>
> (Nikki, 15/5/20)

Do we need connection to enable self-worth that may then value and prompt self-care? How can we care for something we do not value?

Self-care in the time of crisis   171

Image 10.12 'It is an individual responsibility'

Maybe 'connection' is our self-care strategy? I think that this has proven to be such a valuable project in terms of self-reflection. Who knew that it would be so important in actually finding the time and space to think deeply about what is happening in your life, how you feel about it and how you will/can respond? That said, for me anyway, it could have become self-indulgent or self-wallowing if I had not had someone to share these thoughts with. So thank you for proposing that we collaborate!
(Robyn, 14/4/20)

COVID-19 took centre stage as we struggled with the changes in how we lived and what the future might hold. Our weekly posts drew us into deeper contemplation and reflection, the building blocks for creation and generation of the new, essential for us to look beyond crisis to what may be and what we wanted for ourselves. Pondering, questioning, examining took the rhizomes beyond prescribed notions of self-care.

This week something shifted within me. There was a revelation of profound concern that hung over me; a foreboding that I couldn't shift. I sat with one of my witches' cats on my lap and asked myself: When we emerge from this hideous situation, will there be a return to some semblance of normality or will our lives be forever changed, lived through a computer screen? Devoid of the touch of other homo sapiens; working from our homes; ordering all we need online? These thoughts become so overwhelming that I decided to escape the confines of my apartment and walk. I focused on what was around me rather than what was churning inside me. As I came around a corner of the bush track, I spotted a little blue wren who flitted from branch to branch unaware that I had intruded into his space . . . "he was telling me that I was on the right path" . . . I hope/wish/pray that we are all on the right path.

(Robyn, 2/4/20)

Caring for ourselves took on new meaning and urgency as we experienced chaos unfamiliar to anything in our own prior lives.

Image 10.13 'The stability of the familiar'

In 'The Plague' (Camus, 1948) the 'man who spits on cats' provided a symbol of our human absurdity amidst the futile reality of our apparently doomed lives. This week I have been struck by an overwhelming sense of absurdity: oscillating between the demands of what must be done to enable life as we knew it to continue and what is needed for quality of life in facing this terrifying new reality. . . . Maintaining a sense of normality, the stability of the familiar is supportive to our wellbeing. It also allows us to push aside the torrent of fear and anxiety that is rushing along underneath like the proverbial duck and ignore our need to self-care.

(Nikki, 17/4/20)

Challenge and uncertainty were constants within our lives, our need for self-care, while shaping our perceptions were also altering our activity for self-care.

Lessons to be learnt. . . . Over the past three months on well-earned study leave coupled with lockdown restrictions, I supplemented my various 'almost started' research projects with daily doses of self-care reading and reflection. Most websites suggest a good night's sleep, nutritious food, regular exercise and the like. But is that enough? Now (in my final self-care entry) I weave together what I have learnt from the perspective of an older academic who has spent the last 30 years (off and on) at the University of Sydney and who entered this unknown territory with a 'why-not' attitude. . . .

> *Lesson 1: Appreciate those who have come into your life. They are there for a reason. . . .*
> *Lesson 2: We may feel alone but when we connect to others that feeling is diminished. . . .*
> *Lesson 3: Get outside – walk in the bush, along the beach, through city streets – explore the world. It's still a beautiful place! . . .*
> *Lesson 4: Be kind to yourself. There's only one of you! . . .*

What I have learnt about self-care. Nothing earth-shattering but something that I wouldn't have ever contemplated unless you approached me all those months ago.

(Robyn, 25/5/20)

Our conversation shows us exploring the layers of self-care, the spaces for self-care, and the possibilities of self-care. As we explicitly and implicitly posed more questions than answers, we challenged our practices and saw the spaces to challenge practice beyond ourselves.

Self-care is a relatively new notion in humanity appearing in time to be quickly taken possession of by neoliberalism and launched as a capitalist venture whereby our own sustenance is marketed to us as something necessarily luxurious. This introduction came through Foucault's later (1984) works turning from 'the other' of ethical considerations to the 'subject', which was deemed by some as self-obsessed and self-indulgent . . . Foucault's intention was to shift our thinking of morality and ethics from the external to start from ourselves; to look at the "self as a problem, requiring production and manipulation and thereby becoming a basis for ethics" (Boer, 2014). What he neglected was the gaping difference between the advantages of upper-class ancient Greeks on which he developed his thinking and the reality of the working classes, thus enabling self-care to thrive as self-indulgence. But do we have an ethical imperative to self-care (Barnett et al., 2007)? Feminist poet and activist Audre Lorde argued "Caring for myself is not self-indulgence, it is

> *self-preservation, and that is an act of political warfare" (1988). Without self-care who are we?*
>
> (Nikki, 8/5/20)

Taken up by medical professionals "as a way for patients to treat themselves and exercise healthy habits" (Harris, 2017, para. 3), self-care has been positioned to serve many roles. Industrialised by academics as "ways for workers in more high-risk and emotionally daunting professions . . . to combat stress brought on by the job" (para. 3), self-care has become a 'moral obligation' in professions such as psychology and social work (Bohall & Bautista, 2017; Dalphon, 2019; Wilcox & Schroeder, 2017). The onus thus being that individuals must self-care to fulfil their employment obligations. Civil rights and women's movements grew self-care from survival – in relation to equitable healthcare – to become a political act as exemplified by Lorde (1988) to enable true autonomy. Sitting within the dualisms of survival or luxurious indulgence; weapon to change society or individualist obligation to meet society's demands, self-care saw us all too often align in guilt and apology for enacting self-care.

> *I was about to begin this email with an apology, though have stopped myself . . . Yesterday . . . I felt my all-too-familiar, and all too female (Schumann & Ross, 2010), response . . . to apologise (for being human and thus fallible) . . . I recognised that whether I needed to apologise or not was irrelevant. Apologising would do nothing for my self-care, it would simply keep me churning, moving further away from what I needed to do, let alone what I needed to do in order to value and care for myself. So, while it might seem incredibly trivial and inconsequential my greatest act of self-care this week has been to stop myself from apologising.*
>
> (Nikki, 14/5/20)

Contiguity arose as our diverse experiences touched in shared responses to divergent experiences.

> *And, I too was about to start this week's self-care reflection with an apology. Empty-nesting, study leave and a pandemic had started to wear me down. There was a sameness to each day. Did I actually know one day from another?*
>
> *A daily routine had emerged that I resented. What had happened to my spontaneous spirit? I felt curtailed and imprisoned in my own home. So when an invitation to venture to the north coast with a friend was offered, I gladly accepted. Just overnight, she said but it felt like a door to the unknown had been opened and I tentatively stepped out. And step out, I did.*
>
> *Walking along an almost deserted beach in the early morning hours, I encountered the occasional dog walker who nodded and passed by. More content to throw balls into the waves then stop and make idle conversation. I sat in the damp sand and watched the surfers in wet suits patiently waiting for the wave that would carry them back to shore. Why are so many of us drawn to the ocean? I love her tormented moods, her gentle caresses, her great expanse. I know I shouldn't over romanticize the power of the sea but isn't that what so many writers and poets have done? . . .*

Self-care in the time of crisis 175

Image 10.14 'Consider images through an artistic lens'

> *So, you see my self-care this week seemed self-indulgent and I wanted to apologise for it. What do I have to complain about in a world gone to ruin? . . . This is what the Arts offer us – spaces to help us understand "those ideas . . . that lie adjacent to one another, touch one another, or exist in the presence of one another" (Irwin & Springgay, 2008, p. xxviii).*
>
> (Robyn, 15/5/20)

On the Cusp of Returning to Normal

We knew we were opening ourselves to consider self-care from different yet shared positions. COVID-19 changed our lives unrecognisably, casting aside best laid plans, changing how our new life phases would play out. Unexpected was the change not only from the intrusion of crisis but also the impact of shared self-care upon our view of normal life.

> *Tomorrow I will be back to working at work . . . I am not looking forward to it . . . I am not wanting to let go of working from home. I am actually not wanting to let go of isolation. I have enjoyed more about lockdown than I have missed.*

Walking home along our street each evening after our daily walk I feel a sense of déjà vu, a recalling of my own childhood as kids play on the car free road, adults sit on the lawn calling out to neighbours, and aromas of slow cooking waft from each home. I prefer this way of life, the slowness, the smaller yet more meaningful ways of connecting . . .

Best of all is not . . . battling the commute for 90 minutes every morning, knowing I will do the same again at the end of the day. With that comes more time in my day. Initially I didn't even realise, so frantic was the workload . . . This project has prompted me to consider self-care in a way I never have before – consistently, deeply, with purpose and commitment. In doing so I have taken steps to self-care. . . . The most significant step has been drawing a line between work and home every weekend.

. . . I am feeling the hold upon me that will fight a return to work filled weekends. This new reality is both restorative and unsettling in my self-care. It has been enabled by an unprecedented level of self-isolation . . . that is finite. . . .

As I realise this reality is finite, I catch my breath: How will I hold onto time for me when the demands of juggling work while being a solo parent fill every moment of my days?

(Nikki, 24/5/20)

Separating life from work in academia is as impossible as objectivity in research. The vast array of human experience might not be seen within academia, although we are not a homogenous entity. Approaches to self-care and how we engage with our work within our lives varies enormously, necessarily so to accommodate the multitude of contexts and needs.

Unlike you, I am looking forward to a return to the work office. I read, with interest, Michael Koziol's column 'Normalising working from home will kill off society' (Sun-Herald, 24 May 2020). He claims that there is a "cold utilitarianism behind this idea that we can all save time and money by having people stay at home and Zoom into meetings. What corporations might save on floor space and desks and upgrades, the rest of us will lose in the death of society as we know it" (p. 13). Yes, one of the things that I have learnt about self-care is the importance of connection and work provided me with that. Connection with people not the internet! . . . I find that my sense of self-worth is bolstered by helping others. I am a deep-listener and people come to my office with tales that they need to tell. I listen, really listen and I believe that they leave feeling better. That is an uplifting feeling!

(Robyn, 25/5/20)

I also read Michael Koziol's article though had a very different response, I was a bit angered to be honest. Then I read Matt Beard's response to the article on twitter and returned to his article 'Do we have to choose between being a good parent and good at our job?' from 2018. He hit the nail on the head for me. Work life balance has been sold to us as a need to balance time and place when it really needs to be about identity – moving away from separate identities at work to home . . . we need "to redefine what it means to be professional so that it's not unrecognisable to the people who know us in our personal lives". For me, that is what lockdown has triggered . . . We have seen into each other's lives and respected the interruptions, the chaos even, and somewhere in there we have started finding a new way of being, a unified being no longer moving between two worlds. For me, I have come to see self-care in this way. It is not so much about time, nutrition, exercise, while all of those are crucial they will not happen unless the ultimate need in self-care is met, i.e. Identity, and from that is the individual, personally shaped nature of self-care. . . . Lockdown has allowed me a glimpse of balance, a glimpse towards being on top of things rather than always making choices over what will be let to slide and ultimately finding everything slides.

(Nikki, 9/6/20)

Academia has taken the separation of work and life beyond most professions through the "traditions and conditions that have a bias against selfhood and which focus on objectivity" (Black et al., 2017, p. 137). This entrenched separation of self from work leaves no space for self-care. As researchers, we have pushed back on these restrictive traditions and opened awareness to the absence of objectivity through such measures. As academics we need to push back on the separation of work and life to uncover the misnomers in enabling self-care.

Pushback is needed on systems that have created a situation whereby "stress in academia exceeds that found in the general population" (Catalano et al., 2010, n.p., as cited in Black et al., 2017, p. 139). Cartesian separation of reason and emotion established a separation of self from work that neoliberalism has taken to a whole new level in seeking 'care-less' workers (Lynch, 2010), where "(W)orkloads are so heavy and expectations of productivity so high . . . that they can only be achieved by workers who have no relationships or responsibilities that might constrain their productive capacities" (p. 7). Black et al. (2017) align with others in their pushback against these cultures to say "we do care" and "as Pereira (2016) suggests, in order for us to enact our care it is absolutely crucial to resist this tendency of individualisation which pervades performativity in the academy" (Black et al., 2017, p. 148). Self-care cannot move us away from 'care-less'; that must come through connection to care for, and be cared for means to be known not just as a worker, as a person.

We have spoken our lives into the academy (Black et al., 2017). Living inquiry is an act of defiance, a pushback on neoliberal ways of being in academia where self-care is solely in the hands of the self, and work–life balance positions life as subordinate to work. "At the heart of *a/r/tographic* work, deeper discovery of oneself guides the intersection between art-making, living inquiry, and the practices of *educare*; the many ways in which the world draws us forth" (Borhani, 2013, p. 14), and so we are drawn forth conscious of not returning to 'normal' or even the 'new normal', rather allowing the rhizomes to continue to provoke, question, and alert us to new ways of seeing and enacting self-care beyond ourselves.

> *This project that we began almost 3 months ago has allowed me to think, read and write with creative intent; to consider images through an artistic lens and for me, it has been a powerful healing mechanism.*
>
> (Robyn, 15/5/20)

> *The most significant thing that has hit me though is the problematic nature of self-care, that it is an individual responsibility, one that is essential to deal with the trials and tribulations of our society and in being an individual act it is removed from social responsibility. . . . I feel like I am edging towards supporting hot desking, which thankfully COVID-19 has probably killed off as yet another casualty, for which as an introvert I am very grateful. Though is there perhaps more worth in pursuing the common good rather than the personal interest, to draw people together more often, for us as colleagues to know one another better, to be more connected and thus valued . . .*
>
> (Nikki, 15/5/20)

> *Let's continue our conversation.*
>
> (Robyn, 17/5/20)

Image 10.15 Robyn's collage

Self-care in the time of crisis 179

Image 10.16 Nikki's collage

Notes

1 Italics in original
2 McCartney (1970)
3 Anderson-Lopez and Lopez (2014)

References

Ahmad, A. S. (2020, March 27). Why you should ignore all that Coronavirus-inspired productivity pressure. *The Chronicle of Higher Education*. https://www.chronicle.com/article/Why-You-Should-Ignore-All-That/248366

Anderson-Lopez, K., & Lopez, R. (2014). *Let it go! [Recorded by I. Menzel]: On frozen* [DVD]. Disney (Original release 2013).

Arnold, M. (1897). *Isolation: To marguerite*. https://rpo.library.utoronto.ca/poems/isolation-marguerite

Baden-Powell, R. (1908). *Scouting for boys: A handbook for instruction in good citizenship*. Horace Cox.

Barnett, J. E., Baker, E. K., Elman, N. S., & Schoener, G. R. (2007). In pursuit of wellness: The self-care imperative. *Professional Psychology: Research and Practice*, *38*(6), 603–612.

Barone, T. (2001). *Touching eternity: The enduring outcomes of teaching*. Teachers College Press.

Black, A. L., Crimmins, G. & Jones, J. K. (2017). Reducing the drag: Creating formations through slow scholarship and story. In S. Riddle, M. Harmes, & P. A. Danaher (Eds.), *Producing pleasure within the contemporary university* (pp. 137–155). Sense Publishing.

Boer, R. (2014, February 20). Foucault's care. *Political Ideology*. https://politicaltheology.com/foucaults-care/

Bohall, G., & Bautista, M. J. (2017). Self-care as an obligation. In G. Bohall & M. J. Bautista (Eds.), *The psychologist's guide to professional development* (pp. 47–55). Springer.

Borhani, M. T. (2013). Riding the bus, writing on the bus: A self in transition. *UNESCO Observatory Multi-disciplinary Research in the Arts*, *2*(3).

Bosanquet, A. (2019, October 30). This is self-care. *The Slow Academic*. https://theslowacademic.com/2019/10/30/this-is-self-care/

Budak, Ö. (2017). Searching for authenticity and success: Academic identity and production in neoliberal times. In H. Ergül & S. Coşar (Eds.), *Universities in the neoliberal era: Palgrave critical university studies*. Palgrave Macmillan.

Cameron, J. (2009). *The artist's way*. Jeremy P. Tarcher.

Camus, A. (1948). *The plague*. Hamish Hamilton.

Cloud, H. [@DrHenryCloud]. (2015, February 20). There is a difference between solitude and isolation: One is connected and one isn't. Solitude replenishes, isolation diminishes. *Tweet*. https://twitter.com/drhenrycloud/status/568522763771580416?lang=en

Dalphon, H. (2019). Self-care techniques for social workers: Achieving an ethical harmony between work and well-being. *Journal of Human Behavior in the Social Environment*, *29*(1), 85–95.

Deleuze, G., & Guattari, F. (1987). *A thousand plateaus: Capitalism and schizophrenia*. University of Minnesota Press.

Dugan, A. G., & Barnes-Farrell, J. L. (2020). Working mothers' second shift, personal resources, and self-care. *Community, Work and Family*, *23*(1), 62–79.

Foucault, M. (1984). *The history of sexuality, volume 3: The care of the self*. Vintage.

Gentry, J. E. (2002). Compassion fatigue: A crucible of transformation. *Journal of Trauma Practice*, *1*(3–4), 37–61.

Gibson, R. (2015). *The memory of clothes*. Sense.

Gill, R. (2017). Beyond individualism: The psychosocial life of the neoliberal university. In M. Spooner (Ed.), *A critical guide to higher education and the politics of evidence: Resisting colonialism, neoliberalism, and audit culture*. University of Regina Press. https://openaccess.city.ac.uk/id/eprint/15647/

Harris, A. (2015, April 5). A history of self-care: From its radical roots to its yuppie-driven middle age to its election-inspired resurgence. *Slate*. http://www.slate.com/articles/arts/culturebox/2017/04/the_history_of_self_care.html

Irwin, R. L., & Springgay, S. (2008). A/r/tography as practice-based research. In M. Cahnmann-Taylor & R. Siegesmund (Eds.), *Arts-based research in education: Foundations for practice*. Routledge.

Irwin, R. L., & Springgay, S. (2017). A/r/tography as practice-based research. In M. R. Carter & V. Triggs (Eds.), *Art education and curriculum studies*. Routledge.

Kinman, G. (2014). Doing more with less? Work and wellbeing in academics. *Somatechnics*, *4*(2), 219–235.

Kitchener, C. (2020, April 24). Women academics seem to be submitting fewer papers during coronavirus. *The Lily*. https://www.thelily.com/women-academics-seem-to-be-submitting-fewer-papers-during-coronavirus-never-seen-anything-like-it-says-one-editor/

Koziol, M. (2020, May 24). Normalising working from home will kill off society. *Sun-Herald*. https://www.smh.com.au/national/normalising-working-from-home-will-be-the-death-of-society-20200520-p54uyc.html

Liyuan, P. (2014). *Peng Liyuan named UNESCO special envoy for the advancement of girls' and women's education*. https://en.unesco.org/news/peng-liyuan-named-unesco-special-envoy-advancement-girls'-and-women's-education

Lorde, A. (1988). *A burst of light*. Firebrand Books.

Lynch, K. (2010). Carelessness: A hidden doxa of higher education. *Arts and Humanities in Higher Education, 9*(1), 54–67.

McCartney, P. (1970). *Let it be [recorded by the Beatles], on let it be*. Apple.

Moate, R. M., Gnilka, P. B., West, E. M., & Bruns, K. L. (2016). Stress and burnout among counselor educators: Differences between adaptive perfectionists, maladaptive perfectionists, and nonperfectionists. *Journal of Counseling and Development, 94*(2), 161–171.

Mountz, A., Bonds, A., Mansfield, B., Lloyd, J., Hyndman, J., & Walton-Roberts, M. (2015). For slow scholarship: A feminist politics of resistance through collective action in the neoliberal university. *ACME: An International Journal for Critical Geographies, 14*(4), 1236–1259.

O'Dwyer, S. T., Pinto, S., and McDonough, S. (2018). Self-care for academics: A poetic invitation to reflect and resist. *Reflective Practice, 19*(2), 243–249.

Pereira, M. (2016). Struggling within and beyond the performative university: Articulating activism and work in an 'academic without walls. *Women's Studies International Forum, 54*, 100–110.

Posluns, K., & Gall, T. L. (2020). Dear mental health practitioners, take care of yourselves: A literature review on self-care. *International Journal for the Advancement of Counselling, 42*, 1–20.

Potter, A. (2010). *The wo lives of miss Charlotte Merryweather*. Plume Books.

Rogers, D. (2012). Research, practice, and the space between: Care of self within neoliberalised institutions. *Cultural Studies – Critical Methodologies, 12*(3), 242–254.

Schumann, K., & Ross, M. (2010). Why women apologize more than men: Gender differences in thresholds for perceiving offensive behavior. *Psychological Science, 21*(11), 1649–1655.

Siegesmund, R. (2012). Dewey through a/r/tography. *Visual Arts Research, 38*(2), 99–109.

Springgay, S., Irwin, R. L., and Wilson Kind, S. (2005). A/r/tography as living inquiry through art and text. *Qualitative Inquiry, 11*(6), 897–912.

Stoker, B. (1897). *Dracula*. Archibald Constable and Co.

Sturluson, S. (1995). Gylfaginning. In *Prose Edda*. J. M. Dent.

University of Sydney (USyd). (2020, April 7). *Support for students: No-disadvantage assessment*. Media Statement. https://www.sydney.edu.au/news-opinion/news/2020/01/28/coronavirus-infection-university-of-sydney-statement.html

Wilcox, G., & Schroeder, M. (2017). An academic's ethical obligation for self-care. *The Journal of Educational Thought, 50*(2–3), 80–97.

Winefield, H. R., Boyd, C., & Winefield, A. H. (2014). Work-family conflict and well-being in university employees. *Journal of Psychology – Interdisciplinary and Applied, 148*(6), 683–697.

Section 4

Mind, body, and movement as acts of self-care

11 Kia kōrero te tinana katoa (The whole body must speak)

Māori early-career academics and performing one's cultural self for hauora

Jani Katarina Taituha Wilson

Introduction

Image 11.1 The art of kapa haka

> *Whakataetae, or competitive kapa haka takes much commitment from the performer and their whānau[1]; it takes physical training and mental discipline, very much like a sport. It consists of a waiata tira (choral)[2], whakaeke (entrance), mōteatea (lament)[3], waiata-a-ringa (action song), poi (performed with soft balls on the end of a long cord), haka taparahi or maurākau (haka performed with/without weaponry), and a whakawātea (exit). Every item requires distinctive stances, gestures, and emotions.*
>
> *There is a long preparatory phase including a research and composition process by a core group (ohu), recruitment of kaihaka, of which only forty can make the stage, weekly live-ins (noho), physical and mental exhaustion from drilling moves, standing all day, words, and choreography, the need to somehow accrue more stamina, supportive/understanding but sometimes resentful*

DOI: 10.4324/9781003207863-15

family members who never see you, intra-group politics especially over the selection of the lines, and fundraising. This names only a few activities throughout the lead-up to a competition.

Competitive Kapa haka is not the Royal New Zealand Ballet; you do not get paid while you train or for the impending performance; you and whānau invest time, creativity, energy, and money.

During 'kapas' seasons, you leave work early on a Friday; pick up your child from school, and drive for hours and hours to get to training on time. You drive back on Sunday evening, physically depleted, but thinking through ways to improve your singing, your choreography, facial gestures, and checking your words are memorised accurately. You grab moments in your office to practice your poi at work. You pick up a jandal as if it were a patu (wooden club) and flick it around as though performing the haka for the whakaeke. This phase is <u>no less</u> than three months before a competition, and in some cases can be anywhere between six and nine months depending on the contest you're working towards.

Competition day is fierce. We've been on stage second before. A brutal 4 am wake-up call, which is difficult when the young ones've been up watching kapa haka on their smartphones most of the night with no earphones. No breakfast; just shower, straight into hair, makeup, tā moko (tattooing), dressing, photos, more fussing with the hair, karakia (incantations), physical and vocal warm-ups, more makeup and a gazillion photos (this time with the whole hapū! (subtribe)), and travel to the venue. Regardless of when in the programme your kapa are scheduled to perform, it takes no less than four hours to get ready, then get to the competition venue at least an hour early; there you're herded between practice/warm-up/holding tents and skirting around the stage you wish you could see but can't. It's hidden by partitions so the public can't see you in your performance garb. It's like a pageant; your outfits and who's-who in your kapa is a secret until you walk out! From the stage comes the sound design for the day; beautiful singing, fierce haka, syncopated foot stamping, stunning words sung by your competitors; you are their fans, and they might be yours.

When you finally file onto stage, you can hear your whānau chanting your name; your people shouting 'Kia kaha, Ngāi Taiwhakāea!'

It lifts you.

You never want this next half hour to end. Three months training, the endless gas money, the car packed with a hundred blankets; sleeping on the floor of your marae under the photos of your ancestors with eighty other people, the fees, the inattention to your child; all for these few moments.

For twenty-eight minutes, your ancestors borrow your skin; you're just there for the ride as they use your body and voice to enact themselves, singing and doing haka about their feats, travels, hopes, and mistakes. You hold the last action and pūkana (eye dilation) hard. The crowd roars.

Damn. It's over.

You and your kapa head back to the marae on the bus, elated. Your hapū have cooked a huge spread. You all laugh and eat. You mihi (speak, sing acknowledgements) to your whānau for putting up with you, and you all cry. You may not have won the competition, but indeed, you have won.

That night, you watch your performance projected onto the wall of the wharekai (dining hall), and there are 'woohoos' and 'oh, nos!'; you read through the judges' comments in the reports about your performance together. You agree with some.

Tomorrow, you start all over again.

Hau – wind, breeze, breath, vitality
+ <u>Ora</u> – <u>health, living, fit, to be well</u>
Hauora – <u>healthy, wellness, wellbeing</u>

The art of kapa haka is reminiscent of Tānerore – son of Tama-nui-te-rā and Hine-raumati[4] – known for his special dancing; he aimed to shimmer like his parents, particularly his mother, to whom the wiri (trembling of the hands) is a tribute.[5] There is some research linking the holistic cultural, sensorial, disciplinary, and educative benefits of kapa haka to hauora (Whitinui, 2004, 2008, 2010; Rollo, 2007; Paenga, 2008; Rangihaeata, 2011; Biddle, 2012; Pihama et al., 2014; Hollands et al., 2015; Kerehoma, 2017; Kewene, 2017; Kāretu, 1993, 2020; McLachlan et al., 2021). Most of the growing catalogue of this research speaks metaphorically to kapa haka as a tūrangawaewae, a place to stand, even when separated from one's actual home because of the performer's sense of identity and connection to ancestors through it.

Elsdon Best (1974), an early ethnographer and observer of haka, described it as "a series of rhythmical movements of limbs and body, accompanied by a song [. . .] [or] a series of short refrains . . . by both sexes . . . about a multitude of subjects" (p. 134). It is said that when the Polynesian seafarers travelled the Pacific, largely between 1500 BC and 400 AD, percussive instruments were situated at each island *except* for Aotearoa[6] (Anderson, 1933). Consequent to having no drums, the body became the percussive instrument; striking of the chest, thighs, hands, arms, and tramping and stamping in time became compensation for there not being a rhythmic instrument per se. These, and various other gestures, were adjoined to deep sighs, guttural growls, gasps, eye protrusion, glares, pivots, and quivering facial distortions to whakamana (give honour to) a person or an event, past or present.

From a performer's perspective, haka is a moment to restore, reclaim and, celebrate one's cultural identity; a "physical representation of . . . whakapapa [genealogy] . . . that should not be taken lightly" (Timu, 2018, p. 112). Haka connects ritual and entertainment while raising the performing group's mana, or at times even worse, conjuring silence (Mead, 1984; Haami & Wehi, 2013). To *not* physically move onlookers with ihi, wehi, and wana (thrill, fear, and zeal, respectively) – evidence of which is the 'spine tingling', the goosebumps, and the 'body trembling with excitement' (Mead, 1984, p. 24) – is but wasted haka energy.

Haka warms the muscles and stiffens the sinews (Kāretu, 1993); it consolidates performers to the task at hand; it identifies to audiences unique Māori qualities and connections. To performers, as the introductory passage indicated, it is the coming together of months of preparation, investment, and sacrifice. Kapa haka is essentially a time where we make room in our skin for the wairua (spirit) of our mātua tīpuna (ancestors) to perform through our bodies. We are but frames enacting our ancestors, simply conduits through which they pass from the spiritual world and once again into the physical world. Much is made globally of haka, and since the late nineteenth century, haka has been a feast for sport fans, but even in the sport space, haka has been highly political and contested (Jackson & Hokowhitu, 2002; Hokowhitu, 2005; Hapeta et al., 2018). Many people consider haka an allay to sports culture, and rugby in particular.[7] However for Māori, it is simply a way of life; it is our popular culture and celebrates and invigorates our identity.

Kapa haka is performed on a stage that does not discriminate; it can be performed by all shapes, shades, sizes, and sexual orientations. It's a space where the bigger the lady's hips are, the greater the swish of the piupiu (flax garment, known for its 'swishing' sound)! And the haka still has mana (authority, status) even if the shirtless body that presents it jiggles. There are a growing number of [kaihaka] born male who can and do perform as female, and vice versa. Gender fluidity has *always* been a part of haka as tāne are often encouraged to convey emotions which conventional masculinity might consider 'effeminate'. Meanwhile, wāhine may at times demonstrate what might easily be perceived as masculine. Kaihaka are comfortable with the need to morph according to the character. Regardless, kapa haka is a significant part of demonstrating who we were, who we are, and who we want to be through our performance and, as I'll show, important to our hauora.

Mason Durie's (1984) "Te Whare Tapa Wha"[8] is embedded into New Zealand's health policies – at its very simplest – to ensure that Māori are approached in a way that acknowledges the four sides to a person's makeup, towards spiritual, mental, physical, and familial health. It is endorsed in health and law that if we "get it right for Māori, we get it right for everyone" (Toki, 2010; Parry, 2018). In large part, this most well-used mātauranga Māori[9] framework was developed in response to poor reports on Māori wellbeing in the New Zealand health system. Hauora is essentially when all four 'walls' of someone's makeup are well-structured and balanced like the construction of a house, and evidence of stability is optimal health and development. Ignoring any of the important pillars may completely throw the individual out of kilter. But what happens when *all* sides are under threat, when kapa haka – which in many respects could be said to portray all four of the supports – recedes from view? When I started out as a Māori early-career academic (MECA), balance was simply a nice idea.

The Indispensability of the Māori Early-Career Academic

The opening stanza of this chapter illustrates only an iota of what a kapa haka 'campaign' entails. I dedicated a good proportion of my adult life to competitive kapa haka in hopes that my daughter, Manaaki, would see it as a normal part of our life. At the time of writing, she is seventeen and has superseded me; a stunning, commanding performer and leader. The narrative supplied – including the neglect of my child, who, when we lived in Auckland, was packed into the car on Fridays and left to play with her cousins on the marae all weekend – was real. The black-and white-photo provided is of myself, performing *E Ihowa*, the waiata tira written by my nephew, Tūkirunga Perenara, in 2015. In the photo, I was performing with Te Rōpū Kapa Haka o Ngāi Taiwhakāea at the Mātaatua[10] regionals competition held in Rūātoki that year. Like every other campaign, it was a tumultuous operation, also hinted at in the overture passage. However, we were living in Whakatāne in 2015, so at least the travel was not an issue for the depicted season, whereas other seasons, the tyres of my poor 1984 Toyota Corolla tattooed State Highway 2.

I didn't know it at the time the supplied photo was taken, but it was evidence of my last competitive kapa haka performance. Although our kapa attempted a stand at the regionals in 2017, many of our kaihaka chose to join 'higher-profile' teams, which unfortunately left our numbers flailing and forced us to concede that for a time we would concentrate on being an ahurei kapa (festival).

I completed my doctorate in film, television, and media studies in 2012 and found it incredibly difficult to find a job; too qualified for many roles and underexperienced for everything else. I would have been happy sweeping footpaths if it meant we could live in Whakatāne near my family, as Manaaki adored attending our tribal school, Te Kura o Te Pāroa, known for its arts programme and champions in kapa haka. But although I'd completed the doctorate, I was forced to continue to raise her on 'the benefit' as I had during my post-graduate studies; I topped up with editing, proofreading, transcribing, and translating jobs through my friends in the academy and applied for jobs for what seemed to be without ceasing.

I got my first break into academia as a research fellow in public health. In short, it was an eighteen-month-long, undisclosed disaster, and although not ideal, I found myself desperately applying for alternatives in the first months. Amongst the fray, I was working in Auckland but still living at home in Whakatāne, doing kapa haka at the weekends, and composing for the rōpū. We won our inaugural ahurei and later headed to the regionals in Rūātoki. It pelted down with rain that day, perhaps the tears of our ancestors for my last competition.

Only a few months later, I accepted a two-year post-doctoral fellowship, not completely in my area of expertise but closer to it than public health. I had every intention of continuing competitive kapa haka. During the second year, though, I was asked by an influential character to lecture full-time in my area of expertise as well as complete the obligations of my post-doc, with no contractual changes; essentially doing two jobs for the price of one. It wasn't ideal, but as a Māori single mum, desperate to pay off a huge student loan and keep a roof over my daughter's head and food in her stomach, I decided to chase the dangled carrot, in the shape of teaching something I was good at for a year, for free, to avoid having to re-enter the vortex of job seeking again in a year's time. Risking my daughter's wellbeing was not an option. I completed the post-doc and the 'initiation' year of unpaid lecturing, then was relieved to be offered a tenured position.

Indispensability

Making oneself indispensable is an unsaid part of the MECA job, as first impressions and keenness are most important. Here, I chose Manaaki's stability and wellbeing over mine. You must be better than your Pākehā counterparts; a more dynamic teacher, more polished presenter, serve the university more, and way cooler in the eyes of the students. Talk spreads along the kūmara-vine[11] quickly about one's effectiveness (or the opposite), and it's highly likely someone along that vine will know one of your relations, so you must keep dealings above reproach in case it gets back to your parents! You identify the course content isn't up to scratch, so you engage with graduates you didn't teach, then redesign the whole programme based on what they said. You do this without acknowledgement or pay, and it isn't recognised in terms of promotion because it isn't written into your job description. Yet if you don't do it, your student's development and industry readiness will flail. Consequently, the preparation for in-class teaching is hours and hours, and you stay after class to show you are an effective, attentive, manaaki/tiaki (caring, hosting) teacher, and you learn *every* student's name. Marking doesn't appear to be a problem; you write full and robust responses some students call 'shit sandwiches' so that each essay has a plethora of learnings attached to it, even if it's an "A" and you draw emojis in the borders. The quality of your teaching will be assessed at the end of the semester, and you are constantly nervous about that one potential student who doesn't like you or the content. Supervising Indigenous post-graduate students is a most important space with its own special kūmara-vine that speaks to your professional integrity or lack thereof and your personal values. If you receive a call from the marae manager during class time that the kaikaranga didn't show up that morning and you're needed at the marae to karanga (traditional call), you go to serve the marae and ensure tikanga (correct procedures) are upheld. You talk to your parents to make sure this is OK, because on your own marae, you aren't permitted to karanga because your mother and older sisters are still alive.[12] You do not get paid for this, and again it isn't acknowledged by the university as 'service' towards promotion; but this is virtue to show Māori students, their parents, and grandparents who bring them onto this campus, 'we are here, you are safe'. Every spare moment is spent researching, preparing for conferences you don't really have time to attend; you must submit publications so that your manager can vouch for your effectiveness as a potentially world-renowned researcher in your area of expertise. Even though the Pākehā in your faculty don't have this responsibility, you are at the university marae doing dishes, peeling potatoes, reading drafts, giving feedforward, encouraging, supporting, hugging, and eventually your weekends are leading Indigenous post-graduate students to be world changers, all for aroha.

A major sacrifice amidst my early days as a MECA was my beloved kapa haka. Now time-poor for anything that wasn't in my institution, a teenage child at high school playing elite netball and leading her school kapa, which desperately needed help, backed up with layers of work stress and responsibilities, and growing poor health, I had to resort to watching my own kapa from the audience, singing waiata I'd composed. Viewing your kapa is difficult for a kaihaka. You want to participate beside them, not clap for them; but you clap until your hands hurt while holding back tears. You miss your ancestors using your body to enter the physical world again. The audience isn't where you want to be. Is a kaihaka an *actual* kaihaka without haka in their life? The first years of my tenure, although my academic career was indeed moving along, I felt lost, and it was obvious in my home life how it was affecting my wairua and that of my daughter, who now had a MECA mum who was once a kaihaka. I needed to figure out how I might get a kapa haka fix and hopefully head back to hauora. MAI ki Aronui, a network of disciplinary misfits (like me) became part of my therapy.

MAI ki Aronui

MAI is an acronym for Māori and Indigenous, and belongs to a doctoral network called MAI te Kupenga, supported by Ngā Pae o te Māramatanga, New Zealand's Māori Centre of Research Excellence (Ngā Pae, thereafter). Universities and some Whare Wānanga[13] have sites supported by Ngā Pae to ensure that Māori and Indigenous researchers reach the necessary research capacity for the betterment of our communities. This is the dream of Linda Tuhiwai Smith and Michael Walker. All MAI sites were designed to support Indigenous doctoral students, the majority of whom are not native to the cities where their institutions are based, to get through the incredibly isolating experience together as an iwi (tribe), enjoying each other as Indigenous people, whilst encouraging the highest quality of research. As a University of Auckland graduate who came through MAI ki Tāmaki[14], I was challenged with the leadership of the group formerly called MAI ki AUT, which had fallen on hard times and was not functioning. It required immediate change, and within that, I designed an unapologetically Kaupapa-Māori strategy based on some easily definable but not so readily practicable cultural values.[15] Thus, a complete re-launch was required.

Among a plethora of other important elements to the (re-)launch of MAI ki AUT was a name change; part of this was to mark a paradigmatic cultural shift away from the past construction toward the new. Arriving at the new name to navigate the way forward was relatively simple. Te Wānanga Aronui o Tāmaki Makaurau is the reo Māori (Māori language or voice) name of the Auckland University of Technology (AUT), so named after one of the three baskets of knowledge that, according to mātauranga Māori, Tāne[16] brought to the world from the 'heavens'.[17] Importantly, Aronui is the basket said to contain everything to do with the senses (Morrison, 1999; Fraser, 2009) and the arts, but most significantly, holds the humanities, intelligence, incantations, literature, philosophy, and ritual (Kāretu, 2008, pp. 86–88). Ultimately, it is the basket of innovation, the broader defining element of the university. It made sense then, because of the connections to Aronui, to rename MAI at AUT, MAI ki Aronui.

Months prior to the launch, I composed an anthem entitled *Kei konei Aronui*, literally 'Here is Aronui'. Writing this waiata-a-ringa helped me in the conceptual design of MAI ki Aronui whence it came. Knowing it was highly unlikely potential members were kaihaka and many were non-Māori also helped navigate the potential way forward. In terms of the waiata, I choreographed some very basic actions to ensure *all* – regardless of their schooling – were able to participate.

Kei konei Aronui
Kei konei Aronui   Aronui is here
Kei konei mātou   We are here
Tukua atu te aroha e   Passing out our love
Anei ngā tauira   Here are the students

(*Continued*)

(Continued)

Ki te tohu kairangi	Doing the doctorate
Karanga atu e ngā iwi e	Calling out to all tribes
(Aronui) Ngā Wai o Horotiu	The Horotiu waters
(Aronui) Te Pūrengi te whare	Te Pūrengi the house
Te Kaipara te whare manaaki	Te Kaipara is the hosting house
Mai i te Rangitūhāhā	From the heavens
Mai i te kete a Tānemahuta	From Tāne, the god of living things
MAI ki Aronui mātou e	We are MAI ki Aronui
Kei konei Aronui	Aronui is here.

Anthems and particularly waiata-a-ringa are unificatory in nature, as the voices, words, actions, tramping in time, facial gestures, rationale, and sentiment are the same. As a new network then, waiata was fitting. For many, it is uncomfortable to sing and motion in such a way, particularly when it is *not* your culture; indeed, so is the academic environment, which has a culture of its own. Discomfiture must be managed and, I would suggest, reframed. Equally so was the importance of a logo to visually encapsulate and solidify the defining principles of the network. I approached Zak Waipara, an illustrator, and advantageously one of my doctoral students, to design something that encapsulated us as Kaupapa Māori-centric (Māori 'ways') but demonstrates that we are all different people, from different lands, languages, cultures, with various values, all of which are significant to the group and woven together. Ultimately, although not formed yet, MAI ki Aronui became an opportunity to reconnect with my treasured kapa haka, although not to the scale or intensity I was accustomed. At that point, I would have taken kapa haka in any way, in any form, and at any time. It was like a close friend I hadn't seen for decades; I missed it terribly. We opened MAI ki Aronui officially according to our cultural rituals, at Ngā Wai o Horotiu Marae, during which I presented *Kei konei Aronui* to conclude our initial meeting.

Some months into the early tenure of MAI ki Aronui, we began singing *Kei konei Aronui*, utilising it as a waiata tautoko (support song) to follow presentations and workshops as a sign of respect. Eventually, MAI ki Aronui began practicing the actions for jouissance. It was exciting to see the group – Māori and Indigenous doctoral students – take up the challenge of performing *Kei konei Aronui*. But I soon realised it was more than learning to simply perform it; I saw shy, uncomfortable Māori and Indigenous doctoral students' backs straighten; I saw the sense of accomplishment on their faces when they knew the waiata word-for-word; I saw them practicing the actions around the wharekai. They'd ask to run it over and over and over. I saw Māori, Tongan, Samoan, Yemeni, Mexicana, Colombiana, Mangarevan, Mauritian, and other Indigenous people performing *Kei konei Aronui*, and when performing it, they were a "we" in the university context, some for the first time. Regardless of ethnicity, nationality, or discipline, *Kei konei Aronui* is *our* waiata. I saw the group transform by putting them into an uncomfortable situation but working at it. Academia is uncomfortable. Working at it, practicing, and consistently and humbly developing ourselves is how we improve at both. We had our waiata. I was once again a kaihaka doing kapa haka, perhaps at a completely different, uncompetitive level, but doing it returned me to joy and hauora.

MAI ki Aronui ki Karitāne

In 2019, a relatively large group of our members submitted their doctorates, and we discussed perhaps composing a MAI ki Aronui haka to be performed to whakamana them at the soon-approaching annual MAI te Kupenga doctoral conference in Karitāne (Otago). Every year the accomplishments of MAI whānau are celebrated by Ngā Pae at a national level. At this stage, MAI ki Aronui had a growing repertoire of waiata, but were MAI ki Aronui ready for their whole bodies to speak the way Teowai said (Kāretu, 1993)? Could they comprehend the ceremony and tradition associated with haka, and could they invoke the meaning that respected the central message conveyed by the composer? Was it possible for students who were not Māori to bring the ihi, wehi, and wana to the haka? I'd never written a haka before; who might write it? There would potentially be nothing like doing the haka in these students' lives, and even more special that they could be etched into the words. Thus, I found myself putting down the need for competition to return to the fundamentals of haka: the unification and strengthening of a team of people. Aiming MAI ki Aronui towards performing their own haka was our next adventure.

I conveyed the idea to MAI ki Aronui, all of whom jumped at the chance to be able to have *our* haka, to communicate the doctoral journey. Of her own volition, Atakohu Middleton, at that time a doctoral student focusing on reo Māori journalism, challenged herself to write the lyrics, based on her looming submission.

Anei Mātou

Leader:	MAI ki Aronui e nguguru nei	MAI ki Aronui, growl
All:	I au, au, auē hā!	Breathe
Leader:	MAI ki Aronui e nguguru nei.	MAI ki Aronui, growl
All:	I au, au, auē hā!	Breathe
Leader:	Anei mātou!	Here we are!
All:	Anei mātou MAI ki Aronui,	Here we are MAI ki Aronui
	E tau nei, e tau nei	We've arrived
He tāwharau mo ngāi pīkoko,		A shelter for us who hunger,
Whai mātauranga e,		to chase knowledge,
Whāia te pae tawhiti e.		Chasing the distant horizons.
Manawa tītī, ngakau mahaki,		With stamina and humble hearts
MAI ki Aronui e tau nei!		MAI ki Aronui have arrived!
HĀ!!!		*Exhale!!!*

Metaphorically, the body of the *Anei Mātou* haka speaks to the significant characteristics that are needed to complete the doctorate. It refers to manawa tītī, which are mutton birds; they are small, but can fly with incredible strength and endurance to exponentially far distances. But a most important facet of *Anei Mātou* is that MAI ki Aronui is referred to as a shelter for learners who chase knowledge. Importantly, Middleton (2019) found her 'tribe' at MAI ki Aronui.[18] Once I'd choreographed some *very* simple actions, we practiced during our monthly hui (meetings), and the group picked up on it easily. There was, however, some reluctance within the group, particularly by non-Māori. But I assured them that the intention and purpose of the haka is far more powerful than a perfect performance and asked them to channel and welcome our ancestors to use our bodies by giving them room in our skin. The most significant lesson in learning *Anei Mātou* was communicating the emotion. The advice I proffered was simple:

> Focus on the person/people you are honouring;
> Do not look at the crowd;
> Bring all of your frustration, anger, love, passion, and hurt from your own doctoral journey;
> Dredge up the moments you missed out on special occasions to sit at your desk, to scour the databases, and to write;
> Remember all of the struggles;
> The lost hours of sleep; and
> Think of all of the time you spent away from your family to work on it.
>
> *These people are through their doctorates, and you want to be. You're honouring the person for getting to the end.*

The MAI te Kupenga conference date impended quickly, and MAI ki Aronui asked for more practices to drill *Kei konei Aronui* and *Anei Mātou* in the lead up, very much like before a kapa haka competition. After the MAI ki Aronui panel, all eighteen of us (including a baby) performed *Kei konei Aronui*. We were the only site who had our own waiata! The night where our six submitters were acknowledged – including Atakohu, who had completed her thesis early – Toiroa called out, "MAI ki Aronui, e tū", and there began *Anei Mātou,* our haka, performed by our motley Māori and Indigenous crew. It was a momentous occasion for MAI ki Aronui, especially as composer Atakohu – who was seated with the other submitters – stood to perform the haka back to us.
    It lifted us.
    For about eighty seconds, our ancestors borrowed our bodies . . . we hold the last action and pūkana hard. The crowd roared.
    Damn. It's over . . . We had not won a competition, but indeed, we had won.
    Everyone in MAI ki Aronui was exhausted and out of breath, brows were shiny, necks flushed red, the evidence our heart rates were lifted. I looked around at our whānau, who beamed with pride that we accomplished something very special together, to whakamana those who had completed their doctorates with our own haka, and to spur themselves forward to achieve their completion, too.

To sum, and reflecting now as a mid-career academic, the intensity, unrelenting, and tumultuousness of my early academic career was indeed like the strict regime of training – constant self-critique, strategising for betterment, reaching for unobtainable standards, and anxiety – prior to a big kapa haka competition. However, this campaign is much, much longer. Haka requires *and urges* our spiritual, mental, physical, and familial health, and in many ways, academia counters these important touchstones. Working our way to perform *Anei Mātou* in Karitāne was a significant time, because by focusing on getting MAI ki Aronui to the performance, I was forced to address the damaged pillars of my own depleted hauora and, in doing so, was once again a kaihaka. Mine is not an isolated case; there are many other Māori and Indigenous academics who are (mis)managed in such a way that our hauora is at severe risk. We must address this, and fight for our hauora. Perhaps with this chapter, I'm filing onto the stage to the voices of my hapū, *kia kaha Ngāi Taiwhakāea!*

> *You reflect on your performance projected onto the pages of your ever-expanding academic CV; there are many 'woohoos' and a plethora of 'oh, nos!'; you read through reviewer comments about your work . . . You agree with some.*
>
> *Tomorrow, you start all over again.*

Notes

1 The most simple and widely accepted definition of whānau is family, but it is indeed a foundational building block of Māori social organisations (L. T. Smith, 1996) and therefore goes far beyond this. However, due to space limitations, I cannot venture far into this fundamental concept.
2 Waiata tira isn't an aggregate item, but as a choral piece, it essentially sets the tone for the group.
3 Mōteatea is one of a few that can be performed in this slot. Kapa can also perform waiata aroha (traditional yearning songs), pātere (chants), waiata koroua (traditional chants), or waiata tawhito (ancient waiata). But there are generally a lot of words in these items, which is a very different kind of discipline than perhaps a bouncy waiata-a-ringa (action song).
4 Tama-nui-te-rā (male of the sun) is the son god, and Hine-raumati (summer woman) is the goddess of summer.
5 Heat at a distance can be seen as a kind of shimmering, which is reminiscent of Hine-raumati. For this reason, it is said Tāne-rore performed his dances with trembling hands to honour his mother.
6 This is evidence of 'gong-like' percussive instruments called *pahu*, and it is noted that these were not used to mark rhythmic timing but as a 'signal' or siren in war times (Anderson, 1933, p. 197).
7 There is a definitive frenzy when New Zealand's national rugby team performs haka as a challenge to their opposition prior to a game. Buck Shelford's All Blacks of the 1980s resuscitated the haka from 'cringe-town'. Prior to this, for a good proportion of the time, the All Blacks could not play their Māori and Pasifika players because of their skin colour. Forced by political means *not* to play for New Zealand, The New Zealand Native rugby side emerged in the late 1880s, said to be a solution of removing tensions between colonised people and their colonisers, unscrambling the "problem of social amalgamation" through the love of the national game (The Times as cited in Fitzgerald, n.d.).

The 'Natives' performed a pre-game haka, stirring interest, and to distinguish their team from the national team, who wore the same-coloured strip as them.
8 The loose translation for 'Te Whare Tapa Whā' is The Four-Sided House. At its simplest, Durie likens a person's makeup to that of a house: it cannot be held up without the four sides; each side is as significant as the other.
9 The most basic of definitions for mātauranga Māori is traditional Māori knowledge.
10 Te Rōpū Kapa Haka o Ngāi Taiwhakāea is the competitive team based at Te Pāroa Marae, which is our papakāinga (ancestral home) on my grandfather's side. I grew up in Te Patutātahi, not far from there.
11 Kūmara are sweet potatoes. Much like potatoes, they are cultivated in vines that sprout easily and quickly. The said 'kūmara-vine', much like 'Māori Google', is quite simply communication and dissemination of information between Māori.
12 Where I'm from, women can only practice karanga if their mother and older sisters have passed away. However, my kaumātua assured me that because I work in an educational institution, I may use the opportunity to practice and experiment with the art on campus without upsetting tikanga.
13 Whare wānanga are most simply the mātauranga Māori/tribally lead tertiary institutions. In ancient times, the whare nui – the central houses on the marae complex – were considered whare wānanga because issues were discussed with such intensity.
14 The reo Māori name for the University of Auckland is Te Whare Wānanga o Tāmaki Makaurau, which acknowledges an important Ngāti Whātua ancestor.
15 At the time I proposed this chapter, the intitution I worked in underlined Pā Hēnare Tate's values, 'tika', 'pono', and 'aroha' (correct, truth, and love) as the university-wide values. As Pā Tate was a 'man of the cloth', these were adopted directly from 1 Corinthians 13:13, where Paul the Apostle said "these things remain: faith, hope and love".
16 Some tribes say Tāwhaki retrieved the basket.
17 Some tribal stories say it's the tenth heaven, referred to as rangi tūhāhā, literally the spaced heavens.
18 See Middleton's (2019) blog, *The Value of finding your PhD tribe*. https://thesislink.aut.ac.nz/?p=7706.

References

Anderson, J. C. (1933). Memoirs: Māori music with its Polynesian background. *Journal of the Polynesian Society*, *42*(10), 195–252.
Best, E. (1974). *The Māori as he was: A brief account of Māori life as it was in pre-European days* (Rev. ed.). Government Printer.
Biddle, T. (2012). The mediation of tikanga in haka competition. *Te Kaharoa*, *5*(1).
Durie, M. H. (1984). Te Taha Hinengaro: An integrated approach to mental health. *Community Mental Health in New Zealand*, *1*(1), 4–11.
Fitzgerald, M. (n.d.) *Before the all Blacks: The New Zealand natives*. Museum of New Zealand. https://www.tepapa.govt.nz/discover-collections/read-watch-play/history/all-blacks-new-zealand-natives
Fraser, T. N. (2009). *Māori-Tūhoe epistemology: Stages of sustaining tribal identity through Tūhoe performing arts* [Unpublished Doctoral dissertation, Education. University of British Columbia].
Haami, B., & Wehi, N. (2013). *Ka mau te wehi: Taking haka to the world: Bub & Nen's story*. Ngāpō and Pīmia Wehi Whānau Trust.
Hapeta, J., Palmer, F., & Kuroda, Y. (2018). Ka mate: A commodity to trade or taonga to treasure? *MAI Journal*, *7*(2), 170–185.

Hokowhitu, B. (2005). Rugby and Tino rangatiratanga: Early Maori rugby and the formation of "traditional" Maori masculinity. *Sporting Traditions, 21*(2), 75–95.

Hollands, T., Sutton, D., Wright-St. Clair, V., & Hall, R. (2015). Maori mental health consumers' sensory experience of Kapa Haka and its utility to occupational therapy practice. *New Zealand Journal of Occupational Therapy, 62*(1), 3–11.

Jackson, S. J., & Hokowhitu, B. (2002). Sport, tribes, and technology: The New Zealand all blacks haka and the politics of identity. *Journal of Sport and Social Issues, 26*(2), 125–139.

Kāretu, T. (1993). *Haka: The dance of the noble people.* Reed Publishing (NZ) Ltd.

Kāretu, T. (2008). Te Kete Tuawhā, Te Kete Aronui – the fourth basket. *Te Kaharoa, 1*(1), 86–99.

Kāretu, T. (2020). *Matamua ko te Kupu! Te haka tena! Te wana, taku ihi e, pupuritia!* Auckland University Press.

Kerehoma, L. (2017). *He hua rānei tō te kapa haka: kapa haka as a retention tool for Māori students in mainstream secondary schools: A thesis presented in partial fulfilment of the requirements for the degree of Master of philosophy (humanities and sciences) at Massey University, Turitea, Palmerston North, New Zealand* [Doctoral dissertation, Massey University].

Kewene, F. W. (2017). *Verbatim and Maori theatre techniques: Documenting people's experiences of Hauora* [Doctoral dissertation, University of Otago].

McLachlan, A., Waitoki, W., Harris, P., & Jones, H. (2021). Whiti Te Rā: A guide to connecting Māori to traditional wellbeing pathways. *Journal of Indigenous Wellbeing, 6*(1), 78–97.

Mead, S. M. (1984). Nga Timunga me Nga Paringa o te Mana Maori: The ebb and flow of Mana Maori and the changing context of Maori art. *Te Maori: Maori Art from New Zealand Collections,* 20–36.

Middleton. (2019). *The value of finding your PhD tribe.* https://thesislink.aut.ac.nz/?p=7706

Morrison, A. (1999). *Space for Māori in tertiary institutions: Exploring two sites at the University of Auckland* [Unpublished Masters in Education, University of Auckland].

Parry, S. (2018). *Guidance for best practice management in the National bowel screening programme.* Ministry of Health.

Paenga, M. D. T. A. (2008). *Te Māoritanga: Wellbeing and identity. Kapa haka as a vehicle for Māori health promotion* [Doctoral dissertation, Auckland University of Technology].

Pihama, L., Tipene, J., & Skipper, H. (2014). *Ngā Hua a Tāne Rore: The benefits of Kapa Haka (scoping report).* Manatū Taonga – Ministry of Culture and Heritage. https://researchcommons.waikato.ac.nz/bitstream/handle/10289/12603/Nga%20Hua%20A%20Tane%20Rore%20%20The%20benefits%20of%20kapa%20haka%20(D-0570327).PDF?sequence=2

Rangihaeata, P. K. (2011). *Ka ora ngā kōrero hītori o Ngāti Konohi mā roto mai i ngā mahi whakaako waiata i te kapa haka o Whāngārā-mai-tawhiti* [Unpublished MA thesis, (Arts) Victoria University at Wellington].

Rollo, T. M. (2007). *Kapa haka whakataetae: kua tīni haere te kanohi o te mahi kapa haka i te ao hurihuri nei: kapa haka whakataetae, 1972–2006* [Unpublished master's thesis, University of Waikato].

Smith, L. T. (1996). *Kaupapa māori health research.* Te Rōpū Rangahau Hauora a Eru Pomare.

Sweetman, L. E., & Zemke, K. (2019). Claiming Ka Mate: Māori cultural property and the nation's stake. In Gunderson, F., Lancefield, R. C., & Woods, B. (Eds.) *The Oxford handbook of musical repatriation* (pp. 700–722). Oxford handbooks online.

Timu, N. A. (2018). *Ngā tapuwae o te haka – Māori perspectives on haka in sport* [Thesis, Master of Physical Education. University of Otago]. http://hdl.handle.net/10523/8958

Toki, V. (2010). Therapeutic jurisprudence and mental health courts for Maori. *International Journal of Law and Psychiatry, 33*(5–6), 440–447.

Whitinui, P. (2004). The indigenous factor: The role of kapa haka as a culturally responsive learning intervention. *Waikato Journal of Education, 10*.

Whitinui, P. (2008). Kapa Haka counts: Improving participation levels of Māori students in mainstream secondary schools. *Mai Review, 3*(8), 1–14.

Whitinui, P. (2010). Indigenous-based inclusive pedagogy: The art of Kapa Haka to improve educational outcomes for Māori students in mainstream secondary schools in Aotearoa, New Zealand. *International Journal of Pedagogies and Learning, 6*(1), 3–22.

12 Cycling as a form of self-care

Incorporating and sustaining purposeful movement practices to support wellbeing

Nadine Crane

Image 12.1 Bicycle on track

> *I am up before the sun rises. I prepare my bike and organise myself early to capture the first light of the day, either rising over the bay or glinting through the trees, depending on where I have chosen to ride. As I feel and hear the click of my shoes connecting into the pedals and push off down the road, I know the next couple of hours are mine to think, to breathe, to notice and to push myself in ways that break away from my usual pursuits and pressures. I observe my thoughts passing in and out of my mind as my pedals turn over and over. The repetition soothes me and allows my mind to clear as I focus on the now. I enjoy the feeling*

DOI: 10.4324/9781003207863-16

of breathlessness as a result of the physical work. I take the time to be in the moment and appreciate my surroundings. I am grateful for the company of the many animals that pass by and become a part of my experience such as kangaroos, echidnas, birds and deer. I pause to photograph, capturing moments as tangible reminders of something I find beautiful and interesting. My riding album is full of these moments, with photographs signalling and preserving valuable time spent investing in my wellbeing.

My self-care is centred around mind, body and movement through cycling. This is something I discovered whilst looking for ways to strike a balance between work/life and to introduce intentional self-care practices. As a teacher/PhD student/academic, it allows me to disrupt the way in which I previously approached my work and intentionally make space for wellbeing practices. Riding provides me with valuable space to refresh and energise my body and mind. It improves my sense of self and wellbeing. The regular and purposeful acts of cycling enable me to give the energy and focus my academic work demands. Importantly, it allows me to disconnect from my work then reconnect with clarity and passion. In doing so, it provides essential space to undertake my role as a teacher and academic in a sustainable manner.

Within this chapter I aim to provide an overview of how I was introduced to cycling, how I have created regular routines to honour its importance and how it assists me to take a true break to focus on the moment and be in the now. I will also share a summary of the literature highlighting the benefits of cycling and exercise for wellbeing and how outdoor cycling in particular provides me with an opportunity for mindful practices. Additionally, I will share recommendations on how to identify and work with a wellbeing focus involving physical exercise, no matter what your chosen method may be.

From there to here

I am a teacher, PhD candidate and early-career academic. I am also a cyclist. I use this particular form of physical exercise to approach life in a healthy manner, undertake self-care and embrace mindful practices. My discovery of cycling followed an experience with burnout as a classroom teacher, and I have maintained the practice of regular cycling to purposefully provide self-care since then. Throughout my career I have notoriously been a 'busy' person. There isn't a time where I haven't been juggling multiple jobs and roles while pursuing my many interests and passions and undertaking my studies. The lists of positives to this are endless. I have developed expertise, formed important social connections, travelled and experienced much joy in delving into what sparks my soul. I have been challenged, learned new ways of being/thinking/doing, have overcome obstacles and experienced the elation and satisfaction of setting goals and achieving them. Alongside all of this have also been periods of burnout, stress and fatigue. My experience with these feelings led me to physical exercise in the form of cycling, which has become an essential way to ensure I continue to find balance in my work as an academic.

The beginning of balance and self-care routines

As a graduate primary school teacher, I can say I experienced a sense of burnout. This in turn lead me to experience a struggle with my physical health and wellbeing. Such a feeling is not uncommon amongst graduate teachers. Around the time I was entering the profession, Ewing and Smith (2003) discussed how many graduates experience burnout or leave the profession within the first 3 to 5 years. In more recent times, although there has been debate around how well attrition rates are known in Australia (Weldon, 2018), it is still considered to be an issue of concern, with stress being cited as a key factor in those leaving teaching, or predicted to leave within the next 5 years (Rajendran et al., 2020; Thomson, 2020). I can honestly say I had fantastic support from my school as a graduate teacher, and I set about striving to be the best possible teacher I could be. I completely overworked myself and had very little downtime during the week or weekends. Whilst I loved (still love) my job, it had taken its toll due to my own misinterpretation of the best use of my time, equating to work as much as you can, whenever you can. I found myself facing rolling bouts of fatigue and illness as a result, and questioning whether my chosen career, which I loved so much, was beyond me. A trip to the doctor was the trigger to invest in myself and undertake regular physical exercise. This particular doctor took the time to get to know me and noted I did not have a balanced approach to my life. They then proceeded to outline their thoughts on what was needed to improve my overall health and wellbeing, which included the need to partake in physical exercise on a regular basis. Although I had a very active childhood, participating in many sports, once I reached late teenage years this all fell away. At this point in time walking the dog was the only exercise I participated in, and although that was wonderful, it wasn't enough. On the way home from this appointment I decided to address this straight away and stopped by the local gym to join up, and so began my journey with cycling.

Previously I had had no interest in going to a gym. It never crossed my mind, and I had never been inside one. I can confess once I joined, I had no idea what I was doing or even if it was the right thing for me. After my introductory 'welcome' free personal training sessions I decided to give group fitness a go. I had always ridden a bike in some form throughout my life, and as such I naturally gravitated towards the cycling studio. My first experience was a 6:15 a.m. Les Mills RPM cycling class that I attempted before school one morning (good idea?!?). I set my alarm for 5:15 a.m. and sat in the back of the room in the cycle studio with little idea of what was about to happen. The lights went down, the music went up, and I somehow managed to make it through the whole class. It was hard. Harder physically than anything I had done before, but something clicked. I went to school that day and recounted my experience to my colleagues and experienced the pain of delayed-onset muscle soreness for the first time in my life. And then I went back again. And again. I found myself looking forward to classes; they became a complete break for me where I could zone out and feel my physical fitness improving. I eventually made my way from hiding in the back row to the middle of the studio and then became a front-row regular. I met friends along the way. I got introduced to Bodypump and added resistance-training classes to the mix. I tried different classes and eventually developed a weekly routine around my teaching career as I improved my mental wellbeing and physical fitness. It had such a positive impact on me I wanted to encourage others to try. So much so, I eventually became a group fitness instructor so I could share these life changing experiences with others. The purpose of recounting this introduction through the gym is not only in sharing my story of 'finding' cycling, which I will continue to elaborate upon next, but also to note that trying something new or something you never imagined you would enjoy could just be the thing that changes you positively forever. I can certainly attest this has been the case for me.

From indoors to outdoors . . .

During my time as an eager participant at the gym and a as result of enjoying cycling so much, I decided to buy a bike. I began with a basic mountain bike to ride on the bike paths and devoted my Sundays to an outdoor ride in between my gym routines. I quickly discovered the joy of riding outside and increased the distance I was cycling over time. I would find new places to explore and bought myself a computer to track my speed and kilometres travelled. I then purchased a road bike and entered social cycling events, and not long after, I invested in my first mountain bike with suspension for off-road riding. Soon, I came to discover (and love) what is known in the cycling world as the 'n+1' principle, which, according to Velominati (2014), is "the correct number of bikes to own is n+1. While the minimum number of bikes one should own is three, the correct number is n+1, where n is the number of bikes currently owned". Who would have thought there were so many bikes for so many different types of riding?

Needless to say, outdoor cycling opened up a whole new world to me. Weekend riding adventures became the norm. Holidays overseas were planned around cycling destinations. I began racing and joined a women's mountain bike racing development squad, entering a number of cross-country races. I signed up with a local cycling club and was introduced to criterium and road racing through their women's development program. I had become a regular outdoor rider and finally felt I had found 'myself' through my passion for teaching *and* my newfound passion of cycling. Striking the balance between these activities and work helped me to discover how important it was to have valuable time away from my occupation and studies in order to provide myself with self-care.

I must say this journey has not been without internal struggles and pressures, particularly as I have transitioned into an academic career and post-graduate study. The lines between work and non-work time are often blurred or nonexistent, and at times I have had difficulty justifying my riding time when I 'should be' writing more, researching more or working more. This aligns with Cannizzo's (2018) findings that university staff report work hours can be hard to define, and that some report a 'publish or perish' mentality in working in universities. Cannizzo highlights this is particularly noticeable with early-career academics accounting for their career in narratives reflective of 'survival'. In my experience, it is essential to have self-care routines in place to counter-act this narrative and to continue to embrace the rewarding aspects of the wellbeing practices and a higher education–based career.

The cycling academic

As I have transitioned into an academic career through further study and a position lecturing at a university, it is these purposeful self-care practices through cycling in various ways that continue to provide me with the energy and focus required to undertake academic work. I have found that as a post-graduate student, these regular routines offer much-needed physical movement to counteract long periods of time spent at my desk. It is this exercise and movement that assist me to centre myself when I sit down to work, and it gives me a sense of having given myself a break in a meaningful way. Riding with others allows me to forge important social connections. This is in contrast to the bulk of my PhD experience, where I spend a lot of time alone. Riding alone gives me a chance to think or to break thought and in which I get lost in time and my surroundings without others. Both are important to me in different ways.

Studies have shown that PhD students experience varying levels of stress and barriers to completion, with concerns being raised about their mental health and wellbeing (Usher & McCormack, 2021). In acknowledging the complexity of undertaking a PhD and prioritising my wellbeing, I am valuing and making space for my cycling routines in order to continue to enact self-care. This has been particularly important during recent times, with major disruptions to my doctoral journey due to the COVID-19 pandemic. In a study by Dodd et al. (2021), many university students reported COVID-19 significantly impacted their studies. Dodd et al. (2021) have subsequently highlighted that strategies to support health and wellbeing need to be of high priority for higher education students. The practices I have put in place have assisted in managing stress levels driven by an uncertain and rapidly changing world. They also provided much-needed exercise and a sense of 'normality' in my life during the long periods of unprecedented lockdowns we experienced in Melbourne, Australia.

In terms of my academic work as a lecturer, I have tried to strike the balance between my roles, study and the beginning of an academic career. Whilst academic work does allow for some flexibility to fit in my self-care routines, I have also felt pressure to miss them or drop them to continue work that is not clearly defined by set hours. Kenny and Fluck (2014) describe how traditionally academic work was characterised by a "high degree of self-regulation, flexibility and autonomy" (p. 586), but they also note there is growing tension between these features and the more recent demands in academia. This is also discussed by Mountz et al. (2015), who describe the ever-increasing demands of academic life consisting of "the acceleration of time in which we are required to do more and more" (p. 1237). They advocate for *slow scholarship*, which is time to think, process, write, read and research, and a climate that is reasonable and sustainable. Drawing on my past experiences of maintaining a balance with work and my cycling, I am cognisant of the pressures of beginning an academic career and the natural inclination I have had in the past to work beyond what is reasonable and sustainable. As previously mentioned, I find the time on the bike immerses me in a flow state, which I will discuss further in the next section of this chapter. I feel this is a valuable practice to ensure I maintain a realistic balance in my academic career and continue the practices that have served my wholistic health over time.

During my pre-cycling working life, I felt like I was constantly tired. The thought of then jumping on a bike to ride would have been the last thing I thought my body needed, and I was just 'too busy' to even dream of fitting this in. I found that introducing and maintaining regular exercise routines in fact provides me with more energy if the balance is right. It wakes me up, elevates my mood and allows me to focus more purposefully in my work. These positive impacts correlate with research into exercise generally and cycling specifically. What follows is an exploration of the literature in relation to how such practices have been found to be valuable on many levels, and I will cover both indoor and outdoor forms of exercise, as I have found both to be integral parts of my self-care routines in different ways. Additionally, I will discuss how this resonates with my own experiences in more depth and how cycling generally contributes to my sense of wellbeing, as well as the specific mindfulness aspects of cycling that I experience when riding a bike.

Benefits of physical exercise and cycling

According to Klaperski et al. (2019) regular recreational physical exercise is vital in health promotion and disease prevention. They highlight considerable evidence that engaging in physical exercise on a regular basis also improves mental health. This is also supported by Flowers et al. (2018), who write that there is an extensive research base and comprehensive reviews demonstrating that exercise in any form enhances psychological wellbeing by reducing anxiety, enhancing self-esteem, and improving mood. Whilst Klaperski et al. claim there is little known about the particular types of exercise that will maximise both physical and mental health benefits, Rissel (2015) points to numerous reports and reviews in the last 20 years that summarise the health benefits of cycling in particular. Rissel states, "All of these publications have overwhelmingly concluded that there are multiple health benefits from cycling – benefits consistent with those of physical activity generally" (pp. 46–47), and this includes physical activity being important for mental health. This concurs with research that found cycling, and recreational cycling in particular, improves self-concept and positive mood and contributes to wellbeing (Kaplan et al., 2019). These findings align with my own experiences with cycling and exercise, where I have not only seen the positive impacts it has on my physical fitness but, importantly, the clear role it plays in supporting my own mental health. I'm someone who lived the narrative of overwork, and cycling has given me specific space in order to take time out and rejuvenate my mind and body. By freeing my mind for the time it takes to ride, I feel more focussed and refreshed when work is required.

As recounted in my earlier narrative, I engage in both indoor and outdoor forms of cycling. Both of these practices play important roles in my self-care routines, and they also allow me to schedule these around my work commitments. I can choose to ride in a variety of indoor and outdoor settings and can do so alone or with others. I find this variation provides me with benefits. Research has shown both indoor and outdoor cycling to be beneficial in enhancing enjoyment and experiencing pleasure whilst riding a bike. Rissel (2015) highlights there have been many qualitative studies documenting the joy and pleasure that people experience from cycling, and this has been shown to contribute to wellbeing. Additionally, Flowers et al. (2018) found that the therapeutic outcomes of exercise are enhanced, and psychological benefits are increased when green exercise is performed, that is, it is undertaken in natural environments. Although these studies have focussed on outdoor cycling specifically, indoor group cycling classes have also been shown to enhance enjoyment, affective valence and exertion, particularly if there are higher levels of 'groupness' fostered by feeling like an authentic group (Graupensperger et al., 2019). Both of these findings resonate strongly with me, with enjoyment being a key factor in my participation. Whilst the action of cycling is common, the variation in how I undertake cycling provides me with a range of experiences in different settings, offering a real sense of an 'other' to restore balance in my life.

Flow and mindfulness

I return to my original visual narrative to explore the mindfulness and flow I experience through riding outdoors. My riding experience enables me to disconnect from my academic work, to then reconnect with more focus and energy. As discussed, whilst I do participate in group and indoor cycling activities, I also balance this with outdoor riding and solo journeys. I have found all of these contribute positively to my physical and mental health, but importantly, both assist me in achieving a flow state in different ways. My experiences with flow and cycling accord with Meggs and Chen's (2021) assertion that people who are exercising regularly are likely to experience what is known as *flow* or the *flow state*. Flow is defined by Csikszentmihalyi et al. (2014) as an optimal state experienced when an individual is completely present and involved in their current activity to the point of forgetting everything else except for the activity itself. Csikszentmihalyi's research related to flow centred around a series of studies into autotelic activities which are "things people seem to do for the activity's own sake", and this included athletes undertaking exercise (p. 15). Flow was reported as a state that carried people along effortlessly whilst undertaking their activity and drove them to seek that flow experience again and again. The defining feature of flow is an "intense experiential involvement in moment-to-moment" (Csikszentmihalyi et al., 2014, p. 230), and according to Nakamura and Csikszentmihalyi (2014), it is made up of the following elements:

- Merging of action and awareness
- Intense and focused concentration on what one is doing in the present moment
- Loss of reflective self-consciousness
- A sense that one can control one's actions; that is, a sense that one can in principle deal with the situation because one knows how to respond to whatever happens next
- Distortion of temporal experience (typically, a sense that time has passed faster than normal)
- Experience of the activity as intrinsically rewarding, such that often the end goal is just an excuse for the process

Whilst at times during my cycling life I have been involved in racing, I certainly use cycling primarily as an intrinsically rewarding experience that enables me to connect with a flow state. This flow state provides me with the break I need to enact self-care and to also experience mindfulness. Whilst I don't find cycling to be monotonous, McCartney has described that it is perhaps the "monotony of cycling that allows one to enter a truly blissful state of mindlessness where the thoughts begin to recede and appear to have disappeared, completely" (Wallace, 2018). This certainly resonates with my own experiences whereby I can purposefully use cycling to process my thinking, notice my thoughts pass in and out of my mind as I ride and to provide time to completely disconnect by experiencing a state of flow. In this way I sometimes use the space, particularly on outdoor solo rides, to undertake a mindfulness approach. Fortier and Kowal (2007, cited in Meggs & Chen, 2021) describe mindfulness training as emphasising the present moment and a non-judgemental acceptance of internal and external experiences, and propose that mindfulness practices may be helpful in achieving the flow state whilst exercising. It is through these mindfulness practices, and a state of flow, that I am able to then able to feel I have clarity in my mind, and renewed space and energy for my academic work. This accords with McDonough and Lemon's (2018) assertion that there are emerging trends linking mindfulness and academic success and their argument that mindfulness is key in enabling engagement in the complex cognitive and emotional work of higher education spaces.

Enacting this form of self-care

If undertaking self-care in the form of physical exercise is something that is of interest to you, I will now share my ideas on the strategies which may assist you in this journey. In doing so, I will purposefully refer to physical exercise in a broader sense, as I feel one of the most important elements is that you find the type of movement activity that you find enjoyable.

- *Find the right type of physical activity for you:* As outlined in this chapter, I do love cycling, and it has formed the basis of my routines. For you, the thought and practice of riding a bike may not be as enjoyable, so I would encourage you to find the physical activity that really connects with your own interests. According to Flowers et al. (2018), there is an extensive research base and comprehensive reviews demonstrating that exercise in any form enhances psychological wellbeing by reducing anxiety, enhancing self-esteem and improving mood. I would therefore encourage you to find the physical activity that you love doing most, and you can then move towards finding the one which assists you to experience a flow state whereby you discover intrinsic motivation to undertake the activity for the sake of itself.

    If you are new to physical exercise or are not sure where to begin, start small and try different things. I took time to recount my journey from the beginning when I joined the gym, which eventually brought me to cycling. It was also an example of something I had never thought about doing before that then became what I loved to do. I then built my exercise routines around this to include indoor and outdoor activities. Take the time and be patient to really find the type of exercise that provides you with the space and empowerment you need as well as the motivation to stay invested and involved. Also, consider indoor versus outdoor exercise. Both are beneficial to my overall health and fit into my schedule. I find that my most mindful state is achieved through outdoor cycling, although I can certainly achieve a flow state either riding indoors or outdoors. Riding indoors has social benefits for me and is also a time-efficient way to work out that can easily fit around my working day. Consider what works best for you.

- *Start slowly and in small doses.* When introducing physical activity into your life that is new, start small and build slowly. This is important so that you do not over-exert yourself early on and so you build your fitness and strength in a reasonable manner over time. In my narrative, I did recount my experiences in joining a gym, which was new and not something I had given much thought to before. Whilst I did start in the cycle studio, I also tried other group fitness classes to see what I really connected with and enjoyed. I began with just three visits to the gym a week and over time developed a routine that worked best for myself, my work schedule and what I enjoyed doing the most. I followed a similar pattern when introducing myself to outdoor cycling. I began with short rides once a week, then over time built up the distance I was riding. I then introduced other days in the week I would venture outside, swapping an indoor routine with an outdoor 'green' setting. It does take time to find the right combination of exercise that will motivate you to keep participating. Ensure you build your routines slowly so you do not burn yourself out or cause an injury. Flexibility to adjust in response to your work week and commitments will also be useful to build a sustainable routine. Not only does this mean you are more likely to get it 'done', but it also adds variety.

- *Exercising socially, solo, or both?* Find out whether you enjoy the type of exercise you do with others, solo or a combination of both. I have found both to be beneficial and feel I need a balance to ensure my self-care practices meet my needs. I have friends who find it difficult to ride alone and are motivated by the presence of others and some who enjoy their alone time so much they only exercise solo. Your decisions here may also depend on the exercise(s) you find that you really enjoy and perhaps assist you in finding flow. Some will afford you more social opportunities if you are involved in a team sport or a club, whereas others may allow you the option of purely solo sessions like swimming, running or cycling.

- *Carve out time and a schedule for you.* If you choose an activity you love doing, this will be less challenging. In saying this, we all have days where we wonder if we should 'give it a miss'. In these instances, I focus on how great it feels once I have done my ride/exercise and focus on the benefits for the remainder of the day. I always find when I am 10 minutes into it, any hesitation I had disappears quickly, as I am enjoying what I am doing and do 'disconnect' and find my flow. I always ensure that if I am unwell, I rest. If I am busy and it's impossible to fit in, I am realistic and skip workouts. However, I always ensure I pick up the schedule again as quickly as possible, and I prioritise it as a part of my week. Consider the time of day you may undertake these practices. I find that I enjoy exercising first thing in the morning for a number of reasons. This enables me to begin my day with an endorphin lift and to experience what I think is the best part of the day, early morning. You may prefer a completely different time of day or need to vary it according to your other commitments. Whatever it is, purposefully schedule it in, and where possible, schedule other things around it so you have dedicated time to undertake your practices.

To conclude

Throughout this chapter, I have shared my own experiences in enacting self-care through cycling. By undertaking this purposeful activity, I have been able to push back against my own narrative of overworking and provide myself with valuable time to invest in my own physical and mental health. Whilst I have explored a variety of ways in which I enact this form of self-care, it is the flow state experienced from outdoor cycling in particular that provides valuable time engaging in mindful practices. This in turn enhances my sense of self and well-being and enables me to continue to give the energy and focus to my academic work. Whilst cycling may not be for everyone, I hope that I have been able to convey the positive impact physical exercise has had on my work/life balance and how something I had never considered doing was the starting point for this discovery and now my lifestyle. I encourage you to seek something that works for you in the same way in order to engage with physical movement as a purposeful way to honour yourself and your wellbeing practices.

References

Cannizzo, F. (2018). "You've got to love what you do": Academic labour in a culture of authenticity. *The Sociological Review, 66*(1), 91–106. https://doi.org/10.1177/0038026116681439

Csikszentmihalyi, M., Abuhamdeh, A., & Nakamura, J. (2014). *Flow and the foundations of positive psychology*. Springer. https://doi.org/10.1007/978-94-017-9088-8_16

Dodd, R. H., Dadaczynski, K., Okan, O., McCaffery, K. J., & Pickles, K. (2021). Psychological wellbeing and academic experience of university students in Australia during COVID-19. *International Journal of Environmental Research and Public Health, 18*(3), 866. https://doi.org/10.3390/ijerph18030866

Ewing, R., & Smith, L. (2003). Retaining quality beginning teachers in the profession. *English: Practice and Critique, 2*(1), 15–32.

Flowers, E. P., Freeman, P., & Gladwell, V. F. (2018). Enhancing the acute psychological benefits of green exercise: An investigation of expectancy effects. *Psychology of Sport and Exercise, 39*, 213–221. https://doi.org/10.1016/j.psychsport.2018.08.014

Graupensperger, S., Gottschall, J. S., Benson, A. J., Eys, M., Hastings, B., & Evans, M. B. (2019). Perceptions of groupness during fitness classes positively predict recalled perceptions of exertion, enjoyment, and affective valence: An intensive longitudinal investigation. *Sport, Exercise, and Performance Psychology, 8*(3), 290–304. https://doi.org/10.1037/spy0000157

Kaplan, S., Wrzesińska, D., & Prato, C. (2019). Psychosocial benefits and positive mood related to habitual bicycle use. *Transportation Research Part F: Traffic Psychology and Behaviour, 64*, 342–352. https://doi.org/10.1016/j.trf.2019.05.018

Kenny, J., & Fluck, A. (2014). The effectiveness of academic workload models in an institution: A staff perspective. *Journal of Higher Education Policy and Management, 36*(6), 585–602. https://doi.org/10.1080/1360080X.2014.957889

Klaperski, S., Koch, E., Hewel, D., Schempp, A., & Muller, J. (2019). Optimizing mental health benefits of exercise: The influence of the exercise environment on acute stress levels and wellbeing. *Mental Health & Prevention, 15*. https://doi.org/10.1016/j.mhp.2019.200173

McDonough, S., & Lemon, N. (2018). Mindfulness in the academy: An examination of mindfulness perspectives. In N. Lemon & S. McDonough (Eds.), *Mindfulness in the academy: Practices and perspective from scholars* (pp. 1–21). Springer Press. https://doi.org/10.1007/978-981-13-2143-6_1

Meggs, J., & Chen, M. (2021). The effect of a brief-mindfulness intervention on psychosocial exertion and flow-state among sedentary adults. *Perceptual and Motor Skills, 128*(3). https://doi.org/10.1177/0031512520984422

Mountz, A., Bonds, A., Mansfield, B., Loyd, J., Hyndman, J., Walton-Roberts, M., Basu, R., Whitson, R., Hawkins, R., Hamilton, T., & Curran, W. (2015). For slow scholarship: A feminist politics of resistance through collective action in the *neoliberal* university. *ACME: An International Journal for Critical Geographies, 14*(4), 1235–1259.

Nakamura, J., & Csikszentmihalyi, V. M. (2014). The concept of flow. In *Flow and the foundations of positive psychology*. Springer. https://doi.org/10.1007/978-94-017-9088-8_16

Rajendran, N., Watt, H. M., & Richardson, P. W. (2020). Teacher burnout and turnover intent. *The Australian Educational Researcher, 47*(3), 477–500.

Rissel, C. (2015). Health benefits of cycling. In J. Bonham & M. Johnson (Eds.), *Cycling futures* (pp. 43–62). The University of Adelaide Press. https://doi.org/10.20851/cycling-futures

Thomson, S. (2020). TALIS: Stress levels among Australian teachers. *Teacher Magazine*. https://www.teachermagazine.com/au_en/articles/talis-stress-levels-among-australian-teachers

Usher, W., & McCormack, A. (2021). Doctoral capital and well-being amongst Australian PhD students: Exploring capital and habitus of doctoral students. *Health Education, 121*(3), 322–336. https://doi.org/10.1108/HE-11-2020-0112

Velominati. (2014). *The rules: The way of the cycling disciple*. W. W. Norton Company.

Wallace, W. (2018). *Cycling as meditation: Can riding help us achieve mindfulness?* https://cyclingtips.com/2018/07/cycling-as-meditation-can-riding-help-us-achieve-mindfulness/

Weldon, P. (2018). Early career teacher attrition in Australia: Evidence, definition, classification and measurement. *Australian Journal of Education, 62*(1), 61–78.

13 Anatomy of a burnout

Walking, reading and journal writing as practices of self-care to support intellectual life

Lynelle Watts

Introduction

This photograph of my sneakers resting on the grainy tarmac aims to evoke the role this footwear played in my recovery from an episode of burnout in 2012–2013. I walked along the road, seashore on one side, cars whizzing past, and, at a certain point, I would turn, walk back the way I had come, seashore on the other side. Putting these shoes on, I slowly, painfully came to terms with the physical aches, fatigue and mental distress that had been going unacknowledged. I was walking because there did not seem anything more I could manage.

Image 13.1 Walking shoes

DOI: 10.4324/9781003207863-17

The process of this physical, emotional and existential reckoning was captured in voice memos – I was in the habit of recording my thoughts as reflective notes for my doctoral research also happening at this time – so I kept the practice going. I felt a pressing need to engage in dialogue with myself about what was happening to me. This chapter includes excerpts from these recordings to present an anatomy of my burnout event. I am calling it an event to signal a specific moment when it finally became clear that this was not an isolated run of exhaustion due to the time of the academic year. I present a discussion about the practices that supported my return to health and how these became the backbone to my re/engagement in intellectual life and community. Hence, the focus of the chapter is not to rehearse the details leading to the burnout event. Readers may take it as read that burnout is a pernicious risk to people inhabiting neoliberalised university spaces (Alves et al., 2019). Academic environments can often be felt as a permanent provocation to our sense of wellbeing, requiring on going reflexive engagement; itself an effortful and sometimes exhausting practice. As Watts and Robertson (2011) point out:

> All jobs involving intensive interaction with others, as with teaching have the potential to have a negative impact upon employees' wellbeing and burnout, as a consequence of sustained emotional involvement in the workplace, is one common consequence.
>
> (p. 35)

The chapter proceeds in three ways. First, I engage in a critical dialogue between my experience, outlined in snippets of voice memo, and the empirical and theoretical literature on burnout. The chapter casts a wide net across a range of interdisciplinary literatures and discourses – psychoanalysis, psychology, philosophy, education, health and sociology – which come to represent different objective dialogical poles through which to process the event. Second, I move to a consideration of the relationship between individual identity and aspects of intellectual life. Considering the centrality of reflection to recovery and repair I utilise Riddle's (2017) discussion of academic desire to frame this discussion. Third, I conclude the chapter with a reflection on the implications from the previous sections. I use this last section to consider the nature of walking, reading and writing as self-tending practices and supports for engaging scholarly creative work.

Circumambulating the body . . .

Jungian analysts use the word 'circumambulation' to describe "the interpretation of an image by reflecting on it from different points of view" (Sharp, 1991, Circumambulation section). This means staying close to an image for the purposes of building understanding from it. This section engages in a circumambulation of the burnout event via the image at the start of the chapter – the sneakers and the road – and by considering the literature on burnout as a phenomenon.

Walked along the beach, it took an hour to do 3 km, I wore my sunglasses and pulled my hat down low – I couldn't seem to stop leaking tears . . . no sound, just tears, not even crying really. I kept my eyes on my shoes . . . felt like it was all I could do . . . one foot, then another . . . I am so sore . . . sorely tired, can barely walk at all; how did I get here?

(November 2012)

I walked like this for weeks, every day for a few hours. I had not walked in years at this point – I had been working 12-hour days and could never seem to find the time. I had not much else to do as I was on sick leave, having been diagnosed with high blood pressure. I had left a work meeting after becoming very distressed over something I cannot even recall now. I remember a deep sense of shame at what I thought of as a failure of my body – to contain my distress, instead leaking it through the blood pressure machine and into a sick-leave certificate. In research by Arman et al. (2011) this moment is outlined as *the collapse* where "the person comes to a crossroads, often described as a breakdown or a collapse. At such a juncture, the person realises that his/her condition has passed a limit and has become serious, even critical" (p. 299). After my visit to the doctor I recorded this:

I'm sitting here in the car . . . am officially off work now because I hit the wall on Tuesday afternoon . . . the symptoms are awful and I am having difficulty concentrating . . . can't seem to mark [papers], even the slightest bit of mental energy leaves me spent, and in need of a sleep . . .

(November 2012)

High blood pressure was only a tiny slice of what I was experiencing, but it was an objective symptom. We were not calling it burnout – just a little high blood pressure. High blood pressure was an objective symptom, and while this is the case, it is also likely it could hide other aspects of burnout. The fix for having high blood pressure was a few weeks off work to see if it calmed down. I wasn't aware at this point how much calming down I needed to do.

There is a substantial body of work establishing burnout as a syndrome, despite little agreement about what it is (Ekstedt & Fagerberg, 2005). Maslach and Leiter (2016) explain job burnout as comprising three components: overwhelming exhaustion, cynicism and feelings of ineffectiveness associated with perceptions of a lack of accomplishment. The upshot is that exhaustion from excessive work demands, where they overrun the resources of the individual, is a core signal of burnout. Maslach and Leiter (2016) explain that this model of burnout "clearly places the individual stress experience within a social context and involves the person's perception of both self and others" (p. 103). Burnout proceeds in a process. Arman et al. (2011) mention that early accounts of burnout primarily discuss it as being about work outside the home; however, the syndrome has broadened to include experiences of long-term unemployment, caring responsibilities or relational stress. In research exploring the lived experience of burnout, Ekstedt and Fagerberg (2005) found it to traverse a trajectory from inner incentives to succeed at a (life or work) project to an experience of breakdown. Image 13.2 captures the aspects described by participants in the study by Ekstedt and Fagerberg (2005):

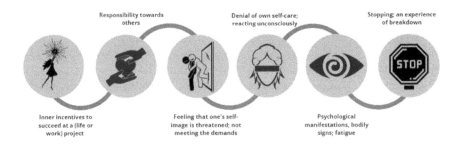

Adapted from Ekstedt and Fagerberg (2005, p. 62)

Image 13.2 Trajectory of a burnout

Burnout is often conceptualised as primarily an individual problem or experience:

> *So I found a paper about burnout – it lists all kinds of things that people report experiencing. I'm shocked, I expected the exhaustion because I had read about it before but this paper asked about people's experience leading up to the burnout . . . [quiet voice, shaky] I have many of these . . . but it gets worse [teary whisper] . . . I have had many of them for two years already . . .*
>
> (November 2012)

A list of symptoms of burnout (Arman et al., 2011, p. 298; see also Ekstedt & Fagerberg, 2005) is presented in Table 13.1. In the second column I have indicated the symptoms I had been experiencing in the previous 2 years before I presented to the doctor that day. Arman et al. (2011) suggest that "[t]here were indications that people affected by burnout tended to shut themselves off from their own suffering" (p. 295). There is a kind of unconsciousness about the condition of oneself that accompanies the process, which Arman et al. (2011, p. 297) characterise as an "existential blindness". This is loneliness of a particular kind. Arendt (2017 [1951]) describes this condition well:

> In solitude . . . I am 'by myself", together with my self, and therefore two-in-one, whereas in loneliness I am actually one, deserted by all others. All thinking . . . is done in solitude and is a dialogue between me and myself; but this dialogue of the two-in-one does not lose contact with the world of my fellow-men [sic] because they are represented in the self with whom

> I lead the dialogue of thought . . . the two-in-one needs the others in order to become [whole] again . . .
>
> (pp. 625–626)

I remember the feeling of being misunderstood. I can see that my internal dialogue about the issue was cut off from myself and from others; I could not hear the inner voice enough to recognise the state of myself.

As to the list of symptoms, with the exception of blood pressure, none of these other symptoms were discussed with the doctor:

Table 13.1 Symptoms of burnout

Symptom	Present
Periods of colds	X
Itching rashes	X
Heart conditions, suspected heart infarction	
High blood pressure	X
Lack of sleep	X
Fatigue	X
Experiences of weakness	X
Powerlessness	X
Lack of concentration	X
Dizziness	
Gastro-intestinal conditions	X
Swelling	X
Fever	
Low tolerance for noise and sound	X
Easily startled	X
Obsessions of various kinds (physical, emotional)	X
Bouts of crying	X
Guilt about relationships (family, friends and work colleagues)	X

The diagnosis of high blood pressure seemed to cover a more fundamental malaise; people around me had other diagnoses – depression, anxiety, being a workaholic, for example. I have included further symptoms in italics – these are my additions to the list. They only emerged in my consciousness over a period of time after the initial event, primarily through walking, journaling and reflection.

> *I am not sure who I thought I was, I can't be sure I haven't been really difficult to be around. God now . . . and now there is the guilt . . .*
>
> (December, 2012)

People frequently discuss burnout in everyday life, usually talking about the exhaustion side of the syndrome. For example, in a recent article in *The Conversation*, Musker (2019) describes burnout and offers advice on how to build one's personal resilience to "inoculate yourself against job interference and prevent it from ebbing into your personal life". Musker (2019, n. p.) also suggests, rather mildly, that "employers have organisational obligations to promote staff wellbeing and ensure staff aren't overworked, overstressed, and headed towards burnout". When an employee does experience symptoms of burnout, their main recourse is almost entirely to access assistance through a general practitioner (GP), at least in the Australian context. This gives people access to any sick leave they are entitled to and mental health plans for counselling services at a lower cost. Such counselling is generally limited in the number of sessions available, and access is by referral from a GP. Other assistance may be available via employee assistance programs (EAP) offered through a person's employer. EAP sessions are also limited depending on the conditions of the employer–provider agreements (Attridge, 2019).

In my case, I accessed sick leave in the first instance. Later I accessed annual leave to extend my time away from the workplace. It was during this period that I put on my sneakers and walked my way out of exhaustion, and, as I walked, I came to understand the true extent of this burnout event.

> Well I have been off work now for four weeks, met E [friend and colleague] for lunch yesterday . . . said I look better, more relaxed. I am not as tired, so that's getting better. I can walk a lot further now. Good news is I am not crying every day anymore.
> (December 2012)

It would be another three years before I could say with some assurance that I had recovered myself. The recovery journey can be seen as reversing the process as illustrated by Image 13.3:

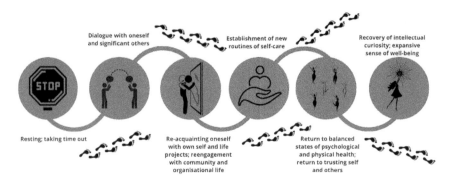

Adapted from Ekstedt and Fagerberg (2005, p. 62)

Image 13.3 Recovery from burnout

Reversing the process included addressing loneliness and isolation from myself as well as reconnecting with family, friends and community. I established new routines of self-care and, along with these, reconnections to significant others, I regained my sense of trust in myself and others. In the next section I consider the intersection of individual identity and organisational contexts and the role of intellectual affect, desire and reflexivity.

I loved my work until I didn't . . .

Sometimes burnout happens not when we dislike what we are engaged in but instead when we *love* what we do. This is true in my case. Greatly committed to education, not least because of its transformative effects in my own life as a mature-age student, I came to scholarly work deeply attached to an idea of the university as a place of ideas and discussion. This attachment began very early in my undergraduate days, when I was inspired by listening to a tutor talk about their honours project while in first year. I have an excerpt from a journal at the beginning of my career as an academic that captures this feeling:

> *So I've been asked to tutor in the first year social work philosophy class – I tried to play it cool but I am seriously excited . . . so much to read, oh god so much to* learn *. . . I cannot believe how lucky I am.*
>
> (May, 2003)

So my long process of initiation into academic life began. Widely considered to be a combination of individual factors and institutional know-how, building an academic identity is a complex process involving induction into institutional and disciplinary norms and practices (Drennan et al., 2017). This development takes time, and there is no single process for undertaking it. As Clegg (2008) asserts, "identity is understood not as a fixed property, but as part of the lived complexity of a person's project and their ways of being in those sites which are constituted as being part of the academic" (p. 329). Cannizzo (2018) explores aspects of this academic identity making in his research on academic labour, concluding that "the present [wider] culture of authenticity encourages academics . . . to seek out a personal connection with their labour" (p. 130). The personal connection for me was in the liberation to be found in reading and talking about ideas with students and colleagues and later with teaching, writing and research practice.

Each person's engagement in academic identity making is different. We all inhabit different communities within the institution of higher education. Not only that, where we are in our journey of becoming-academic will exert different engagements with the organisation of scholarly work (Cannizzo, 2018). Becoming a scholar was once described to me as a long process involving finding one's voice through teaching, writing, reading and through the kinds of research questions a person might pursue or get involved with. The assumption underpinning this description from a senior colleague was that of assumed longevity and security of tenure within the academy – something that I aspired to but had yet to experience, being still in the phase of short-term contracts and undertaking my doctoral studies on the job. Universities remain very hierarchical institutions, and knowing where one is in this system is part of the impact of the organisational culture and climate that also contributes to one's sense of identity. This has increased in recent years with the emphasis on early- to mid-career designations for research scholars. Cannizzo's (2018) research points to different ways of producing a sense of self as an academic in relation to increasing managerial governance. One way is to evoke nostalgic longings for a past age of value-driven work; such longings may also point to desires and values experienced in the present. Another way is to accept the managerial demands for productivity "in terms of 'survival' – a future-oriented discourse that normalises compliance with managerial imperatives as an unavoidable externality" (Cannizzo, 2018, p. 104).

Riddle (2017) also reflects on these discourses in academic life through his discussion of the oft-heard advice to early-career researchers about doing what sustains you as an academic, exhortations that evoke notions of desire, creativity and collegiality. Riddle (2017) raises the question of how *we* as academics "might seek for a more permissive and pleasurable approach to the performativities of producing ourselves as academics?" (p. 32). Here Riddle is revealing the existence of desire within the space of academic organisational life characterised by enterprise practices via technologies of audit and performance metrics. Like many scholars in the academy, Riddle is asking how one might resist, survive and, with others, transform the increasingly managerial conditions of academic life to create spaces that Mountz et al. (2015, p. 1238) describe as "cultivating caring academic cultures and processes". Scholars have also explored how to engage in academic work mindfully, building spaces that are collegial, creative and inspired (Gardner & Grose, 2015; Lemon & McDonough, 2018).

There is another aspect to the desire for engaging in creative and scholarly work: that of intellectual affect. Intellectual affect includes "delight, wonder, awe, fascination, courage, surprise, worry, doubt, curiosity, concern, tenacity, and hope" (Goldie, 2012, p. 122). Goldie (2012) suggests that these emotions are key to engagement in the practices of inquiry. My view is that this basic intellectual affect towards creative, scholarly work is a wellspring that feeds engagement in the practices of academic life. It is possible to hear this intellectual affect in the way academics speak with passion for their work (Back, 2016; McPherson & Lemon, 2018; Wels, 2019). This aspect of academic life requires a delicate balance of collegiality and solitude in order to flourish. This wellspring can dry up. I did not realise intellectual affect could disappear, let alone result in intellectual depression (Goldie, 2012).

> *Q [partner] said the other day that I should go back to work as I am starting to look bored. I am not bored . . . I don't care, I am really struggling to feel anything . . .*

no ideas here . . . how can I go back? What if I've worn out the circuits? What if it never comes back? What is the point of it anyway?

(January, 2013)

Riddle (2017) also warns about "the dangers of desire, where we might find ourselves desiring our own oppression . . . and behaving in ways that run counter to our ethical principles through a desire to be known as successful academic subjects" (p. 27). This issue of ethics is important to considering how one might be deeply engaged in work which is meaningful and how this might be sustainable or how it might tip towards unsustainability, as it did in this event. While Clegg's (2008) research is primarily concerned with understanding the lived experience of academic identity making, we can also see such occupational identity projects in the context of wider aspects of identity. Much of my recovery required re-engagement with other aspects of my identity subsumed under the demands of the academic life. Laden (2001) describes practical identity as having a personal and a social side. The personal side is typified by strong reciprocal relationships that place us in a unique web of social ties – with our family and friends, for example. The social side of our practical identity is less reciprocal and involves aspects of us that are socially salient to others as well as ourselves – our gender, ethnicity; able-bodiedness; our occupation. According to Korsgaard (1996), practical identity is the site from which our values emerge, in response to the necessitations of life.

In this way our values are inextricably tied to action – actions emerge via the vicissitudes of navigating the competing necessitations we experience. There is an intimate connection between values, action and reflection with respect to our ethical commitments to ourselves and others. Korsgaard (1996) suggests that the "test of reflective endorsement is the test used by . . . moral agents to establish the normativity of all their particular motives and justifications" (p. 89). Capacities to engage in reflection, also referred to as reflexivity (Archer, 2003), are seen as the key connection between values and action. What I experienced was a dulling of my intellectual affect, and consequently, my reflective capacities as the demands of the work increased and the spaces in which to engage in creative and deliberate scholarship disappeared. This condition is well described by Ball (2012, cited in Riddle, 2017, p. 28) when he asserts that in responding to the accountability requirements and metrics of the 21st-century university, we "become transparent but empty, unrecognisable to ourselves". What disappeared was any inner stillness and, subsequently, space for my own inner conversation (Wiley, 2010). As this continued I increasingly tied aspects of my identity to the role until this side of my practical identity subsumed almost all other aspects, including that of my participation in relationships with family and friends. The organisational context has few hurdles to taking what it will from academic labourers, and as a result, there are few natural barriers to the increasing demands. Image 13.4 offers a visual slice of the process:

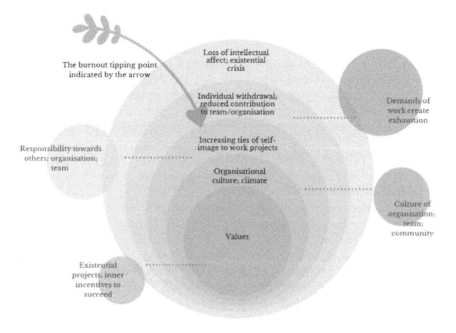

Image 13.4 Anatomy of a burnout

Abedini et al. (2018), in their research with medical residents, make a distinction between circumstantial and existential burnout. Circumstantial burnout is tied to the environment (Abedini et al., 2018), whereas existential burnout involves more internal aspects in which the person considers themselves in relation to their role. It emerges that recovery can entail different practices (Abedini et al., 2018). For circumstantial burnout addressing workload challenges, re-energising one's personal life including relationships with family, friends, starting new hobbies and practicing self-care such as mindfulness and exercising regularly generally aids recovery. Existential recovery requires a different focus. Recovery from existential burnout entails, first, recognition and validation of the experience from peers; finding connections with others and reconnecting to the meaning of the work (Abedini et al., 2018). There were elements of both circumstantial and existential burnout in my burnout event, and this called for the whole suite of self-tending care practices to aid recovery of wellness but also for a reimagining of my existential projects:

> *Okay so I am trying not to give myself a hard time about not being more productive . . . I have barely turned my computer on since going on leave . . . I still cannot read more than a few paragraphs of anything . . . remembered a conversation about this thing called sharpening the saw – apparently you cannot keep at the work if your*

saw is blunt . . . when they told me the name of the book I thought oh god I have that book on my shelf at home . . . and yep my saw is blunt alright.

(January, 2013)

Sharpening the saw . . . practices of recovery

Sharpen the saw is the seventh habit outlined by Stephen Covey (1989). It refers to "a balanced program for self-renewal in the four areas of one's life: physical, social/emotional, mental, spiritual (Covey, 2021). This section discusses the self-tending practices that I utilised to begin and sustain my recovery. Taking my lead from Stephen Kemmis (2019), practices can be considered as:

> a form of human action in history, in which particular activities (doings) are comprehensible in terms of particular ideas and talk (sayings), and when the people involved are distributed in particular kinds of relationships (relatings), and when this combination of sayings, doings and relatings 'hangs together' in the project of the practice (the ends and purposes that motivate the practice).
>
> (p. 13)

Here practices are aimed at care of the self; self-tending if you will. Already in the chapter I have situated the event within the context of particular 'doings' – too much work, for example – and explicated some of the talk – 'sayings' about the event using various literatures about burnout, intellectual affect and academic life. I have utilised the framework suggested by Covey (1989) to structure the discussion.

Physical

Walking as a practice for scholarly life has a long history (Thomas, 2020). Walking became a crucial activity. Indeed, walking initiated the process of recovery. There is something about this slow, human-paced speed that brought me into my own body. Walking in nature is known to be restorative (Olafsdottir et al., 2020). I walked around the bush in my neighbourhood; by the ocean and on the beach. I experimented quite a bit with different kinds of walking. Initially I walked to music to ignore the sound of my own breathing, and later, tuning into my breathing became an important way of grounding myself. Sometimes I walked in silence so I could hear the bush and birdsong. I experimented with pace – brisk, ambling, fast and slow. I walked looking at my feet, saying to myself "I will just get to the next tree; just walk for another few minutes then you can turn back". Sometimes, I walked slowly so I could admire the canopy, watch the breeze swaying along the leaves, light dancing across my eyes, filling my retinas with green energy. Other times, I walked just noticing the ocean and sand on my feet. Throughout all this I tried to feel my way back into my body . . . looking up, watching my feet, feeling into my body through my heels, toes, shins, back and hips – an important practice of noticing my way back into my body post-burnout. Now I think of walking as crucial restoration, and it has become a staple of my practice for balancing the demands of academic life.

Social/emotional

Reconnecting with family, friends and colleagues was another aspect of recovery. Part of this was learning to trust others as well as trust myself. I cannot overstate how important this aspect is. One of the effects of burnout is depersonalisation (Maslach & Leiter, 2016), which involves a kind of non-caring attitude towards others. However, alongside this is a deep distrust of oneself; distrust in the sense of being able to say when something is too much as much as when one's needs are not being met. This is that invisibility to oneself discussed earlier. The burnout literature implies this is just in the workplace. However, I found this attitude extended beyond the workplace to permeate many aspects of my relationships with others. I had to recover my patience and compassion for others, and the only way to do so was to find a way to get my own needs for understanding and empathy met. Much of this came from my family, friends and close colleagues, folks who shone a light for me in the dark and often let me lean on their sense of who I was or had been. Family members went walking with me; took me dancing; listened for what seems like a long time; wrote a list of affirmations for me until I found my balance again. A close friend wrote a list of my achievements in the workplace to help me offset my feelings of failure and shame, because during the darkest days I couldn't see these at all. Other people helped me with new hobbies and interests. Sometimes people just sat with it and let me feel whatever I needed to. People shared their own experiences and sometimes offered up practices that helped them in their own dark nights of the soul. It seems ironic, but alongside this support I needed individual counselling sessions, as this helped in being able to take up social connections, largely because it provided a space for processing the experience and supported the return of my emotional life. The feeling of being understood allowed the spaces inside me to expand in understanding and empathy for others.

Mental

This aspect refers to learning, reading, writing and teaching. By the time of the event my engagement in learning and reading for work had shrunk to almost nothing, and teaching had lost its shine almost completely. This was very different to how I was previously, when reading was my way of supporting and feeding my curiosity and love of learning. I no longer read for pleasure by this stage; I also had trouble locating what I thought about things because I was so reactive, was easily startled and had little concentration. Writing and recording my thoughts about what I was experiencing was my route to recovery. I wrote and also kept an audio journal. When I look back on these records I can pinpoint the moment when I felt myself return to myself – it was during a recording when I could finally make fun of myself. I joined Twitter that year and found a whole new community of people writing and talking about writing and academia. This, possibly more than anything, helped with the return of intellectual affect by giving me a space to let my curiosity run wild. With the return of curiosity, my commitment to learning and teaching returned as well. Now I use curiosity as a bit of a bellwether measure for how to gauge my wellbeing in terms of the work–life balance.

Spiritual

Spiritual can have many meanings (Hodgson & Watts, 2017). Canda and Furman (2009, p. 5) suggest that spirituality means "a universal quality of human beings and their cultures related to the quest for meaning, purpose, morality, transcendence, wellbeing, and profound relationships with ourselves, others, and ultimate reality". I discussed earlier how I had tied my meaning and purpose too closely to my idealised notion of what academic life is or what being in the role meant. This had the effect of making my life smaller, not larger. The burnout event precipitated an existential crisis for me about the meaning and purpose of work, a crisis that spread throughout my life, causing me to question my fundamental assumptions about my values and my relationships to others. Building this aspect took the longest and most sustained effort to recover. Meditation, walking, nature, reading, writing, building connections to others all contributed. I knew I had made it back from the edge when beauty began once more showing up all around me.

Conclusion

Narelle Lemon (2018) describes how finding balance in academia can be a negotiation of front-, back- and offstage spaces and how mindfulness practice was a route for her in an ongoing process of balancing. This ongoing balancing act for academics is crucial for wellbeing but also for preventing burnout events. Burnout in academic life has become something of a commonplace, and the mental health and quality of life of academics is the subject of discussion within the academic literature (Alves et al., 2019; Khan et al., 2019). Not all of it is the responsibility of the individual; organisational culture and climate also play a part. The question I had when starting this reflection on this burnout event was what happens to our abilities to engage in such front-, back- and offstage negotiations within academic life when we burn ourselves out? Self-tending practices involved reseating connections to myself, others and the wider world through walking, reading, writing and learning and spending time in natural spaces. These practices continue to form a route through which to balance my life and work.

References

Abedini, N. C., Stack, S. W., Goodman, J. L., & Steinberg, K. P. (2018). "It's not just time off": A framework for understanding factors promoting recovery from burnout among internal medicine residents. *Journal of Graduate Medical Education, 10*(1), 26–32. https://doi.org/10.4300/jgme-d-17-00440.1

Alves, P. C., Oliveira, A. D. F., & Paro, H. (2019). Quality of life and burnout among faculty members: How much does the field of knowledge matter? *PLoS One, 14*(3), e0214217. https://doi.org/10.1371/journal.pone.0214217

Archer, M. S. (2003). *Structure, agency and the internal conversation*. Cambridge University Press.

Arendt, H. (2017 [1951]). *The origins of totalitarianism*. Penguin Classics.

Arman, M., Hammarqvist, A.-S., & Rehnsfeldt, A. (2011). Burnout as an existential deficiency – lived experiences of burnout sufferers. *Scandinavian Journal of Caring Sciences, 25*(2), 294–302. https://doi.org/10.1111/j.1471-6712.2010.00825.x

Attridge, M. (2019). A global perspective on promoting workplace mental health and the role of employee assistance programs. *American Journal of Health Promotion, 33*(4), 622–629. https://doi.org/10.1177/0890117119838101c

Back, L. (2016). *Academic diary: Or why higher education still matters*. Goldsmiths Press.

Canda, E. R., & Furman, L. D. (2009). *Spiritual diversity in social work practice: The heart of helping*. Oxford University Press.

Cannizzo, F. (2018). "You've got to love what you do": Academic labour in a culture of authenticity. *The Sociological Review, 66*(1), 91–106. https://doi.org/10.1177/0038026116681439

Clegg, S. (2008). Academic identities under threat? *British Educational Research Journal, 34*(3), 329–345. https://doi.org/10.1080/01411920701532269

Covey, S. R. (1989). *The seven habits of highly effective people: Restoring the character ethic*. Simon and Schuster.

Covey, S. R. (2021). *Habit 7: Sharpen the saw®*. https://www.franklincovey.com/habit-7/

Drennan, J., Clarke, M., Hyde, A., & Politis, Y. (2017). Academic identity in higher education. In P. Teixeira & J. C. Shin (Eds.), *Encyclopedia of international higher education systems and institutions* (pp. 1–6). Springer Netherlands. https://doi.org/10.1007/978-94-017-9553-1_300-1

Ekstedt, M., & Fagerberg, I. (2005). Lived experiences of the time preceding burnout. *Journal of Advanced Nursing, 49*(1), 59–67. https://doi.org/10.1111/j.1365-2648.2004.03264.x

Gardner, P., & Grose, J. (2015). Mindfulness in the academy – transforming our work and ourselves "one moment at a time". *Collected Essays on Learning and Teaching, 8*, 35–46. https://doi.org/10.22329/celt.v8i0.4252

Goldie, P. (2012). Loss of affect in intellectual activity. *Emotion Review, 4*(2), 122–126. https://doi.org/10.1177/1754073911430133

Hodgson, D., & Watts, L. (2017). *Key concepts and theory in social work*. Palgrave Macmillan.

Kemmis, S. (2019). Introducing the theory of practice architectures. In S. Kemmis (Ed.), *A practice sensibility: An invitation to the theory of practice architectures* (pp. 7–29). Springer. https://doi.org/10.1007/978-981-32-9539-1_2

Khan, F., Khan, Q., Kanwal, A., & Bukhair, N. (2019). Impact of job stress and social support with job burnout among universities faculty members. *Paradigms, 12*(2), 201–205. https://doi.org/dbgw.lis.curtin.edu.au/10.24312/paradigms120214

Korsgaard, C. M. (1996). *The sources of normativity*. Cambridge University Press.

Laden, A. S. (2001). *Reasonably radical – deliberative liberalism and the politics of identity*. Cornell University Press.

Lemon, N. (2018). I am not playing the academic hunger games: Self-awareness and mindful practices in approaching research. In N. Lemon & S. McDonough (Eds.), *Mindfulness in the academy: Practices and perspectives from scholars* (pp. 129–154). Springer Publishers.

Lemon, N., & McDonough, S. (Eds.). (2018). *Mindfulness in the academy: Practices and perspectives from scholars*. Springer.

Maslach, C., & Leiter, M. P. (2016). Understanding the burnout experience: Recent research and its implications for psychiatry. *World Psychiatry: Official Journal of the World Psychiatric Association (WPA), 15*(2), 103–111. doi:10.1002/wps.20311

McPherson, M., & Lemon, N. (2018). It is About fun stuff! Thinking about the writing process in different ways. In N. Lemon & S. McDonough (Eds.), *Mindfulness in the academy: Practices and perspectives from scholars* (pp. 113–127). Springer.

Mountz, A., Bonds, A., Mansfield, B., Loyd, J., Hyndman, J., Walton-Roberts, M., Basu, R., Whitson, R., Hawkins, R., Hamilton, T., & Curran, W. (2015). For slow scholarship: A feminist politics of resistance through collective action in the neoliberal university. *ACME: An International Journal for Critical Geographies, 14*(4), 1235–1259.

Musker, M. (2019). *Workplace burnout is all too common: Here's how to tell if you're affected*. https://www.abc.net.au/news/2019-06-04/workplace-stress-burnout-symptoms-and-signs-diagnosis/11174404

Olafsdottir, G., Cloke, P., Schulz, A., Van Dyck, Z., Eysteinsson, T., Thorleifsdottir, B., & Vögele, C. (2020). Health benefits of walking in nature: A randomized controlled study under conditions of real-life stress. *Environment and Behavior, 52*(3), 248–274. https://doi.org/10.1177/0013916518800798

Riddle, S. (2017). Do what sustains you. In S. Riddle, M. K. Harmes, & P. Danaher (Eds.), *Producing pleasure in the contemporary university* (pp. 25–36). SensePublishers.

Sharp, D. (1991). *Jung lexicon: A primer of terms and concepts*. https://www.psychceu.com/Jung/sharplexicon.html

Thomas, E. (2020). *Five philosophers on the joys of walking*. https://blog.oup.com/2020/02/five-philosophers-on-the-joys-of-walking/

Watts, J., & Robertson, N. (2011). Burnout in university teaching staff: A systematic literature review. *Educational Research, 53*(1), 33–50. https://doi.org/10.1080/00131881.2011.552235

Wels, H. (2019). Academia in the fast lane vs. organisational ethnography and the logic of slow food. In L. Donskis, I. Sabelis, F. Kamsteeg, & H. Wels (Eds.), *Academia in crisis: The rise and risk of neoliberal education in Europe* (pp. 111–128). Brill Rodopi.

Wiley, N. (2010). Inner speech and agency. In M. S. Archer (Ed.), *Conversations about reflexivity* (pp. 17–38). Routledge.

Index

Page numbers in *italics* indicate a figure and page numbers in **bold** indicate a table on the corresponding page.

#10minsofmaking 108, *109*

academic life/work 35, 41, 74, 93, 123, 127, 131–134, 154–159, *155, 157–158*, 217–219, 221–223
academic wellbeing xvi
academic writing 37
Ackerman, D. 61
acting, in a play 17, 75–76
activism, act of 3, 17, 29, 79, 123, 137, 140
affect 21, 24–26, 30
'aha' moments 60, 62
Ahmad, A. S. 163
Ahmed, S. 132
Anderson, G. 140
Aotearoa 187
Arat, A. 39
Arendt, H. 214
Armstrong, J. 141
Art as Contemplative Practice (Franklin) 78
art education practice 24
artist–audience relationship *143*
art journaling 46; art-to-journal 42; journal-to-art 42; reflection in *38*
art making 107, 142, 149, 177; for development of the soft skills 42; to explore our imagination 42; production of knowledge and 25, 28
art paper, for drawing and painting 46
art practice 12, 23, 140–142; *see also* collages and posters
a/r/tographic conversation 13, 24, 153, 162, 177
arts-based methods 34, 131
artworks 21, 23–26, 29, 37, 42–43, 46–47, 142–144, 147

Auckland University of Technology (AUT) 191

Barcan, R. 139
Barnett, R. 138
Barone, T. 165
Beckman, K. 59
Best, E. 187
Biesta, G. 141
Black, A. L. 177
Black Indigenous People of Color (BIPOC) 83
body/mind/emotion centres 89, 91, 95
Bourdieu, P. 139, 149
breaking points 121, 129, 131
brushes 47
Buddhist concept of sati 39
burnout 16, 211–212; in academic life 217–221; mental recovery from 222–223; physical recovery from 221–222; recovery from *216*; social/emotional recovery from 222; spiritual recovery from 223; symptoms of 214–215, **215**; as a syndrome 213; trajectory of *214*
Butler-Kisber, L. 142

calm, feelings of 2, 8, 56, 67, 77–80, 213
Calvocoressi, G. 80–81
Cannizzo, F. 202–203, 217
care-ful making 23–25, 29–30
carnival 139–140
channels of expression and interruption 131–133
Chen, M. 205
circumambulation, use of 212–217
Clegg, S. 217

cognitive functions 83
collaborations 59, 81–82
collaborative community 8, 77, 81–83
collaborative expression 7
collaborative running 89–91, 95, 97, 100; race/races 91–102; training and preparation 90–91
collaborative self-care 102–103
collaborative work 11, 122
collages and posters 142–143; creation or manipulation of objects and images 149–150; passageway posters 144–145, *145*; photographic collage *137*; postcard 145–147, *146*; Robyn's collage *178*; of Zoom backgrounds 147–149, *148*
collective care 54
coloured pencils 45–47, 50
communication 2, 59, 82, 131, 140–141
community: collaborative 8, 77, 81–83; wellbeing 80–82
compassion 3, 16, 74, 222
conceptual gateways 59
connectedness, experiences of 58–59
Contu, A. 150
conversation 25, 29–30, 88, 90, 93, 113, 146–148, 153, 174, 219
Conversation, The (Musker) 216
Court, K. 116
Covey, S. 221
COVID-19 pandemic 28, 105, 125, 138, 171, 175, 178, 203; experience of social isolation 170; impact on academic work/life 105, 126; job security and 133
craft/crafting 2–3, 83, 105, 108, 149
Cranny-Francis, A. 59
creative research methods: a/r/tographic conversation 13; collage 142–143; craft 2–3, 83, 105, 108, 149; dance 17; dataviz project 113–114, 116; journaling 33–50; photography 131; poetic inquiry 1–17; poetry 1–2, 78–81, 83–84, 131; visual narrative 55–56; writing 46
creative self 76, 84, 162
creative writing 78–79, 81–82, 128
creativity 8, 17, 59, 75–76, 83–84; a/r/tography 13, 24, 153, 162, 177; being novice 83; craft/crafting 2–3, 83, 105, 108, 149; dances *185*, 185–188; data visualisation, construction of 117; dataviz project 113–114, 116; flow and 79–80; as interruption 11; meditative process of 79; photography 131; poetic inquiry 1–17; poetry 1–2, 78–81, 83–84, 131; stepping off the creative edge 82–83;
visual narratives 1, 17, *55*, 56, 64, 91, 130, 138–139, 205; wellbeing via 80–82; writing 1, 5, 7, 9, 16–17, 23–25, 34–35, 43–44, 46, *67*, 74, 78–81, 83–84, 88–90, 93, 95, 97, 99–101, 116, 121–124, 128, 131–134, 142, 188, 191, 202, 217, 222–223; *see also* journaling
critical thinking 39, 59
Csikszentmihalyi, M. 58, 61, 75, 79–80
Csikszentmihalyi, V. M. 206
Cs of human capabilities 59
cumulative damages 129
curiousness 60–61
cycling *199*, 199–200; benefits of 204–205; flow and mindfulness 205–206; outdoor 202, 205; riding with others 203; self-care practices through 203–204
cynicism 213

Daher, N. 107
Dallas Marathon, 2019 89; commitment to participate 94–96, *94*; individual and collective wellbeing 95; metaphor of marathon 98–99; race route 91–93, *92–93*; regaining equilibrium *99*, 99–101; regeneration 96–97; *see also* collaborative running
dance 17
data visualisation, construction of 117
data visualisation knitted object 105, *106*, 107
da Vinci, L. 148
dear 154
de Botton, A. 141
deep thinking 114
Deleuze, G. 162
DeSalvo, L. 82
DIY art therapy 35–37
'doing' research 24
doing*thinking* 21, 23, 28; with affect and space 25–26; movement in 27–29
Donaghue, N. 121
drawing 17
Drawing on the Right Side of the Brain (Betty Edwards) 34
Drew, P. 142
Dürer, A. 148
Durie, M. 188
Dweck, C. S. 61

Ekstedt, M. 214
electronic journal 42–43; *see also* journaling
Ellsworth, E. 24
embodiment 7, 17, 31, 58, *66*, 90

embracing curiosity 6
emotional meaning 3
emotions 1, 38, 54, 59–60, 63–64, 68, 82, 84, 91, 95
employee assistance programs (EAP) 216
engagement 39
ethics: of care and caring 123; of care and rest 133
exhaustion, feeling of 7, 16–17, 74, 121, 125–126, 130–132, 142, 212–214, 216
expertmaterial/s work 26–27

faculty: development 9, 89; wellbeing 76
Fagerberg, I. 214
Faulkner, S. 90
fear: feeling of 6; uncertainty and isolation, issue of 159–167
fearlessness, feeling of 6, 57–58
feelings of ineffectiveness 16, 213
feminist consciousness 90, 95, 101
feminist knowledge 28
feminist methodologies 121, 123, 131; see also neoliberal university
feminist pedagogy 11, 130–132
feminist protest 132–133
feminist snap 129, *130*, 132
Feynman, R. 60–61, 67
Field Guide to Getting Lost, A (Solnit) 57
Fine Arts Work Centre (FAWC) 77–78, 80
flexibility 39, 155, 157
flow 79–80, 205–206
Flowers, E. P. 204
Fluck, A. 203
folding, acts of 17
Foucault, M. 173
Franklin, M. 78
Fremantle Art Centre (FAC) Print Award 26

game 139
Garrett, H. J. 54
Gill, R. 121
Glaveanu, V. P. 62
Golden, N. A. 60
graphite pencils 46
Greene, M. 141, 149
groupness, levels of 205
Guattari, F. 162

haka (traditional posture dance): art of *185*, 187; kapa haka (haka team) 14, 186–190, 192–193, 194, 195, 196; hauora (wellbeing) 14, 186–187, 188, 190, 195; MAI ki Aronui 190–195; waiata (song, to sing) 185, 188, 190, 191–194, 195

Hall, M. P. 81
handwriting, as movement 5, 49
Hanney, R. 58
Harré, N. 123
hauora, cultural self for 187–188, 190, 195
Henderson, L. 124
Hensher, P. 49
higher education 17, 24, 54, 74, 88, 102, 105, 107, 113, 138, 147, 150, 203, 217
Higher Education Academy case studies 124
holism, cultivation of 76
holistic learning experience 58
holistic wellbeing 9, 89
House of Cards (Urquhart) 145
Hoyser, C. E. 81
hyperbolic paraboloid 55–56; corners *64*; embodiment 66; folding 63, *65*; location of parabolic and hyperbolic surface curves *65*; math-making experience 56–67, *67*; playful polyhedral construction 66

identity of maker 23
Indigenous art centres 28
Indigenous Knowledges 28
individualism 122
information-processing 34
innovator, attributes of 55
integrative experience 60
intimate journals 41
intrinsic learning 60
intrinsic motivation 57, 207
irreversible experience 60
Irwin, R. 24

journaling 5, 80, 215; for creating revitalising space 36; electronic journal 42–43; focus areas 41; mindfulness and 39–41; mindful self-care and 35–37; paper journal 43–46; for reflection and reflexivity 37–39; right and left 33–35; tools 46–50; types 41–42; use of photographs and collage 47
journals 34–35, 41–50, 166
joy 6, 53–55, 58, 62, 67–68, 80, 110, 113, 124, 128, 200, 202, 205

K–12 students 74
Kapa haka 185, 185–188
Kaupapa Māori-centric (Māori 'ways') 192
Kei konei Aronui 191–192, 194
Kelly, W. 141
Kemmis, S. 221

Kenny, J. 203
Kinman, G. 159
Klaperski, S. 204
knitting 17; positive impact of 105; as a relaxing leisure pursuit 116–117; social benefits 106; *see also* data visualisation knitted object
knowledge 23–25, 28, 30, 35, 53–54, 56–60, 123–125, 149, 162, 191, 194
knowledge workers 145
Kruger, B. 142
Küpers, W. 138

Land, R. 59–60
Langer, E. J. 39
lectio and *visio divina* 81
Leiter, M. P. 213
Lemon, Narelle 206
lined paper 44, 46
Lorde, A. 79
Loveless, N. 21–22

Maeda, J. 53–54
MAI 191–193
MAI ki Aronui 191–195
MAI ki AUT 191
MAI ki Tāmaki 191
MAI te Kupenga 191
MAI whānau 193
Ma, J. 59
making, process of 2, 23; art making 25, 28, 42; collective math-making 53–54; fearlessness and 57; and flexing a hyperbolic paraboloid 55; image-making 12; materialities of 25; with mathematics 6; meditative math-making 53, 57, 59–67; as representation of self-care 4–6
Manguel, A. 61
Māori 187–188
Māori early-career academic (MECA) 188–190
Māori wellbeing 188
marathon training program 94–97; *see also* Dallas Marathon, 2019
Maslach, C. 213
material-discursive enactments 25
mathematics 6, 53–54, 57–58, 60
math-making, in higher education: epistemological and ontological comparisons 61–62; meditative 17, 53–68; metaphors 54–55
Maths in Motion (MiM) 58
mātua tīpuna (ancestors) 187
McDiarmid, D. 142

McDonough, S. 206
meaning making with arts 140–142
meditation 79, 223
meditative math-making 17, 53–68, *67*
Meggs, J. 205
memoir 42
memories 165–166, *165–166*
mental recovery from burnout 222–223
meshwork nets and grid 24
metacognitive thinking 117
Meyer, J. 59–60
Miller, J. 76
mindfulness 39–41, 205–206
mixed-media paper 45
Mona Lisa 148
moral slumber 78
Mōteatea 185, 195n3
Mountz, A. 123–124, 203
movements of care 4
multipotentialites 58

'n+1' principle 202
Nakamura, J. 206
Napier, N. K. 60
nature journaling 42, 50
negative emotion 1
neoliberalism 74–76, 84, 88, 102, 121–122, 128, 131, 134, 139, 154, 159, 173, 177
neoliberals 74–75, 84, 88, 102, 121–122, 128
neoliberal university 74, 121–122, 212; academic career in 122–124; academy's individualistic and competitive games 123; transformative shift in 123–126
nourishing gesture of refusal 11, 133
novelty producing, practice of 39
novelty seeking 39
nurturing, practice of 7, 9

on/with making 25
Organisation of Economic and Development (OECD) 53–54
other-care 9, 88–90, 101

Pallasmaa, J. 58
Palmer, P. J. 57, 74–76, 79–80
pandemic 10, 105, 107–108, 110–111, 113, 116–117, 125, 138–139, 143, 153, 174, 203
paper bags 26–29
paper journal 43–46; chronological entries 46; planning entries 44; selection of paper 45–46; tools for 45; *see also* journaling

Pasztory, E. 142
pedagogy 11, 74–75, 78, 80–81, 130–132
pencils: coloured 46; graphite 46; watercolour 47
Pennebaker, J. 82
Pereira, M. 177
photography 131
physical exercise, therapeutic outcomes of 204–205
physical feminism 90, 92, 101
physical recovery from burnout 221–222
Piaget, J. 54
Plague, The (Camus) 172
planner journaling 41
play 6
playfulness 60
poetic inquiry 1–17
poetry 1–3, 78–84, 131
Postcards Project 145–147, *146*, 149; see also collages and posters
power of relationships 7
practice: in research-creation 21, 23; transdisciplinary-ness 23, 53–55, 58–59, 67; translating and transforming 23
prairie fire *96*, 96–97
praxis 24
pre-cycling working life 204
presentness, literature on 57–59
private-practice workplaces 25
promisingness, state of 53
publishing process 35
pursuit of newness 53–55, 61, 67–68

queer knowledge 28

reading 2, 16, 80–82, 156, 158, 166–167, 170, 190, 212, 217, 222–223
rebuilding connections with others 16, 169–171, *171*
recovery 16, 95, 211–212, 216, 219–223
recreational runners 99
reflection 1–2, 34, 37–39, 59, 89, 116–117, 123, 142, 144, 153, 156, 162, 166, 171, 173–174, 212, 215, 219, 223
reflective journaling 37–39
reflective thinking 117
reflexive journaling 37–39, 41
reflexivity 24, 30, 37–38, 217, 219
Reimagining the Academy: ShiFting Towards Kindness, Connection, and an Ethics of Care (Dwyer and Black) 123
relational act, in self-care 3, 9, 13, 57, 89, 102, 138, 153
relationship building 220

research-creation 4, 21, 23, 29–30
research inquiry 23
research journals 34–35
research-recreation 30
resilience 129–130
resistance 53, 58, 88, 90, 101, 103, 121–123, 126, 131–132, 139–140, 202
resistance-training classes 202
retaliation 140
rhetorical feminism 90–91, 97, 101
rhizomes 153, 162, 166–167, 171, 178
Rhodes, M. 82
Riddle, S. 212
Riley, J. 106, 116
risks 6, 12, 14, 29–30, 42, 53, 61–62, 64, 78–79, 88, 125, 133, 149–150, 174, 195, 212
Rissel, C. 204
Robertson, K. 107, 117
Robertson, N. 212
running 9, 17, 27, 87–103, 122, 156, 208

SAGE Encyclopedia of Social Science Research Methods, The 37
Sax, D. 50
sculptures *141*
self 122; consequences for 62; creative 84; division of 75; exploration of 78; inner 79; light and the dark of 75; mapping of 30, 34; person's sense of 57; sense of 83, 129
self-alienation 75
self-awareness 78
self-care 1, 3, 17, 29, 48, 54, 76, 78, 90, 110, 117, 121–122, 153–159, *158*, 160–162, *163*, 164–167, *175*; approaches to 176–177; balancing 201–202; boundaries as integral to 167–168, *168*, 177; connection and 169–171, *171*; diverse experiences 174–175; ethical considerations 173; form of 206–208; gender and 168–169; individualist requirements for 159; mind, body, and movement as acts of 14; as moral obligation 174; need for 73–74; perceptions of 172–173; poetic representation of 4–6; practices through cycling 203–204; see-able 30; and self-soothing strategies 128–130, *130*; shared 175–176; spaces for 173
self-compassion 16, 83
self-discovery 3, 6, 53, 62
self-expression 78, 105
self-knowledge 75–77

self-/other-care 88, 90, 101
self-renewal 221
self-tending practices 16, 212, 220–221, 223
self-transformation 57
Shahjahan, R. A. 80
Sharpen the saw (Stephen Covey) 221–223
Shirgley, D. 148
singing, act of 17, 186, 190, 192
sketch paper 45
skunk *98*
slowing down 11, 17, 116, 121, 130, 134, 156
Smith, C. 150
Smyth, J. 82
snap 128–134
social/emotional recovery from burnout 222
social knitting 116; *see also* knitting
social world 139
Socratic *Know thyself* 61
space for wellbeing 15, 200
spirituality/spiritual 16, 73–75, 82–83, 91, 141, 188, 195, 221, 223
spiritual leave 75
spiritual recovery from burnout 223
STEAM education 53, 58–59
Stinson, M. 64
studies in higher education 24, 138
supercomplexity, concept of 139

tactile organic shapes 77, *77*
Taylor, C. 24
teacher burnout and distress 74
Teams Platform 105
tenure/tenure-track faculty 89
thesis artworks 24
thinking*doing* 21, 23, 28
thresholdness, concept of 59–60
toxic/toxicity 13, 121–122, 126, 144, 154
transdisciplinarity 23, 53–55, 58–59, 67
transformational value 2, 62
transformation, issue of 6, 54
transformative experience 60
trauma healing 82
Tree of Yggdrasill *169*, 170
troublesome experience 60

Ulus, E. 150
universities 138–139; *see also* neoliberal university
"university as an infinite game" metaphor 123
university campus life *see* academic life/work
unmaking and remaking 25

van Berkum, R. 106
Velominati 202
victimization, by university management 140
Vinebaum, L. 107, 117
visual narratives 1, 17, *55*, 56, 64, 91, 130, 138–139, 205

Wacquant, L. J. D. 149
Wagner, T. 55, 61–62
waiata (song or to sing) 185, 188, 190, 193, 195n3
Waipara, Z. 192
wairua (spirit) 187
walking 128, 131, 142, 161, 174, 176, 201, 211–212, 215, 221, 223
walking shoes *211*
Wapnick, E. 58, 61
waterbrush 47
watercolour: paints 47; paper 45; pencils 47
Watts, J. 212
wellbeing 1, 9, 53–55, 58, 60, 62, 73–74, 90, 110, 117, 122, 139, 156, 203, 223; holistic, sustainable 9; personal and professional 82; practicing strategies of 30; via community and creativity 80–82
well-be(com)ing 12, 137–138, 147, 149
whimsical experience 56
White, S. 76
'why-not' attitude 173
'wicked problem' of integration 59
Willats, S. 143, 147
work–life balance 36, 154, 157, 159, 177, 223
writing 1, 5, 7, 9, 16–17, 23–25, 34–35, 43–44, 46, 67, 74, 78–81, 83–84, 88–90, 93, 95, 97, 99–101, 116, 121–124, 128, 131–134, 142, 188, 191, 202, 217, 222–223
writing lives 9, 88
writing utensil 46